BEHAVIORAL
SCIENCE

Cleocin t 1%

Board Review Series

BEHAVIORAL SCIENCE

BARBARA FADEM, Ph.D.

Department of Psychiatry
University of Medicine & Dentistry of New Jersey
New Jersey Medical School
Newark, New Jersey

WILLIAMS & WILKINS
BALTIMORE · HONG KONG · LONDON · MUNICH
PHILADELPHIA · SAN FRANCISCO · SYDNEY · TOKYO

Editor: Alexander Kugushev
Developmental Editor: Mark W. Crowe
Designer: Dan Pfisterer
Production Coordinator: Barbara J. Felton

Copyright © 1991
Williams & Wilkins
428 East Preston Street
Baltimore, Maryland 21202, USA

Printed in the United States of America

Library of Congress Cataloging in Publication Data

Fadem, Barbara.
    Behavioral science / Barbara Fadem.
      p.   cm. — (Board review series)
    Includes index.
    ISBN 0-683-02952-5
    1. Psychiatry—Outlines, syllabi, etc. 2. Psychology—Outlines, syllabi,
etc. 3. Psychiatry—Examinations, questions, etc. 4. Psychology—Examinations,
questions, etc. I. Title. II. Series.
    [DNLM: 1. Behavior—examination questions. 2. Behavior—outlines. 3. Behavioral
Sciences—examination questions. 4. Behavioral Sciences—outlines.   WM 18 F144b]
RC457.2.F34   1991
616.89—dc20
DNLM/DLC
for Library of Congress   90-12956
                                                CIP

                                      91 92 93 94
                    1   2   3   4   5   6   7   8   9 10

PREFACE

The close relationship between the mind and the physical health of the individual is becoming more and more apparent. Those of us involved in education in psychiatry in medical schools wish that our students could learn about this relationship in great depth. As teachers in medical school, however, we know how overloaded and overwhelmed with information our students are by the time they must be evaluated by standardized testing services such as the National Board Examinations Part I. This book has been written as a learning tool to help students rapidly recall information they have learned in didactic lectures in behavioral science and psychiatry courses; it is not intended to be a substitute for a behavioral science textbook.

The author wishes to thank the staff members of Williams & Wilkins who helped initiate and produce this text, including Charles Duvall, the director of NOVUS Books, Alex Kugushev, and developmental editor, Mark Crowe. The author also acknowledges with thanks those faculty members at the University of Medicine & Dentistry of New Jersey who reviewed sections of the text, including Drs. J. Anne Bartlett, A. Wallace Deckel, Jacob Lindenthal, John Lagos, Michael Miller, Sheldon Miller, and Diane Shrier. Most of all, the author thanks Dr. Steven Simring, Director of Medical Student Education for the Department of Psychiatry at the New Jersey Medical School, for practical help with the text, enthusiasm, and encouragement.

HOW TO USE THIS BOOK

Typically, very little time is available to you when reviewing for the National Board and similar examinations. My goal is to minimize the time you invest and maximize your return on the effort. The following features are intended to facilitate achievement of this goal:

- The text is organized in 8 sections and 24 chapters. The 8 sections group the principal themes tested at the National Board Examinations. The 24 chapters allow you to locate easily specific topics that need reviewing.
- To achieve speed and efficiency in reviewing, the material in each chapter is divided into units organized visually and numerically and is indented in order of hierarchical importance.
- Some 500 Board-type questions are distributed in the 24 chapters and in a Comprehensive Examination. These questions reflect the changes introduced into National Board Examinations in 1991, placing a strong emphasis on A- and B-type questions. Some K-type questions are included because they are useful for self-testing.
- Careful answers to each question are given.
- A Comprehensive Examination is included. It contains a few, strategically selected questions from each of the 8 sections and is designed to be used flexibly. You can either refer to it as a pretest to determine weaknesses or use it as a final confidence-building self-test.
- Tables in most chapters present important material in a concise, easy-to-remember manner.

TRY TO "CUSTOMIZE" THE EFFORT, TAILORING IT TO YOUR OWN LEARNING STYLE. You may be a reader, a scanner, a self-tester, or a visual memorizer. Through the above means I have tried to provide for each individual's particular learning mode.

You may wish to start by taking the Comprehensive Examination to diagnose areas of weakness. This should provide a focus for the main review effort. If you need to review the material, it is arranged in short sections by subject. Each short section contains a few statements and most statements contain an emphasized word or phrase that highlights the most important point in that statement. By scanning the emphasized words and phrases in each short section, you can get both a good idea of the subject matter covered as well as a speedy review of the material.

In chapters in which you feel that you remember the material fairly well, start by taking the examination at the end of that chapter. After testing yourself you may decide that you don't need to review the material in the chapter. If you decide to review, follow the approach described previously.

CONTENTS

1

The Genetic Bases of Psychiatric Disorders

I. Types of Genetic Studies

Different types of studies can help to identify genetic factors in psychiatric disease.

A. Family Risk Studies

—The term **pedigree** denotes a family tree showing the occurrence of traits and diseases within a family.

—A pedigree helps to assess the **mode of inheritance** of a trait or disease.

—**Family risk studies** compare the prevalence of a disease in the relatives of the **proband**, or affected individual, with its prevalence in the general population.

B. Adoption Studies

Adoption studies using twins reared together or apart are used to distinguish the effects of genetic and environmental factors in disease.

—Twin studies may involve **monozygotic** (derived from a single fertilized ovum) or **dizygotic** (derived from two fertilized ova) twins.

—If genetic in origin, a disorder would be expected to occur more often in monozygotic than in dizygotic twins.

—If both twins have a trait, they are **concordant** for that trait.

II. Genetic Origins of Schizophrenia

A. Incidence and Prevalence of Schizophrenia (see also Chapter 10)

1. *Incidence*

   The incidence of schizophrenia is about 1 per 1000 population per year.

2. *Prevalence*

   The chances of an individual becoming schizophrenic in his or her lifetime (lifetime prevalence) is about 1%.

   —The prevalence of schizophrenia is approximately equal in males and females.

   —Although older studies reported that more blacks than whites were schizophrenic, schizophrenia is now thought to be equivalent in whites and blacks.

Table 1.1. Risk of Developing Schizophrenia in Relatives of Schizophrenics

Group	Incidence (%)
Children with one schizophrenic parent	10–12
Dizygotic twin of a person with schizophrenia	9–26
Children with two schizophrenic parents	35–46
Monozygotic twin of a person with schizophrenia	35–58

—Past diagnoses of blacks as schizophrenic are believed to have resulted from biases that led to misdiagnosis of black bipolar patients.

B. Genetic Factors

Strong evidence indicates that genetic factors are involved in schizophrenia. Although environmental factors probably affect the expression of genetic factors in schizophrenia, these are most likely outweighed by genetic influences.

—The closer the genetic relationship of an individual to a schizophrenic patient, the more likely he or she is to be concordant for, or develop, the disease (Table 1.1).

—Increased severity of the disease is directly related to a high concordance rate for schizophrenia in twins.

—Low platelet monoamine oxidase (MAO) activity is a possible genetic marker for schizophrenia.

—Even though one monozygotic twin may be normal and one schizophrenic, their platelet MAO activity has been shown to be similar.

III. Genetic Origins of Affective (Mood) Disorder

The **affective disorders** include both unipolar and bipolar disorders (see Chapter 11). Genetic factors have been shown to be involved in the etiology of both conditions.

A. Unipolar Disorder

Unipolar disorder is characterized by single or multiple episodes of depression.

—The lifetime incidence of unipolar disorder is about 20% in women and 10% in men.

B. Bipolar Disorder

In bipolar disorder, episodes of both elevated mood (mania) and depressed mood are seen.

—The lifetime incidence of bipolar disorder is about 1.2% in women and 1% in men.

—Although evidence of specific genetic markers had been identified in bipolar disorder, recent studies suggest a weaker relationship between these markers and this condition than originally believed.

—Markers on the **X chromosome**, including color blindness, have been associated with mood disorders.

C. Relationship Between Unipolar and Bipolar Disorder

The **concordance rate** for bipolar disorder is higher than that for unipolar disorder.

Table 1.2. Incidence of Mood Disorders in Specific Populations

Group	Incidence (%)
Children with one bipolar parent	27
Dizygotic twin of a bipolar patient	20
Children with two bipolar parents	50–75
Monozygotic twin of a bipolar patient	67

Table 1.3. Psychiatric Problems Found in Relatives of Patients with Personality Disorders

Personality Disorder of Patient	Problem Seen in Relatives
Antisocial	Alcoholism
Avoidant	Anxiety disorder
Borderline	Mood disorder
Histrionic	Somatization disorder (Briquet's syndrome)
Obsessive-compulsive	Depression

—Of individuals with bipolar disorder, about 50% have at least one parent with a mood disorder.

—The degree of relatedness to persons with bipolar illness is related to the incidence of the illness (Table 1.2).

—In unipolar patients, the likelihood of having a relative with bipolar illness is no higher than in the general population.

IV. Genetic Origins of Personality Disorders

There is evidence for **genetic factors** in antisocial, obsessive-compulsive, schizotypal, histrionic, and schizoid personality disorders (see Chapter 14).

—The concordance rate for personality disorders is higher in monozygotic than in dizygotic twins.

—Schizoid, paranoid, and schizotypal personality disorders (Cluster A illnesses) occur more frequently in relatives of individuals with schizophrenia.

—Patients with borderline personality disorder are more likely to have relatives with mood disorders than other groups.

—Relatives of patients with specific personality disorders have been shown to demonstrate characteristic psychiatric problems (Table 1.3).

V. Genetic Origins of Neuropsychiatric Disorders

A. Alzheimer's Disease

There is evidence for a genetic component in Alzheimer's disease (see Chapter 13).

—In one study, 40% of cases had a family history of Alzheimer's.

—A high concordance rate for Alzheimer's has been seen in twins.

—An anomaly on chromosome 21, the same chromosome involved in Down's syndrome, has been seen in Alzheimer's patients.

B. Other Disorders

—Tourette's syndrome, Huntington's disease, Wilson's disease, and infantile autism also have genetic components.

Table 1.4. Genetic Defects in Neuropsychiatric Diseases

Syndrome	Genetic Defect
Alzheimer's	Anomaly on chromosome 21
Cri-du-chat	Part of chromosome 5 missing
Down's	Nondisjunction or trisomy (more common) of chromosome 21
Huntington's	Abnormal gene on short arm of chromosome 4
Klinefelter's	More than one X chromosome; one Y chromosome
Turner's	One X chromosome; no Y chromosome
Lesch-Nyhan	Autosomal recessive transmission

—In Huntington's disease, there is an autosomal dominant pattern of inheritance; if one parent has the disease, each offspring has a 50% chance of getting the disease (Table 1.4).

—Forms of mental retardation that have genetic components include Down's, Klinefelter's, Turner's, cri-du-chat, and Lesch-Nyhan syndromes (Table 1.4).

VI. Genetic Origins of Alcoholism

There is evidence for a genetic component in alcohol abuse (see Chapter 8).

—Alcoholism is **four times more prevalent** in children of alcoholics than in the children of nonalcoholics.

  —This ratio persists even if the children are not raised by their biological parents.

  —A Swedish study found a concordance rate for alcoholism in monozygotic twins two times higher than in dizygotic twins.

—Sons of alcoholics are more at risk than daughters.

Review Test

THE GENETIC BASES OF PSYCHIATRIC DISORDERS

DIRECTIONS: For each of the questions or incomplete statements below choose the answer that is **most correct**.

1.1. All of the following are true about the development of schizophrenia EXCEPT:

A. Genetic factors are important.

B. Environmental factors are important.

C. Genetic influences probably outweigh environmental influences.

D. The closer the genetic relationship of an individual to a schizophrenic patient, the more likely that individual is to develop the disease.

E. The incidence of schizophrenia in a child of two schizophrenic parents is about 90%.

1.2. All of the following are true about affective disorders EXCEPT:

A. The lifetime incidence of unipolar disorder is equivalent in men and women.

B. In bipolar disorder episodes of both elevated and depressed mood are seen.

C. The likelihood of having relatives with bipolar disorder is no higher in unipolar patients than in the rest of the population.

D. Bipolar patients have relatives with both bipolar and unipolar illness.

E. The concordance rate for bipolar disorder is higher than that for unipolar disorder.

1.3. The incidence of mood disorders in the offspring when there is one bipolar parent is approximately

A. 10%.
B. 15%.
C. 27%.
D. 38%.
E. 42%.

1.4. Which of the following personality disorders has been linked to alcoholism in relatives?

A. Histrionic
B. Borderline
C. Obsessive-compulsive
D. Avoidant
E. Antisocial

1.5. All of the following are true EXCEPT:

A. Borderline patients have more relatives with mood disorders than control groups.
B. There is a high incidence of schizoid personality disorder in the families of patients with schizophrenia.
C. There is a high incidence of schizotypal personality disorder in the families of patients with schizophrenia.
D. The concordance rate for personality disorders is equivalent in monozygotic and in dizygotic twins.
E. There is evidence for genetic factors in antisocial personality disorder.

1.6. All of the following are true about the genetics of neuropsychiatric disorders EXCEPT:

A. In cri-du-chat syndrome, part of chromosome 5 is missing.
B. A high concordance rate for Alzheimer's disease is seen in twins.
C. An anomaly on chromosome 21 has been linked to Alzheimer's disease.
D. Lesch-Nyhan syndrome involves autosomal dominant transmission.
E. There is probably a genetic component in infantile autism.

1.7. All of the following are true about the genetics of schizophrenia EXCEPT:

A. The lifetime prevalence is about 10%.
B. The prevalence of schizophrenia is about equal in males and females.
C. The incidence is about 1 per 1000 population per year.
D. The prevalence is equivalent in white and black individuals.
E. The monozygotic twin of a schizophrenic patient has a 35 to 58% chance of having the disease.

1.8. All of the following are true about the genetics of alcoholism EXCEPT:

A. The concordance rate is higher in monozygotic than in dizygotic twins.
B. Alcoholism is more prevalent in the children of alcoholics than in the children of nonalcoholics.
C. There is evidence for a genetic component in alcohol abuse.
D. Daughters are more at risk than sons.
E. Environmental factors are involved in alcohol abuse.

Answers and Explanations

THE GENETIC BASES OF PSYCHIATRIC DISORDERS

1.1. E. The incidence of schizophrenia in children of two schizophrenic parents is about 45%.

1.2. A. The lifetime incidence of unipolar disorder is higher in women than in men.

1.3. C. When there is one bipolar parent, the incidence of mood disorders in the offspring is approximately 27%.

1.4. E. Alcoholism in relatives is seen in patients with antisocial personality disorders.

1.5. D. The concordance rate for personality disorders is higher in monozygotic than in dizygotic twins.

1.6. D. Lesch-Nyhan syndrome involves autosomal recessive transmission.

1.7. A. The lifetime prevalence of schizophrenia is about 1%.

1.8. D. Sons of alcoholics are more at risk than daughters.

2

The Anatomy and Biochemistry of Behavior

I. Anatomy of the Nervous System
   A. **The Neuron**
      The nerve cell or **neuron** is the basic unit of the nervous system. Neurons generally have two types of projections—axons and dendrites.
      —The **axon** usually carries messages away from the neuron, is covered with a myelin sheath, and has a terminal enlargement called the axon terminal, or **bouton**.
         —Myelin greatly increases the conduction efficiency of the axon.
         —The axon terminal is one site for the synaptic vesicles that contain neurotransmitters.
      —Many, few, or no **dendrites** may emerge from the neuron cell body.
         —Often dendrites consist of many branches and contain spikes known as **dendritic spines**.
            —The dendritic spines are sites of reception of neurotransmitter messages from the axons of other neurons.
   B. **Glial Cells**
      Glial cells are non-neuronal cells in the nervous system. They contribute to the **blood-brain barrier**, which prevents substances from passing from the blood into the nervous system.
      —The four types of glial cells in the central nervous system are **astrocytes, ependymal cells, oligodendrocytes,** and **microglia**.
         —Astrocytes, oligodendrocytes, and ependymal cells are known as **macroglia**.
      —The two types of glial cells in the peripheral nervous system are **Schwann cells** and **satellite cells**.
   C. **Peripheral and Central Nervous System**
      The human nervous system consists of the central nervous system (CNS) and peripheral nervous system (PNS).
      —The **CNS** includes the **brain** and **spinal cord**.
         —The CNS receives, processes, and sends sensory and motor information to the body.
         —All behavior is a reflection of the function of the CNS.
      —The **PNS** comprises **cranial nerves, spinal nerves,** and **peripheral ganglia**.

—The PNS carries sensory information to the CNS and carries motor information away from the CNS.

D. Autonomic Nervous System

The autonomic nervous system (ANS), which consists of **sympathetic** and **parasympathetic** divisions, innervates the internal organs.

—The ANS mediates motivational states and emotions with their corresponding visceral responses, such as heart rate, blood pressure, and pupil size.

II. Functional Brain Anatomy and Psychopathology

A. Cerebral Cortex

The cerebral cortex is more developed in humans than in other mammals.

—The cerebral cortex can be divided anatomically into four lobes—**frontal, temporal, parietal,** and **occipital**.

—The cerebral cortex can also be divided based on the arrangement of neuron layers or **cryoarchitecture**.

—The cerebral cortex can also be divided by **modalities**, including motor, sensory, and association areas.

B. Cerebral Hemispheres

The brain has two **cerebral hemispheres**, which are connected by the corpus callosum, anterior commissure, hippocampal commissure, posterior commissure, and habenular commissure. The two hemispheres show lateralization of function.

—The right hemisphere is associated with **spatial relations, musical and perceptual ability,** and the **perception of social cues**.

—The left, or dominant, hemisphere is usually associated with **language function** in both right- and left-handers.

C. Brain Lesions

Brain lesions caused by accident, illness, or surgery are associated with particular behavioral and cognitive deficits (Table 2.1).

III. Neurotransmission

A. Synapses

Information in the nervous system is transferred through synapses or connections between neurons. The space between the synapses is known as the **synaptic cleft**.

B. Receptors

Receptors—proteins present in the membrane of the neuron—can recognize specific neurotransmitters. Receptors may be presynaptic or postsynaptic.

—Presynaptic receptors function to bind neurotransmitters that are produced either by their own neuron (autoreceptors) or another neuron (heteroreceptors).

—Postsynaptic receptors may change the ionic conduction of membranes.

C. Neurotransmitters

Neurotransmitters are chemicals that exert their effects on specific pre- or postsynaptic receptors.

Table 2.1. Neuropsychiatric Consequences of Brain Lesions

Location of Lesion	Result
Frontal lobes	Impulsivity, inappropriate behavior, labile affect, depression, shallow affect, reduction in motivation, problems with attention and memory
Temporal lobes	Dominant lesions—expressive aphasia Bilateral lesions—impaired memory, Klüver-Bucy syndrome Nondominant lesions—dysphoria, irritability, decreased visual and musical ability Dominant lesions—euphoria, auditory hallucinations, poor verbal comprehension, thought disorders
Hippocampus	Poor new learning; implicated specifically in Alzheimer's disease and amnestic disorders
Amygdala	Docility and changes in sexual behavior (Klüver-Bucy syndrome)
Parietal lobes	Bilateral lesions—problems with intellectual processing of sensory information Nondominant lesions—problems with visual-spatial processing, denial of illness, and neglect of the left side Dominant lesions—verbal processing, agraphia, right-left disorientation
Occipital lobes	Visual hallucinations and illusions, blindness, disturbances of spatial orientation
Other brain areas important in psychiatry:	
Thalamus	Increased pain perception, impaired memory and arousal
Basal ganglia	Disorders of movement, thought, affect, and cognition, Parkinson's and Huntington's diseases
Cerebellum	Atrophy may be seen in schizophrenia, bipolar disorder, epilepsy, and autism
Reticular system	Sleep-arousal mechanisms affected
Hypothalamus	Problems with eating, sexual activity, body temperature, and sleep-wake cycle
Limbic system	Emotion, memory, mediation between cortex and lower centers affected

1. *Classification*

    The three classes of neurotransmitters are **biogenic amines, amino acids,** and **peptides**.

2. *Mechanism of Action*

    —In chemical synapses, a neurotransmitter is released by the presynaptic neuron, travels across the synaptic cleft, and acts on specific receptors on the postsynaptic neuron.

    —Although a single neurotransmitter is released by all processes of a single neuron, a neuron can contain more than one type of neurotransmitter, eg, both biogenic amine and peptide neurotransmitters.

    —Neurotransmitters can be excitatory if they increase the chances that a neuron will fire, or inhibitory if they decrease these chances.

    —Reuptake of neurotransmitters by the presynaptic neuron can occur.

    —If this reuptake is blocked, a higher concentration of neurotransmitter is available in the synaptic cleft.

D. **Neurotransmitters in Disease**

   Availability of specific neurotransmitters is associated with common **psychiatric and neuropsychiatric disease states** (Table 2.2).

IV. Biogenic Amines: Overview

—The **biogenic amines,** or **monoamines,** are involved in 5 to 10% of the synapses of the human brain.

Table 2.2.   Disease States and Associated Neurotransmitters

Disease or Syndrome	Neurotransmitter
Schizophrenia	↑ Dopamine *↓ Parkinson*
Depression	↓ Norepinephrine, seratonin, and dopamine
Anxiety	GABA, norepinephrine, and serotonin
Alzheimer's	↓ Acetylcholine ↑ *parkinsons*

—The biogenic amines consist of **dopamine** and **norepinephrine** (catecholamines); **serotonin** (an indoleamine); **histamine** (an ethylamine); and **acetylcholine** (a quaternary amine).

A. Dopamine

1. *The Role of Dopamine*

   Dopamine is involved in the pathophysiology of schizophrenia, Parkinson's disease, and mood disorders.

2. *Synthesis, Transport, and Storage*

   —The amino acid tyrosine is converted to the precursor for dopamine by the action of tyrosine hydroxylase.

   —Following synthesis, dopamine is transported and stored in synaptic vesicles.

   —When stimulated, dopaminergic neurons release dopamine into the synaptic cleft.

3. *Dopamine in Psychiatric Disease*

   —A hyperdopaminergic state may be involved in the etiology of schizophrenia.

   —The clinical success of antipsychotic drugs that block dopamine receptors supports this hypothesis.

   —Also, the brains of schizophrenics show increased numbers of dopamine receptors at autopsy.

   —This increase in the number of dopamine receptors may be secondary to and thus confounded by antipsychotic drug treatment that the schizophrenic patient may have received.

   —Manic patients may show dopamine hyperactivity; depressed patients may show dopamine hypoactivity.

4. *Dopaminergic Tracts*

   Three dopaminergic tracts important in neuropsychiatry are the nigrostriatal tract, the tuberoinfundibular tract, and the mesolimbic-mesocortical tract.

   —The **nigrostriatal tract** is involved in the tonic regulation of muscle tone and movement.

   —The nigrostriatal tract degenerates in Parkinson's disease.

   —Treatment with antipsychotic drugs, which block postsynaptic dopamine receptors receiving input from the nigrostriatal tract, can result in parkinsonism-like symptoms.

   —Dopamine acts on the **tuberoinfundibular tract** to inhibit the release of prolactin from the anterior pituitary.

   —Blockade of dopamine receptors by antipsychotic drugs prevents the inhibition of prolactin release and results in elevated prolactin levels in patients who take these drugs.

—The **mesolimbic-mesocortical tract** may have a role in emotional expression since it projects into brain areas involved in complex behavior.

5. *Tardive Dyskinesia*

Tardive dyskinesia is a serious side effect of antipsychotic drugs.
—It is thought to occur when the postsynaptic dopamine receptors become supersensitive to compensate after they have been blockaded over an extended period by antipsychotic drugs.

6. *Metabolism of Dopamine*

Free dopamine is metabolized by **monoamine oxidase (MAO)**.
—**Homovanillic acid (HVA)** is a metabolite of dopamine that is often measured in psychiatric research.
—Higher levels of plasma HVA are seen in unmedicated schizophrenics than in medicated schizophrenics or normal controls.
—There is an association between cerebrospinal fluid levels of HVA and suicidal behavior.
—Decreased HVA can be seen when patients improve clinically following treatment with neuroleptics.

B. Norepinephrine

1. *Role of Norepinephrine*

Norepinephrine may play a role in the sleep-wake cycle, arousal, anxiety, and pain.
—Norepinephrine is also important in mood and anxiety disorders.

2. *Noradrenergic Neurons*

Noradrenergic neurons contain norepinephrine.
—Noradrenergic neurons are located in the locus ceruleus.
—Approximately 10,000 noradrenergic neurons per side innervate all of the neocortex.

3. *Noradrenergic Receptors*

Alpha (α) and beta (β) are two classes of noradrenergic receptors. Each of these consist of two subtypes—α_1 and α_2, and β_1 and β_2.
—The α_1-**receptors** are postsynaptic, whereas α_2-**receptors** are mainly presynaptic.
—The β_1- and β_2-**receptors** are usually postsynaptic but may also be presynaptic.

4. *Metabolites of Norepinephrine in Psychiatric Illness*

The most significant metabolite of norepinephrine in the CNS is **3-methoxy-4-hydroxyphenylglycol (MHPG)**.
—MHPG in urine is lowered in patients with severe depressive disorders.
—Decreased MHPG in CSF has been correlated with attempted suicide.

C. Serotonin

1. *Role of Serotonin and Its Metabolites in Psychiatric Illness*

—Serotonin is involved in the pathophysiology of **affective disorders**; for example, low levels are associated with depression.

—The **monoamine hypothesis** of mood disorder states that depression results from too little noradrenergic or serotonergic activity.

—Serotonin is also involved in anxiety and in violence.

—Serotonin is metabolized by MAO to 5-hydroxyindoleacetic acid (5-HIAA).

—Low concentrations of 5-HIAA in CSF have been correlated with suicidal depression and antisocial, aggressive, or impulsive personality traits.

—High concentrations of 5-HIAA in urine are seen in patients with carcinoid tumors and occasionally in those taking phenothiazines.

—Serotonin is also involved in sleep.

—If the **dorsal raphe nucleus** (which contains almost all of the brain's serotonergic cell bodies) is destroyed, sleep is reduced for some time.

2. *Formation and Storage of Serotonin*

Conversion of the amino acid tryptophan to serotonin (also known as 5-hydroxytryptamine [5-HT]) is accomplished by the enzyme tryptophan hydroxylase as well as an amino acid decarboxylase.

—Serotonin is stored in synaptic vesicles and released into the synaptic cleft upon stimulation.

—In the synaptic cleft, serotonin binds to serotonergic receptors.

—Deactivation of serotonin is achieved by its reuptake into the presynaptic terminals.

—Serotonin-1 receptors mediate the inhibitory actions of serotonin; serotonin-2 receptors are excitatory.

3. *Antidepressants and Serotonin*

Tricyclic antidepressants and **monoamine oxidase (MAO)** inhibitors are thought to increase the presence of norepinephrine and serotonin in the synaptic cleft.

D. Histamine

1. *Role of Histamine*

Histamine is involved in the control of sleep and waking.

—Histamine cells are present in the hypothalamus. Projections of these cells go to the thalamus, cerebral cortex, and limbic system.

—Abnormalities in histamine metabolism have been seen in schizophrenic patients.

2. *Blockade of Histamine Receptors*

—Blockade of histamine-1 receptors is the mechanism of action of allergy medication (antihistamines).

—Because histamine-1 receptor blockade contributes to sedation and weight gain, histamine may be used in the treatment of anorexia nervosa.

E. Acetylcholine

1. *Role of Acetylcholine*

Acetylcholine, the transmitter used by nerve-skeleton-muscle junctions, has been implicated in mood and sleep disorders.

—Cholinergic neurons synthesize acetylcholine from acetylcoenzyme A and choline.

—Acetylcholinesterase degrades acetylcholine into choline and acetate.

—Degeneration of cholinergic neurons is involved in Alzheimer's disease, Down's syndrome, and Parkinson's disease.

2. *Acetylcholine Receptors*

Cholinergic receptors are divided into two main types—**nicotinic and muscarinic receptors**.

—Block of muscarinic receptors with drugs such as antipsychotics and tricyclic antidepressants results in the side effects of blurred vision, dry mouth, urinary hesitancy, and constipation.

—Some depressed patients may have supersensitive muscarinic receptors.

—Block of cholinergic receptors can result in delirium.

V. Amino Acid Neurotransmitters

Amino acid neurotransmitters account for up to 60% of the synapses in the human brain. Amino acid neurotransmitters include **γ-aminobutyric acid (GABA), glycine,** and **glutamic acid**.

A. GABA

GABA, the best studied of the amino acid neurotransmitters, is the principal neurotransmitter mediating presynaptic inhibition in the CNS.

GABA and the Action of Psychoactive Drugs

—The **benzodiazepines** are antianxiety drugs that act through GABA receptors.

—Benzodiazepines increase the affinity of GABA for its binding site, allowing more chloride to enter the neuron.

—When chloride ions enter the neuron, the neuron becomes hyperpolarized and inhibited and neuronal firing decreases.

—**Barbiturates** may also act through GABA receptors.

B. Amino Acid Neurotransmitters and Neuropsychiatric Illness

—Decreased GABA activity may be involved in the development of epilepsy and anxiety.

—Loss of GABA-ergic neurons has been reported in Huntington's and Parkinson's diseases.

—Glycine is an inhibitory neurotransmitter in the spinal cord.

—Glutamic acid is an excitatory neurotransmitter and may be involved in epilepsy and neurodegenerative illnesses.

VI. Neuropeptides

A. Neuroactive Peptides

A **peptide** is a protein that consists of fewer than 100 amino acids. Although about 50 neuroactive peptides have been identified, many more may exist.

—Peptides, like other neurotransmitters, are present in **axon terminals.**

B. Endogenous Opioids

Endogenous opioids mediate the effects of stress and pain on the organism.

—**Enkephalins** and **endorphins** are endogenous opioids that affect thermoregulation, seizure induction, alcoholism, and schizophrenia.

Table 2.3. Neuropeptides and Possible Associated Psychopathology

Neuropeptide	Psychopathology
Cholecystokinin	Schizophrenia, eating and movement disorders
Neurotensin	Schizophrenia
Somatostatin	Huntington's, Alzheimer's, mood disorders
Substance P	Pain, Huntington's, mood disorders
Vasopressin	Mood disorders
Vasoactive intestinal peptide	Dementia, mood disorders

C. Other Neuropeptides

The peptides **adrenocorticotropic hormone (ACTH)** and **corticotropin-releasing hormone (CRH)** may be involved in the regulation of stress, memory, and mood.

—Other neuropeptides have also been implicated in psychopathology (Table 2.3).

Review Test

THE ANATOMY AND BIOCHEMISTRY OF BEHAVIOR

DIRECTIONS: For each of the questions or incomplete statements below choose the answer that is **most correct.**

2.1. The Klüver-Bucy syndrome is associated with damage to the

A. frontal lobes.
B. temporal lobes.
C. parietal lobes.
D. occipital lobes.
E. basal ganglia.

2.2. Sleep-arousal mechanisms are affected by damage to the

A. cerebellum.
B. basal ganglia.
C. thalamus.
D. reticular system.
E. amygdala.

2.3. Increased pain perception is associated with damage to the

A. thalamus.
B. corpus callosum.
C. basal ganglia.
D. reticular system.
E. hypothalamus.

2.4. Parkinson's disease is associated with damage to the

A. cerebellum.
B. hypothalamus.
C. basal ganglia.
D. frontal lobes.
E. temporal lobes.

2.5. The primary neurotransmitter implicated in Alzheimer's disease is

A. dopamine.
B. norepinephrine.
C. serotonin.
D. GABA.
E. acetylcholine.

2.6. The primary neurotransmitter thought to be involved in schizophrenia is

A. norepinephrine.
B. serotonin.
C. dopamine.
D. GABA.
E. acetylcholine.

2.7. Which of the following neurotransmitters is an indoleamine?

A. Acetylcholine
B. Dopamine
C. Norepinephrine
D. Serotonin
E. Histamine

2.8. All of the following are true EXCEPT:

A. Mania is associated with dopamine hyperactivity.
B. Free dopamine is metabolized by monoamine oxidase (MAO).
C. There is more plasma homovanillic acid (HVA) in unmedicated schizophrenics than in controls.
D. There is an association between levels of HVA and suicidal behavior.
E. Increased HVA is seen with clinical improvement in patients treated with neuroleptics.

2.9. All of the following are true about serotonin EXCEPT:

A. It is involved in the pathophysiology of affective disorders.
B. It is stored in synaptic vesicles.
C. It is metabolized by MAO to HVA.
D. It is involved in anxiety.
E. It is involved in sleep.

2.10. The major area of the brain implicated in Alzheimer's disease and amnestic disorders is the

A. amygdala.
B. parietal lobes.
C. hippocampus.
D. thalamus.
E. basal ganglia.

2.11. All of the following are true about neurotransmission EXCEPT:

A. Receptors are proteins in the membranes of neurons.
B. Presynaptic receptors may bind neurotransmitters.
C. Postsynaptic receptors change the ionic conduction of membranes.
D. Neurotransmitters exert their effects only on postsynaptic neurons.
E. Postsynaptic receptors bind neurotransmitters.

2.12. Which of the following is true about neurotransmission?

A. Amino acid neurotransmitters account for 15% of the synapses in the human brain.
B. The biogenic amines are involved in 50% of the synapses in the human brain.
C. A neuron can contain only one neurotransmitter.
D. A single neurotransmitter is released by all processes of a single neuron.
E. Reuptake of neurotransmitters by the presynaptic neuron does not occur.

2.13. All of the following are true about dopamine in the brain EXCEPT:

A. At autopsy, the brains of schizophrenics show increased numbers of dopamine receptors.
B. Blockade of dopamine receptors results in decreased prolactin levels.
C. Antipsychotic drugs that block postsynaptic dopamine receptors cause Parkinson-like symptoms.
D. Dopamine inhibits the release of prolactin.
E. Patients with mania may show dopamine hyperactivity.

2.14. Norepinephrine is likely to play a role in

A. the sleep-wake cycle.
B. arousal.
C. anxiety.
D. pain.
E. all of the above.

2.15. Which of the following is true about GABA?

A. It is primarily an excitatory neurotransmitter.
B. It is an amino acid neurotransmitter.
C. It mediates postsynaptic inhibition in the central nervous system.
D. Increased GABA activity has been reported in Huntington's disease.
E. Increased GABA activity is seen in epilepsy.

2.16. All of the following are true about the endogenous opioids EXCEPT:

A. They mediate the effects of stress and pain on the organism.
B. Alterations in opioid levels may be involved in seizures.
C. They include the enkephalins.
D. They include glutamic acid.
E. Alterations in opioid levels may be involved in alcoholism.

2.17. Which of the following neuropeptides has been implicated in the pathology of schizophrenia?

A. Somatostatin
B. Neurotensin
C. Substance P
D. Vasopressin
E. Vasoactive intestinal peptide

2.18. All of the following neuropeptides have been implicated in the psychopathology of mood disorders EXCEPT:

A. cholecystokinin.
B. vasopressin.
C. substance P.
D. somatostatin.
E. vasoactive intestinal peptide.

2.19. Types of glial cells in the central nervous system include all of the following EXCEPT:

A. satellite cells.
B. astrocytes.
C. oligodendrocytes.
D. ependyma.
E. microglia.

2.20. All of the following are commonly thought to be functions of the right hemisphere of the brain EXCEPT:

A. perception of social cues.
B. musical ability.
C. spatial relations.
D. language.
E. perceptual ability.

DIRECTIONS: For each of the questions or incomplete statements below, **one** or **more** of the answers or completions given are correct. Choose answer:

A. if only **1, 2,** and **3** are correct.
B. if only **1** and **3** are correct.
C. if only **2** and **4** are correct.
D. if only **4** is correct.
E. if **all** are correct.

2.21. Which of the following is/are true about the human nervous system?

1. The peripheral nervous system includes the spinal nerves.
2. The autonomic nervous system innervates the internal organs.
3. The autonomic nervous system is involved in the control of heart rate.
4. The peripheral nervous system conducts motor information away from the central nervous system.

2.22. Which of the following connect(s) the two cerebral hemispheres?

1. The corpus callosum
2. The anterior commissure
3. The hippocampal commissure
4. The posterior commissure

2.23. Which of the following is/are true about the neurotransmitters?

1. MHPG levels in urine are decreased in patients with severe depressive disorders.
2. MHPG is decreased in the cerebrospinal fluid of patients who have attempted suicide.
3. Norepinephrine is important in mood disorders.
4. MHPG is a metabolite of serotonin.

2.24. Blockade of histamine-1 receptors is associated with

1. sedation.
2. weight loss.
3. antiallergy activity.
4. increased anxiety.

2.25. Degeneration of cholinergic neurons is involved in

1. Down's syndrome.
2. Parkinson's disease.
3. Alzheimer's disease.
4. Pick's disease.

Answers and Explanations

THE ANATOMY AND BIOCHEMISTRY OF BEHAVIOR

2.1. B. The Klüver-Bucy syndrome is associated with damage to the temporal lobes.

2.2. D. Sleep-arousal mechanisms are affected by damage to the reticular system.

2.3. A. Damage to the thalamus is associated with increased pain perception.

2.4. C. Parkinson's disease is associated with damage to the basal ganglia.

2.5. E. Acetylcholine is implicated in Alzheimer's disease.

2.6. C. A hyperdopaminergic state is thought to be involved in the etiology of schizophrenia.

2.7. D. Serotonin is an indoleamine; dopamine and norepinephrine are catecholamines.

2.8. E. Decreased HVA can be seen in patients who improve clinically following treatment with neuroleptics.

2.9. C. Serotonin is metabolized by MAO to 5-HIAA.

2.10. C. The major area of the brain implicated in Alzheimer's disease and amnestic disorders is the hippocampus.

2.11. D. Neurotransmitters exert their effects on specific pre- or postsynaptic receptors.

2.12. D. The biogenic amines are involved in 5 to 10% of the synapses of the human brain; amino acid neurotransmitters account for up to 60% of the remainder. A neuron can contain more than one neurotransmitter, and reuptake of neurotransmitters by the presynaptic neuron can occur.

2.13. B. Blockade of dopamine results in increased prolactin levels.

2.14. E. All are correct.

2.15. B. GABA is an inhibitory amino acid neurotransmitter. GABA is the principal neurotransmitter mediating presynaptic inhibition in the central nervous system. Decreased GABA activity may occur in epilepsy, and loss of GABA-ergic neurons has been seen in Huntington's and Parkinson's diseases.

2.16. D. The endogenous opioids include the enkephalins and endorphins.

2.17. B. Neurotensin and cholecystokinin have been implicated in the pathology of schizophrenia.

2.18. A. Vasopressin, substance P, somatostatin, and vasoactive intestinal peptide have been implicated in mood disorders.

2.19. A. The four types of glial cells in the central nervous system are astrocytes, oligodendrocytes, ependyma, and microglia.

2.20. D. Dominance for language in both right and left handers is usually in the left hemisphere of the brain.

2.21. E. All are correct.

2.22. E. All are correct.

2.23. A. MHPG is a metabolite of norepinephrine.

2.24. B. Blockade of histamine-1 receptors is associated with sedation, weight gain, and antiallergy activity.

2.25. A. Degeneration of cholinergic neurons is seen in Parkinson's disease, Alzheimer's disease, and Down's syndrome.

3

The Pharmacology of Behavior and Electroconvulsive Therapy

I. Antipsychotic Drugs

A. Overview

Drugs used in the treatment of psychosis are known as **antipsychotics, neuroleptics,** and **major tranquilizers.**

—Antipsychotic drugs are used primarily in the treatment of schizophrenia.

—The advent of antipsychotics is largely responsible for the reduction in psychiatric inpatients from 500,000 in 1950 to 100,000 in 1985.

—Antipsychotic drugs are also used to treat psychosis and agitation that are associated with other psychiatric and organic disease.

B. Classification

—The three most important classes of antipsychotic drugs are the **phenothiazines, thioxanthenes,** and **butyrophenones.**

—The phenothiazines include the **aliphatics, piperazines,** and **piperidines.**

—Each antipsychotic can be classified by its potency (Table 3.1).

C. Action and Usefulness

Antipsychotics act by blocking central dopamine receptors.

—Significant improvement is seen in approximately 70% of patients following treatment with antipsychotics.

—Although negative symptoms of schizophrenia (see Chapter 10)—such as withdrawal—may improve with continued treatment, antipsychotics are most effective against positive symptoms such as hallucinations and thought disorders.

D. Side Effects and Drug Interactions

Low-potency antipsychotic drugs are associated with non-neurologic side effects (Table 3.2); high-potency antipsychotic drugs are associated with neurologic side effects (Table 3.3).

—One of the most serious side effects of antipsychotic drugs is **tardive dyskinesia,** which results in permanent abnormal involuntary movements.

Table 3.1. Potencies of Common Antipsychotic Drugs

Generic Name	Trade Name	Group	Potency
Thioridazine	Mellaril	Piperidine phenothiazine	Low
Chlorpromazine	Thorazine	Aliphatic phenothiazine	Low
Haloperidol	Haldol	Butyrophenone	High
Perphenazine	Trilafon	Piperazine phenothiazine	High
Trifluoperazine	Stelazine	Piperazine phenothiazine	High

Table 3.2. Non-Neurologic Side Effects of Antipsychotic Drugs

Side Effect	*Low Potency* Comments
Sedation	Chlorpromazine most sedating
Orthostatic hypotension	Caused by adrenergic blockade; more common with chlorpromazine
Anticholinergic effects:	
Peripheral	Dry mouth, blurred vision, constipation, urinary retention
Central	Severe agitation, disorientation
Endocrine	Increase in prolactin results in breast enlargement, galactorrhea, impotence, amenorrhea, decreased libido
Skin	Skin eruptions, photosensitivity, blue-gray skin discoloration with chlorpromazine
Ophthalmologic	Irreversible retinal pigmentation may result from thioridazine treatment; chlorpromazine may result in deposits in lens and cornea
Cardiac	ECG abnormalities; piperidines most cardiotoxic in overdose
Hematologic	Leukopenia, agranulocytosis—usually in first 3 months
Liver	Jaundice, elevated liver enzymes—usually in first month and usually associated with chlorpromazine
Weight gain	Significant common adverse effect

—Antipsychotic drug treatment is associated with a variety of other side effects (see Tables 3.2 and 3.3).

—Drug interactions occur between antipsychotics and antidepressants, CNS depressants, antihypertensives, anticholinergics, antacids, nicotine, epinephrine, propranolol, and warfarin.

II. Other Drugs Used to Treat Psychosis

Other drugs used to treat psychosis include **reserpine** and **clozapine**.

—**Carbamazepine, lithium, propranolol,** and **benzodiazepines** have also been used to treat psychosis, but usually only when patients are unable to take antipsychotics.

III. Antidepressant Drugs

A. Classification

The **heterocyclic** antidepressants (tricyclic and tetracyclic drugs), the **monoamine oxidase inhibitors (MAOIs),** the sympathomimetics (the amphetamines), and atypical antidepressants are used to treat depression.

—The heterocyclics and MAOIs have little or no effect as euphoriants or stimulants in nondepressed people.

B. Heterocyclics

The **tricyclic antidepressants**, which structurally resemble the phenothiazines, are the primary drugs used to treat depression.

High Potency ⟨ *Low sedation & Anticholin*
high EPS

Table 3.3. Neurologic Side Effects of Antipsychotic Drugs

Side Effect	Comments
Parkinsonian effects	Occur in 15% of patients within 3 months; associated with muscle rigidity, shuffling gait, stooped posture, drooling, tremor, mask-like facial expression
	More common in women and older patients
Tardive dyskinesia	Usually occurs after at least 6 months; abnormal movements of tongue, head, body, and face
	More common in women and older patients; may not be reversible
Neuroleptic malignant syndrome	High fever, sweating, increased pulse and blood pressure, muscular rigidity
	More common in men; mortality, 15–25%
Akathisia	Motor symptoms; subjective feeling of agitation
Dystonias	Slow, sustained muscular contractions or spasms
	Most common in young men
Seizures	Slowing and increased synchronization of the EEG; decreased seizure threshold

(handwritten across table header: High Potency)

—Generally, heterocyclics block reuptake of norepinephrine and serotonin at the synapse, increasing the availability of these neurotransmitters and causing various side effects (Table 3.4).
  —Heterocyclics also block muscarinic acetylcholine and histamine receptors.
—The heterocyclics often result in anticholinergic effects such as dry mouth, blurred vision, urinary retention, and constipation.
—Other adverse effects of the heterocyclics include precipitation of manic episodes, orthostatic hypotension, neurologic effects such as tremor, cardiac effects, allergic reactions, weight gain, and impotence.
  —**Nortriptyline** is the heterocyclic least likely to cause orthostatic hypotension.
  —The heterocyclic **amoxapine** is associated with parkinsonian-like symptoms, hyperprolactinemia with associated galactorrhea, anorgasmia, and ejaculatory disturbances and is most dangerous if an overdose is taken.
—Overdoses of heterocyclics may be fatal.

C. **Monoamine Oxidase Inhibitors**

Monoamine oxidase inhibitors are also used to treat depression.
—MAOIs may be particularly useful for eating disorders, pain syndrome, agoraphobia with panic attack, and post-traumatic stress syndromes.
—MAOIs inhibit monoamine oxidase in an irreversible reaction, thereby increasing norepinephrine and serotonin availability at the synaptic cleft.
—MAOIs are as safe as the heterocyclics if dietary precautions are followed, ie, avoiding foods rich in tyramine, such as beer and wine, broad beans, aged cheese, beef or chicken liver, orange pulp, and smoked or pickled meats or fish.
  —Ingestion of tyramine-rich foods can lead to a hypertensive crisis in patients taking MAOIs.
—**Side effects** of MAOIs are similar to those of the heterocyclics and include anticholinergic effects, sedation, and cardiac complications.

Table 3.4. Effects of Heterocyclic Antidepressants

Generic Name	Trade Name	Side Effects	
		Anticholinergic	Sedation
Imipramine	Tofranil	+ + +	+ +
Desipramine	Norpramin	+	+
Amitriptyline	Elavil	+ + +	+ + +
Nortriptyline	Pamelor	+ +	+ +
Amoxapine	Asendin	+ +	+ +
Doxepin	Sinequan, Adapin	+ + +	+ + +
Maprotiline	Ludiomil	+ +	+ +

Key: + = Slight effect; + + = moderate effect; + + + = strong effect.

D. Atypical Antidepressants

Atypical antidepressants include trazodone (Desyrel), alprazolam (Xanax), fluoxetine (Prozac), and lithium.

—**Trazodone** is less anticholinergic and has a greater margin of safety than other antidepressants and may be used as an adjunct with tricyclic antidepressants.

—**Alprazolam** is used mainly as an antianxiety agent.

—**Fluoxetine**, a new antidepressant, is equal in efficacy, has minimal anticholinergic and cardiovascular side effects, and may be unique in that it may cause weight loss when compared with tricyclic antidepressants.

—Although **lithium** in the form of lithium carbonate or citrate is used mainly to treat the mania of bipolar disorder, it also has antidepressant activity and may be used in combination with other antidepressants in patients with unipolar depression.

—The therapeutic mechanism of action of lithium is uncertain.

—Side effects of chronic lithium use include renal effects, cardiac conduction abnormalities, gastric distress, tremor, and mild cognitive impairment.

IV. Antianxiety Drugs

A. Classification

Antianxiety drugs include the benzodiazepines, such as diazepam (Valium) and chlordiazepoxide (Librium), carbamates, such as meprobamate (Miltown), and the barbiturates.

—Antianxiety drugs are also known as **anxiolytics** or **minor tranquilizers**.

B. Benzodiazepines

Benzodiazepines can be short-, intermediate-, or long-acting and may be used to treat disorders other than anxiety (Table 3.5).

—Benzodiazepines act by increasing the affinity of the GABA receptor for GABA.

—Sleepiness is the most common adverse effect of the benzodiazepines.

—Other side effects of benzodiazepines include blurred vision, weakness, nausea, and vomiting.

—Tolerance and dependence may occur with chronic use of the benzodiazepines.

—Benzodiazepines are also used as muscle relaxants and anticonvulsants.

C. Carbamates

The carbamates, including meprobamate, ethinamate, and carisoprodol, are drugs that have been used as anxiolytics in the past.

Table 3.5. Characteristics of the Benzodiazepines

Generic Name	TradeName	Duration of Action	Other Uses
Alprazolam	Xanax	Intermediate	Antidepressant, panic
Chlordiazepoxide	Librium	Long	—
Clonazepam	Klonopin	Intermediate	Seizures
Diazepam	Valium	Long	Muscle relaxant
Flurazepam	Dalmane	Long	Insomnia
Halazepam	Paxipam	Long	—
Lorazepam	Ativan	Intermediate	Akathisia
Oxazepam	Serax	Short	—
Prazepam	Centrax	Long	—
Triazolam	Halcion	Short	Insomnia

—The carbamates have more abuse potential and are more likely to induce dependence than the benzodiazepines.

—Use of carbamates is indicated only when benzodiazepines are not an option.

D. Barbiturates

Barbiturates are more likely to be abused and have a lower therapeutic index (the ratio of minimum toxic dose to maximum effective dose) than the benzodiazepines and thus are less frequently used as antianxiety agents.

—Overdoses of antianxiety drugs such as barbiturates may be lethal.

—Side effects of the barbiturates include sedation.

—Tolerance and dependence develop with chronic use.

V. Electroconvulsive Therapy

A. Uses of Electroconvulsive Therapy

Electroconvulsive therapy (ECT) is an effective, safe treatment for some psychiatric disturbances.

—ECT involves inducing a generalized seizure by passing an electric current across the brain.

—ECT may alter neurotransmitter function in a manner similar to that of antidepressant drug treatment.

—ECT is most commonly used to treat major depression.

    —Other possible indications for ECT are schizophrenia with acute, catatonic, or affective symptoms and acute mania.

—Some signs of improvement typically begin after a few ECT treatments.

—A maximum response to ECT is usually seen after 5 to 10 treatments.

B. Problems Associated with Electroconvulsive Therapy

—Problems associated with ECT (such as broken bones) have been virtually eliminated with the use of general anesthesia and muscle relaxants during treatment sessions.

    —Unilateral electrode placement has also reduced problems associated with ECT.

—The major side effect of ECT is memory loss.

    —In most patients, memory impairment after ECT is no longer present 6 months after treatment.

Review Test

THE PHARMACOLOGY OF BEHAVIOR AND ELECTROCONVULSIVE THERAPY

DIRECTIONS: For each of the questions or incomplete statements below choose the answer that is **most correct**.

3.1. Which of the following is the most sedating of the antipsychotic drugs?
A. Haloperidol
B. Chlorpromazine
C. Perphenazine
D. Thioridazine
E. Trifluoperazine

3.2. Which of the following heterocyclic antidepressants is least likely to cause sedation?
A. Desipramine
B. Imipramine
C. Amitriptyline
D. Doxepin
E. Amoxapine

3.3. The heterocyclic antidepressant least likely to cause orthostatic hypotension is
A. desipramine.
B. imipramine.
C. amitriptyline.
D. doxepin.
E. nortriptyline.

3.4. Parkinsonian-like symptoms are associated mainly with
A. desipramine.
B. imipramine.
C. amitriptyline.
D. amoxapine.
E. nortriptyline.

3.5. All of the following are true about the benzodiazepines EXCEPT:
A. The most common adverse affect is drowsiness.
B. Blurred vision may occur.
C. Tolerance may occur.
D. They are rarely addictive.
E. They may be used as muscle relaxants.

3.6. All of the following are true about antianxiety agents EXCEPT:
A. The carbamates are antianxiety drugs.
B. The carbamates have less abuse potential than the benzodiazepines.
C. Barbiturates are more likely to be abused than benzodiazepines.
D. Overdoses of antianxiety drugs may be lethal.
E. Antianxiety drugs may be used to treat disorders other than anxiety.

3.7. All of the following are true about electroconvulsive therapy EXCEPT:
A. The most common indication is schizophrenia.
B. It involves induction of a generalized seizure.
C. It is a relatively safe treatment.
D. It is an effective treatment for depression.
E. Maximum response is usually seen after 5 to 10 treatments.

3.8. All of the following are true about the antipsychotics EXCEPT:
A. A major group is the phenothiazines.
B. Their major use is in the treatment of schizophrenia.
C. They may be used to treat agitation associated with organic diseases.
D. A side effect is elevated liver enzymes.
E. They are also known as minor tranquilizers.

3.9. All of the following are true about the antidepressants EXCEPT:
A. They structurally resemble phenothiazines.
B. They frequently induce euphoria in nondepressed patients.
C. They often have anticholinergic effects.
D. The heterocyclics block reuptake of serotonin at the synapse.
E. The heterocyclics block reuptake of norepinephrine at the synapse.

3.10. All of the following are true about the MAO inhibitors EXCEPT:

A. The inhibition of MAO is reversible.
B. Tyramine-rich foods must be avoided.
C. They are used to treat depression.
D. Their side effects are similar to those of the heterocyclics.
E. A hypertensive crisis may occur if certain foods are eaten.

3.11. All of the following are side effects of treatment with lithium EXCEPT:

A. cardiac conduction abnormalities.
B. gastric distress.
C. tremor.
D. mild cognitive impairment.
E. food allergy.

3.12. Which of the following benzodiazepines has a long duration of action?

A. Alprazolam
B. Diazepam
C. Triazolam
D. Oxazepam
E. Clonazepam

3.13. All of the following are side effects of the antipsychotics EXCEPT:

A. orthostatic hypotension.
B. dry mouth.
C. amenorrhea.
D. weight loss.
E. breast enlargement.

DIRECTIONS: For each of the questions or incomplete statements below, **one** or **more** of the answers or completions given are correct. Choose answer:

A. if only **1, 2,** and **3** are correct.
B. if only **1** and **3** are correct.
C. if only **2** and **4** are correct.
D. if only **4** is correct.
E. if **all** are correct.

3.14. Which of the following is/are high potency antipsychotic(s)?

1. Chlorpromazine
2. Haloperidol
3. Thioridazine
4. Trifluoperazine

3.15. Which of the following is/are true about antipsychotics?

1. They are more effective against the negative than the positive symptoms of schizophrenia.
2. They act by blocking central dopamine receptors.
3. The low potency type are more likely to cause neurologic side effects than the high potency type.
4. Approximately 70% of patients improve significantly following treatment.

3.16. Which of the following is/are true about tardive dyskinesia?

1. It is more common in men than in women.
2. It includes abnormal movements of the tongue.
3. It usually occurs within 3 months of starting drug treatment.
4. It is a consequence of antipsychotic drug treatment.

3.17. Drug interactions occur between antipsychotics and

1. antihypertensives.
2. antacids.
3. antidepressants.
4. nicotine.

3.18. Drugs used to treat psychosis in patients unable to take antipsychotics include:

1. lithium.
2. benzodiazepines.
3. carbamazepine.
4. propranolol.

Answers and Explanations

THE PHARMACOLOGY OF BEHAVIOR AND ELECTROCONVULSIVE THERAPY

3.1. B. The most sedating of the antipsychotic drugs is chlorpromazine.

3.2. A. Of the heterocyclic antidepressants listed, desipramine is the least likely to cause sedation.

3.3. E. The heterocyclic antidepressant least likely to cause orthostatic hypotension is nortriptyline.

3.4. D. Treatment with amoxapine may result in parkinsonian-like symptoms.

3.5. D. Dependence may occur with chronic use of the benzodiazepines.

3.6. B. The carbamates have more abuse potential and are more likely to cause dependence than the benzodiazepines.

3.7. A. The most common indication for electroconvulsive therapy is major depression.

3.8. E. The antipsychotics are also called major tranquilizers and neuroleptics.

3.9. B. The antidepressants have little or no effect as euphoriants or stimulants in nondepressed people.

3.10. A. The inhibition of MAO is not reversible.

3.11. E. Cardiac conduction abnormalities, gastric distress, and tremor are side effects of lithium treatment.

3.12. B. Benzodiazepines with a long duration of action include diazepam, chlordiazepoxide, flurazepam, halazepam, and prazepam.

3.13. D. Orthostatic hypotension, dry mouth, amenorrhea, breast enlargement, and weight gain are side effects of the antipsychotics.

3.14. C. Haloperidol, perphenazine, and trifluoperazine are high potency antipsychotics.

3.15. C. Antipsychotics are more effective against the positive than the negative symptoms of schizophrenia. High potency antipsychotics are more likely to cause neurologic side effects than are low potency antipsychotics.

3.16. C. Tardive dyskinesia is more common in women than in men and usually occurs after 6 months of treatment with an antipsychotic.

3.17. E. All are correct.

3.18. E. All are correct.

4

The Beginning of Life, Growth, and Development

I. Pregnancy

A. Conception

Child development begins at conception and is influenced by factors that occur during pregnancy and childbirth as well as those that occur during postnatal life.

—Approximately 90% of children are wanted at conception.

B. Emotions

—A woman's sense of maternal competence is strongly influenced by her own mother as a role model.

—Mood swings are common during pregnancy.

—Concerns over loss of physical attractiveness increase as pregnancy progresses.

C. Sexuality

—Most obstetricians do not suggest cessation of coitus until about 4 weeks prior to expected delivery.

—During pregnancy, some women have an increased sex drive, which may be due to pelvic vasocongestion.

—In other women, sex drive may be reduced because of physical discomfort or the association of motherhood with decreased sexual activity.

—Coitus may be avoided during pregnancy as a result of fears of harming the fetus.

—Diminution in sexual activity can put a strain on the marriage.

—Husbands' extramarital affairs, if they occur, are most likely during the last 3 months of the wife's pregnancy.

II. Childbirth

A. Birth Rate and Infant Mortality

—The birth rate in the United States was 15.4 per 1000 population in 1987 (3,615,000 babies born).

—The infant mortality rate in the United States is currently about 12 per 1000 live births.

25

—The infant mortality rate in the United States decreased from 20 per 1000 in 1970 to 12 per 1000 in 1987.

—Low socioeconomic status correlates with high infant mortality.

—The mortality rate for white infants is lower than that for black infants.

—The rate for cesarean section increased from 5% in the 1960s to 20% in the 1980s.

B. Prematurity

Prematurity is defined as gestation of less than 34 weeks or birth weight under 2500 g.

—Prematurity occurs in about 7% of all births.

—Prematurity correlates with teenage pregnancy, low socioeconomic status, and poor maternal nutrition.

—Prematurity puts the child at risk for emotional and behavioral problems, mental retardation, and learning problems such as dyslexia.

C. The Mother-Infant Relationship

—Bonding between mother and infant may be adversely affected if the child is of low birth weight, is ill, is separated from the mother after delivery or if there are problems in the mother-father relationship.

—Women prepared for childbirth by training techniques such as Dick-Read's "natural childbirth" and Lamaze's "psychoprophylactic childbirth" have shorter labors and fewer medical complications, need less medication, and have better immediate relations with their infants.

D. Postpartum Reactions

One in every 2 to 3 women may develop a depressed mood known as **baby blues** or **postpartum blues** following the birth of a child.

—Postpartum blues result from changes in hormone levels, the stress of childbirth, awareness of increased responsibility, disappointment over the baby's appearance, and fatigue.

—Five to 10% of women suffer a more severe major depression after childbirth.

  —About 0.1 to 0.2 % of these severely depressed women will develop a postpartum psychosis characterized by hallucinations or delusions and severe anxiety.

—Social factors related to long-lasting postpartum reactions include lack of experience in child care and lack of social support from husband and relatives.

III. Infancy: Birth to 15 Months

A. Attachment Between Mother and Infant

The principal psychological task of infancy is the formation of an intimate attachment to the mother or primary caregiver.

1. *Separation of Mother and Infant*

   —If separated from the mother or primary caregiver between 6 and 12 months of age, the child first protests loudly at the loss.

—With continued absence of the mother, the infant is at risk for **anaclitic depression**, in which the infant becomes withdrawn and unresponsive.

2. *Studies of Attachment*

Three researchers known for their studies of attachment in infants are Harlow, Bowlby, and Spitz.

—**Harry Harlow** showed that infant monkeys reared by surrogate artificial "mothers" (ie, in relative isolation) do not develop normal mating, maternal, and social behavior as adults.

—Harlow found that males may be more affected than females by such isolation.

—If young monkeys are raised in isolation for under 6 months, normal young monkeys can rehabilitate the isolated monkeys by playing gently with them.

—If young monkeys are isolated for over 6 months, no recovery is possible.

—**John Bowlby** demonstrated that maintenance of a continuous relationship, including physical contact between mother and infant, is crucial to the child's development.

—**Rene Spitz** documented that children without proper mothering (eg, those in institutions) show severe developmental retardation, poor health, and higher death rates in spite of adequate physical care.

B. Characteristics of the Infant

—At birth, the infant possesses simple reflexes such as the startle reflex, the palmar grasp reflex, the Babinski reflex, and the rooting reflex.

—Although there is an innate reflexive smile present at birth, the **social smile** that develops at 5 to 8 weeks of age is one of the first markers of the infant's responsiveness and attachment to another individual.

—**Stranger anxiety** is the infant's tendency to cry and cling to the mother when a stranger approaches.

—In normal infants, stranger anxiety develops at 7 to 9 months of age and signals the fact that the infant has developed a specific attachment to the mother and can distinguish her from a stranger.

—Infants exposed to multiple caregivers are less likely to show stranger anxiety than those exposed to only one caregiver.

C. Individual Differences Between Infants

It is likely that there are endogenous differences in infants in temperament and reactivity to stimuli.

—Differences between infants have been described in activity level, cyclic behavior patterns such as sleeping, approach or withdrawal to new stimuli, adaptability, intensity of reaction, threshold of responsiveness, mood, distractibility, and attention span.

—In many people, these differences are quite stable for at least the first 25 years of life.

D. Developmental Theorists: Overview

A number of individuals—including Freud, Erikson, Piaget, and Mahler—studied children and adopted ways of categorizing milestones of growth and development (Table 4.1).

Table 4.1. Major Developmental Theorists: Chronological Age and Developmental Stage

Age (years)	Stage			Associated Characteristics
	Freud	Erikson	Piaget	
0–1	Oral	Basic trust vs. mistrust	Sensorimotor (0–2 years)	Object permanence
1–3	Anal	Autonomy vs. shame and doubt	Preoperational (2–7 years)	Separation anxiety
3–5	Phallic-oedipal	Initiative vs. guilt	Preoperational (2–7 years)	Imaginary companions
6–11	Latency	Industry vs. inferiority	Concrete operations (7–11 years)	Logical thought
11–20	Genital	Identity vs. role diffusion	Formal operations	Abstract thought

E. Sigmund Freud and Erik Erikson

—According to Freud, during the first year of life, or the **oral phase**, the major site of gratification for the child is the mouth.

—Erik Erikson noted that children establish a sense of **basic trust versus** a sense of **mistrust** by the end of the first year.

  —In order to establish trust, a child must have the expectation that its basic needs will be taken care of and that it can rely on its caretakers to respond to its signals in a fairly consistent manner.

F. Margaret Mahler

—Margaret Mahler described early infant development as the **normal autistic phase**.

  —In this stage, from birth to 1 month of age, the infant has little interaction with the environment.

—Mahler's normal autistic phase is followed by the **symbiotic stage**.

  —The infant's sense of oneness with the mother or caregiver lasts from about 1 to 4 or 5 months of age.

—Following the symbiotic phase, Mahler described the stage of **separation-individuation**.

  —The first phase of separation-individuation is the **period of differentiation** at 5 to 9 months when the mother is first perceived as a separate entity.

  —The second phase is the **practicing phase**, which occurs at 10 to 16 months.

    —In the practicing phase, the child moves away from the mother but returns from time to time.

G. Jean Piaget

—Piaget described birth to 2 years as the **sensorimotor stage**.

  —In this phase, mastery of the child's environment comes through **assimilation**—the ability to understand new stimuli in the environment—and **accommodation**—the ability to alter one's behavior when a new stimulus is presented.

—The capacity to maintain internal representations without currently seeing the object is, according to Piaget, **object permanence**.

—Object permanence develops at 18 months to 2 years of age.

IV. The Toddler Years: 15 Months to 2½ Years

A. Attachment Between Mother and Toddler

The major theme of the second year of life is to separate from the mother or primary caregiver.

—The child develops physical and emotional distance from the mother and begins to behave like a separate person by about 18 months of age; however, the process of separation-individuation is not complete until about age 3.

—Although the toddler is separate from the mother, the child comes back to the mother for help, comfort, and reassurance.

—Mahler called the period of moving away and returning for comfort at 16 to 24 months **rapprochement**.

—Separation anxiety peaks at 18 months.

B. Characteristics of the Toddler

The second year of life is characterized by increasing motor and intellectual development.

—With this increasing control over his or her actions at about 2 years of age, "the terrible twos," the child becomes increasingly autonomous; the favorite word is "no."

—Toilet training occurs at around 2 years of age and can be a source of parent-child conflict.

—Positive reinforcement and modeling is more effective than punishment in achieving toilet training.

—Core gender identity, an individual's sense of being male or female, is established between 18 and 30 months of age.

C. Developmental Theorists and the Toddler

—This age is Erikson's stage of **autonomy vs. shame and doubt**: the child resolves its internal drive for independence with parental control.

—The term autonomy is used when the child has command of his or her impulses and has achieved separateness from the mother.

—If autonomy is not achieved because of excessive parental control, the child will feel that the outside world looks down on him or her.

—Freud's **anal stage** of development occurs during the toddler years.

V. The Preschool Child: 2½ to 6 Years

A. Physical and Psychological Characteristics of the Preschool Child

—During the preschool years there is marked physical growth.

—The child reaches half of adult height between 2 and 3 years of age.

—The child's vocabulary increases rapidly.

—Relationships to others change markedly.

—The birth of a sibling is likely to occur in the preschool years.

—Although the child may learn cooperation and sharing with a new sibling, sibling rivalry may also occur.

B. Fears in the Preschool Child

—The child can distinguish fantasy from reality, although the line between them may still not be drawn sharply.

—Sleep disturbances such as nightmares are common at this age.
  —Night terrors are a form of nightmare in which the child is terrified by a dream but may not fully wake up and will not recall the episode.
  —When a night terror occurs, although the child's eyes may be open he or she may not recognize familiar people.
—The child may also develop transient phobias such as fears of robbers or monsters.
—Preschool children may become overly concerned about illness and may point out every injury.

C. Sexuality and the Preschool Child

Children between 2½ to 6 years are very aware of the genitalia and of physical sex differences.
—Children act out sexual fantasies about sex differences in games of "doctor."
—Freud called this period of development the **phallic** or **oedipal stage**.
—The genitals become a focus of pleasure.
—The **oedipal conflict** arises and involves feelings of intense rivalry with the same-sex parent and love for the parent of the opposite sex.
—This stage is resolved when the child begins to identify with the same-sex parent.

D. Formation of the Conscience

By the end of the preschool years, the child's **conscience** (Freud called this the **superego**) begins to be formed.
—With the development of the conscience, the child learns how he or she is allowed to behave.
—The child also learns that aggressive impulses can be used in acceptable ways such as playing competitive games.

1. *Erikson*

   Erikson termed this period the stage of **initiative vs. guilt**; the child begins to take risks, although there may be fear of punishment and a sense of guilt.
   —If the stage of initiative is resolved successfully, the child is more likely to become a dependable, self-disciplined, and responsible adult.

2. *Piaget*

   Piaget considered this stage to be the beginning of the **preoperational phase** (ages 2 to 7 years), the period when the child begins to think in symbolic terms.

E. Play in the Preschooler

—Role play is important to children of this age.
—Rather than playing with each other, children of this age play alongside each other in parallel play.
—Among children 3 to 10 years old, almost half have imaginary companions.
  —Imaginary playmates help to relieve loneliness and reduce anxiety.

F. Illness and Death in Childhood

The developmental stage is closely associated with the child's reaction to illness.

—During the **toddler years**, hospitalized children fear separation from the parent more than they fear bodily harm, death, or pain.

—During the **preschool years**, the phallic stage, the child becomes more fearful of bodily harm, eg, castration.

   —The preschool age child may not understand fully the meaning of death and may expect that a dead friend or relative will come back to life.

—**School-age children** are often aware when they have a life-threatening illness.

VI.   Latency: 7 Years to Puberty

A. Physical and Psychological Characteristics

—The child develops increased motor coordination and the ability to perform complex motor tasks and activities.

—Formation of the conscience is completed.

—The child acquires the capacity for logical thought.

   —This corresponds with Piaget's **stage of concrete operations.**

—The demands for success in school are important to further personality development.

—The child acquires a sense whether he or she is competent or not competent in interactions with the world.

   —This corresponds with Erikson's **stage of industry vs. inferiority.**

B. The Family and the Outside World

—The child makes new identifications with teachers and group leaders.

—Family becomes less important and the outside world, including peers, becomes more important.

C. Sexuality in Latency-age Children

—Psychosexual issues are not primary during latency.

—The child identifies with the same-sex parent and no longer wants the opposite-sex parent as a love object.

—School-age children prefer to play with children of the same sex.

VII.   Adolescence: 11 to 20 Years

A. Physical Characteristics

Adolescence is distinguished biologically by **puberty**, a process of change marked by development of secondary sex characteristics and acceleration in skeletal growth.

B. Psychological and Social Characteristics

Psychologically, adolescence is identified by cognitive growth and formation of the personality; socially, adolescence is a time of preparation for entering the adult world and accepting adult responsibilities.

—Adolescence is Erikson's stage of **identity consolidation vs. role confusion**, in which a sense of an independent self is developed.

—Strong sexual impulses and attempts at independence occur.

C. Phases of Adolescence

The three phases of adolescence are early (11 to 14 years), middle (14 to 17 years), and late (17 to 20 years).

1. *Early Adolescence (11-14)*
   —Dramatic endocrine changes occur in early adolescence.
     —Girls mature at about 12 years of age, 2 years before boys.
   —Early adolescents are very sensitive to the opinions of peers.
   —Any deviation from expected patterns of development such as acne, obesity, or late breast development may lead to psychological problems.
   —Sex drives are vented by masturbation and physical activity.

2. *Middle Adolescence (14-17)*
   During middle adolescence, male-female roles, body image, and popularity often preoccupy the adolescent.
   —At this stage, boys equal and exceed girls in height and weight.
   —Most girls have reached menarche (begun to menstruate).
   —Heterosexual crushes are common.
   —Transient homosexual experiences may occur.

3. *Late Adolescence (17-20)*
   In most individuals, a well-defined moral and ethical sense and control of one's behavior develop by late adolescence.
   —According to Piaget, by late adolescence the child has developed the ability for abstract reasoning called the stage of **formal operations**.
     —Not all individuals achieve the potential for formal operational thought.
     —Most adults function between Piaget's stages of **concrete operations** *(Logical)* and **formal operations**. *(abstract)*
   —Concern with humanitarian issues, ethics, and world issues occurs in late adolescence.
   —Normally, an identity crisis develops at the end of adolescence; if this stage is not negotiated successfully, the adolescent does not have a solid identity and suffers from **identity diffusion** or **role confusion**.
     —With role confusion, an individual does not have a sense of self and does not know one's place in the world.
     —Behavioral abnormalities such as criminality may occur.
     —Another manifestation of role confusion includes joining cults.

VIII. Teenage Pregnancy

A. Demographics

Teenage pregnancy is a severe social problem; in the United States, teenagers give birth to about 600,000 babies and have 300,000 abortions per year.
—The average age for first sexual intercourse in the United States is 16 years.
—Eighty percent of males and 70% of females have had coitus by age 19.
—Nearly 50% of unmarried mothers are teenagers.

B. Contributing Factors

—Teenagers are erratic in the use of contraceptives.
—Characteristics of teenagers who become pregnant include a divorced home, depression, low academic achievement and goals, and poor future planning.
—Pregnant teenagers are at high risk for obstetric complications.

Table 4.2. Characteristics of Physical and Sexual Child Abuse

	Physical Abuse	Sexual Abuse
Incidence per year	1,000,000: 2000–4000 deaths	125,000: 5000 of incest
Abuser	Usually female	Usually male, eg, father, stepfather, other relatives, and friends; less commonly strangers
Age of child:	32% under age 5 years	Peak age is 9–12 years
	27% aged 5–9 years	25% under age 8 years
	27% aged 10–14 years	
	14% aged 15–18 years	
High risk factors:	Poverty	Single-parent home
	Social isolation	Marital conflict
	Parents abused as children	Alcoholism
	Prematurity, low birth weight	
	Hyperactivity	

IX. Child Abuse

A. Incidence

Child abuse includes frank physical and sexual abuse as well as emotional neglect such as harsh rejection and severe deprivation of parental love (Table 4.2).

—Reported child abuse is increasing in the United States.

　—Nationwide, at least 1 million children are abused yearly, and 2000 to 4000 deaths result from child abuse and neglect.

—When child neglect or abuse is suspected, the physician should intervene, report the case to the appropriate agency, admit the child to the hospital when necessary, confer with members of the child abuse committee, and arrange for follow-up by social service agencies.

B. Characteristics of the Abused Child

—Prematurity and low birth weight are risk factors for abuse and neglect.

—Parents perceive the children they abuse as slow, different, bad, or difficult to discipline.

—Hyperactive children are particularly likely to be abused by parents.

C. Characteristics of the Child Abuser

—More women than men batter young children.

—Abuse is more common in poor, socially isolated families.

—Ninety percent of abusive parents were themselves abused as children.

D. Sexual Abuse of Children

Sexual abuse of children, both male and female, has become increasingly widespread; more than 125,000 cases of sexual abuse are reported per year.

—Fifty percent of sexual abuse cases are committed by family members, usually males.

—Factors associated with sexual abuse include a passive or sick mother, an alcohol abusing father, and crowded living conditions.

—Sexual abuse predisposes the child to later anxiety, phobias, and depression and inability to deal with his or her own and others' aggression.

Review Test

THE BEGINNING OF LIFE, GROWTH, AND DEVELOPMENT

DIRECTIONS: For each of the questions or incomplete statements below, choose the answer that is **most correct**.

4.1. Which of the following develops first in the infant?

A. Stranger anxiety
B. The social smile
C. Rapprochement
D. Core gender identity
E. Phobias

4.2. The birth rate in the United States in 1987 was about

A. 15 per 100 population.
B. 15 per 1000 population.
C. 2.5 per 1000 population.
D. 25 per 1000 population.
E. 35 per 1000 population.

4.3. The infant mortality rate in 1987 in the United States was about

A. 1 per 1000 live births.
B. 5 per 1000 live births.
C. 12 per 1000 live births.
D. 21 per 1000 live births.
E. 40 per 1000 live births.

4.4. All of the following are likely to adversely affect bonding between mother and child EXCEPT:

A. separation of mother and child after delivery.
B. problems in the mother-father relationship.
C. a pregnancy that is longer than the expected term.
D. low birth weight.
E. illness in the child.

4.5. The principal psychological task of infancy is

A. the formation of an intimate attachment to the mother.
B. the development of speech.
C. the development of stranger anxiety.
D. the development of a conscience.
E. the ability for logical thought.

4.6. All of the following are true about latency EXCEPT:

A. It is characterized by completion of the formation of a conscience.
B. The child acquires the capacity for logical thought.
C. Girls begin to identify with their mothers.
D. The family becomes more important to the child.
E. Children play with others of the same sex.

4.7. All of the following are true about adolescence EXCEPT:

A. The personality is formed.
B. Its start is marked by puberty.
C. Crushes are common.
D. Joining cults frequently is a manifestation of role confusion.
E. Identity crises frequently develop at its start.

4.8. The number of deaths due to child abuse or neglect in the United States each year is approximately

A. 250.
B. 500.
C. 1000.
D. 2000.
E. 4000.

4.9. Which of the following is true about pregnancy?

A. A woman's sense of maternal competence is strongly related to the role model provided by her own mother.
B. Extramarital affairs are most likely to occur in the first third of pregnancy.
C. Obstetricians frequently prohibit coitus during the last two-thirds of pregnancy.
D. Sixty to 70% of children are not wanted at conception.
E. Mood swings rarely occur during a normal pregnancy.

4.10. All of the following are true about prepared childbirth EXCEPT:

A. There are fewer medical complications.
B. Labors are longer.
C. Mothers have better immediate relations with their infants.
D. Less medication is needed during childbirth.
E. The "prophylactic childbirth" technique was developed by Lamaze.

4.11. In the United States, high infant mortality correlates with

A. living in the Northwestern states.
B. Asian race.
C. black race.
D. geographic mobility.
E. all of the above.

4.12. Prematurity puts a child at risk for

A. mental retardation.
B. emotional problems.
C. dyslexia.
D. child abuse.
E. all of the above.

4.13. All of the following are involved in the development of the "baby blues" EXCEPT:

A. changes in hormone levels.
B. breast feeding.
C. awareness of increased responsibility.
D. stress of childbirth.
E. fatigue.

4.14. Which of the following is true about postpartum reactions?

A. Postpartum blues occur in about 10% of women.
B. Major depression occurs in about 25% of women after childbirth.
C. Postpartum psychosis occurs in about 8% of women.
D. Lack of social support is common in severe postpartum reactions.
E. Experience in child care is not related to the occurrence of postpartum reactions.

4.15. Which of the following is/are characteristic of the infant who is separated from the mother?

A. At first, the infant protests loudly at the loss.
B. After a time the infant becomes depressed and unresponsive.
C. The incidence of physical illness is higher in infants in institutions.
D. Anaclitic depression may occur.
E. All of the above.

4.16. Harry Harlow's studies of development in infant monkeys showed that all of the following are true about infant monkeys reared by surrogate artificial mothers EXCEPT:

A. The negative effects are long-lasting.
B. They do not develop normal mating behavior as adults.
C. They do not develop normal maternal behavior as adults.
D. They do not develop normal social behavior as adults.
E. They are more likely to be adversely affected if they are female.

4.17. All of the following are true about stranger anxiety EXCEPT:

A. Infants tend to cry and cling to the mother when a stranger approaches.
B. It develops at 3 to 4 months of age.
C. It signals that the child can distinguish mother from a stranger.
D. It is more likely to occur in infants exposed to multiple caregivers.
E. It occurs in normal infants.

4.18. All of the following are true about infant mortality EXCEPT:

A. The mortality rate for white infants is lower than that for black infants.
B. Low socioeconomic status is associated with high infant mortality.
C. The overall infant mortality rate in the United States is about 12 per 1000 live births.
D. With respect to other countries, the infant mortality rate in the United States has increased since 1970.
E. The birth rate in the late 1980s was about 12 per 1000.

4.19. All of the following are true about the toddler years EXCEPT:

A. This is Erikson's stage of industry versus inferiority.
B. They are characterized by increasing motor development.
C. Toilet training usually takes place.
D. Core gender identity is established.
E. The favorite word is "no."

4.20. All of the following are true about the preschool child EXCEPT:

A. Fantasy can usually be distinguished from reality.
B. Nightmares are common.
C. The child begins to think abstractly.
D. Imaginary companions are characteristic.
E. The child becomes aware of physical sex differences.

4.21. During the preschool years

A. There is primary interest in the genitals.
B. The oedipal conflict occurs.
C. The conscience begins to be formed.
D. The child engages in role playing.
E. All of the above.

4.22. Which of the following is true about teenage sexuality in the United States?

A. The average age of first sexual intercourse is 19 years.
B. Teenagers are generally responsible in the use of contraceptives.
C. Approximately 15 percent of unmarried mothers are teenagers.
D. Pregnant teenagers are at high risk for obstetric complications.
E. Teenagers give birth to about 50,000 babies per year.

4.23. All of the following are characteristic of teenagers who become pregnant EXCEPT:

A. depression.
B. low academic goals.
C. living in a rural area.
D. a divorced home.
E. poor planning for the future.

4.24. All of the following are true about sexual abuse of children EXCEPT:

A. The abuser is usually male.
B. The peak age of the sexually abused child is 9 to 12 years.
C. There are approximately 5000 cases of incest reported per year.
D. The sexual abuser is usually a stranger to the child.
E. Alcohol abuse by the sexual abuser is common.

4.25. Which of the following is/are high risk factors in the physical abuse of children?

A. Parents abused as children
B. Social isolation
C. Poverty
D. Prematurity
E. All of the above

4.26. Which of the following is/are consequences in the adult of childhood sexual abuse?

A. Depression
B. Anxiety
C. Phobias
D. Inability to deal with the aggression of others
E. All of the above

DIRECTIONS: For each of the numbered phrases below, choose the developmental theorist with which it is most closely associated. Answers may be used once, more than once, or not at all.

A. Freud
B. Erikson
C. Piaget
D. Mahler

4.27. Separation/individuation

4.28. Trust versus mistrust

4.29. Assimilation and accommodation

4.30. Stage of symbiotic development

4.31. Oral phase

4.32. Period of differentiation

4.33. Practicing phase

4.34. Sensorimotor stage

4.35. Normal autistic phase

4.36. Object permanence

DIRECTIONS: For each of the questions or incomplete statements below, **one** or **more** of the answers or completions given are correct. Choose answer:

A. if only **1, 2,** and **3** are correct.
B. if only **1** and **3** are correct.
C. if only **2** and **4** are correct.
D. if only **4** is correct.
E. if **all** are correct.

4.37. Rene Spitz documented that children in institutions
1. show severe developmental retardation.
2. have generally good health.
3. have high death rates.
4. receive inadequate physical care.

4.38. Reflexes that the infant possesses at birth include:
1. the startle reflex.
2. the palmar grasp reflex.
3. the rooting reflex.
4. the Babinski reflex.

4.39. There are inborn differences in infants in
1. mood.
2. autonomic reactivity.
3. activity level.
4. sleeping patterns.

4.40. Which of the following is/are appropriate intervention(s) by the physician in suspected cases of child abuse?
1. Report the case to an appropriate agency.
2. Confer with members of the child abuse committee at the hospital.
3. Admit the child to the hospital.
4. Arrange for social services follow-up.

4.41. Which of the following is/are true about illness in childhood?
1. Toddlers frequently fear separation from parents more than they fear bodily harm.
2. Preschool age children usually understand the meaning of death.
3. Preschool age children frequently believe that the dead person will come back to life.
4. Older children are rarely aware that they have a life-threatening illness.

Answers and Explanations

THE BEGINNING OF LIFE, GROWTH, AND DEVELOPMENT

4.1. B. The social smile is the first of these to appear in the infant.

4.2. B. The birth rate in the United States in 1987 was about 15 per 1000 population.

4.3. C. In 1987, infant mortality in the United States was about 12 per 1000 live births.

4.4. C. The initial bonding between mother and child can be adversely affected by illness of the child, low birth weight, separation of mother and child, and problems in the mother and father relationship. There is no evidence that a pregnancy that is longer than term adversely affects bonding.

4.5. A. The principal psychological task of infancy is the formation of an intimate attachment to the mother.

4.6. D. During latency, peers become more important to the child and the family becomes less important.

4.7. E. Identity crises frequently develop during late—not early—adolescence.

4.8. E. The number of deaths due to child abuse or neglect in the United States each year is approximately 4000.

4.9. A. The role model provided by a woman's own mother strongly influences her sense of maternal competence.

4.10. B. Labors are shorter, there are fewer medical complications, mothers have better immediate relations with their infants, and less medication is needed during prepared childbirth.

4.11. C. The mortality rate for white infants is lower than that for black infants.

4.12. E. Prematurity puts a child at risk for a variety of developmental problems as well as for child abuse.

4.13. B. Changes in hormone levels, fatigue, stress of childbirth, and awareness of increased responsibility contribute to the development of the baby blues.

4.14. D. Although postpartum blues may occur in two of every three women, postpartum psychosis is rare and occurs in less than 1% of women after childbirth. Lack of social support is common in severe postpartum reactions.

4.15. E. All are correct.

4.16. E. Infant monkeys reared by surrogate artificial mothers have many social problems and are more likely to be adversely affected if they are male.

4.17. B. Stranger anxiety develops in normal infants at 7 to 9 months of age and is seen less frequently in children exposed to multiple caregivers.

4.18. D. With respect to other countries, the infant mortality rate in the United States has decreased since 1970.

4.19. A. The toddler years are Erikson's stage of autonomy vs. shame and doubt.

4.20. C. In the preschool child, fantasy can be distinguished from reality although the line between them may not be sharply drawn. Generally, the child does not begin to think abstractly until the end of latency or early adolescence.

4.21. E. All are correct.

4.22. D. The average age of first sexual intercourse in the United States is 16 years. In general, teenagers are irresponsible in the use of contraceptives and nearly 50% of unmarried mothers are teenagers. Teenagers give birth to about 600,000 babies per year.

4.23. C. Teenagers who become pregnant frequently are from divorced homes, are depressed, show poor future planning, and have low academic goals for themselves.

4.24. D. The peak age of the sexually abused child is 9 to 12 years. The sexual abuser, usually a male, is likely to abuse alcohol and is frequently known to the child.

4.25. E. All are correct.

4.26. E. All are correct.

4.27. D. The stage of separation/individuation, as described by Margaret Mahler, occurs during infancy and follows the symbiotic phase.

4.28. B. Erik Erikson noted that children establish a sense of trust or mistrust by the end of the first year of life.

4.29. C. During Piaget's sensorimotor stage, mastery of the child's environment is achieved through assimilation and accommodation.

4.30. D. Mahler's symbiotic stage occurs from 1 to 4 or 5 months of age.

4.31. A. According to Freud, the oral phase occurs during the first year of life.

4.32. D. According to Mahler, the first phase of separation/individuation is the period of differentiation.

4.33. D. Also according to Mahler, the second phase of separation/individuation is the practicing phase.

4.34. C. Piaget described birth to 2 years of age as the sensorimotor stage.

4.35. D. Mahler described 0 to 1 months of age as the normal autistic phase.

4.36. C. According to Piaget, object permanence develops at 18 months to 2 years of age.

4.37. B. Despite receiving adequate physical care, children in institutions are frequently physically ill and show severe developmental mental retardation.

4.38. E. All are correct.

4.39. E. All are correct.

4.40. E. All are correct.

4.41. B. Preschool children cannot usually comprehend the meaning of death and may believe that the dead person will come back to life. Older children frequently are aware when they have a life-threatening illness.

5

Adulthood, Aging, and Death

I. Early Adulthood: 20 to 40 Years

The three major phases of adulthood are **early, middle,** and **late (old age).**

A. Characteristics

In early adulthood, one's role in society is defined, biological development peaks, and the independent self develops.

—At about age 30, there is a period of reappraisal of one's life.

—According to **Daniel Levinson**, this is an age of transition.

B. Responsibilities and Relationships

—Responsibilities of early adulthood include development of an intimate relationship with another individual.

—According to Erikson, if the individual does not develop the ability to have an intimate relationship he or she suffers emotional isolation.

—By age 30, most people are married and have children.

—Having a child is costly; the cost of raising a child for a middle class family is about $100,000.

—During their mid 30s, many women alter their lives by going back to work or school or resuming their careers.

II. Middle Adulthood: 40 to 65 Years

A. Characteristics

Erikson noted that the individual either maintains a continued sense of productivity or develops a sense of emptiness and stagnation.

—People of this age generally are the members of society who possess power and authority.

—For many people, middle adulthood is a time of great satisfaction.

B. Midlife Crisis

Seventy to 80% of men in their middle 40s or early 50s show a moderate to severe change in work or marital relationships.

—These changes—which include changing jobs, infidelity, severe depression, increased use of alcohol or drugs, or a change in lifestyle—are termed the **midlife crisis**.

—Although they have not been as well studied, women may also experience a midlife crisis.

39

—The midlife crisis is associated with an awareness of one's own aging and death.

—Severe or unexpected changes in one's life at this time such as the death of a spouse, job loss, or serious illness predispose an individual toward a midlife crisis.

—Characteristics of men or women likely to have a midlife crisis include problems between their own parents, anxiety, impulsiveness, and withdrawal of the same-sex parent during the individual's adolescence.

—According to Daniel Levinson, age 50 to 55 is another period of transition; a crisis may occur if the individual is unable to change a life pattern that he or she finds unendurable.

C. Climacterium and Menopause

The **climacterium** is the diminution in physiologic function that occurs during midlife in men and women.

—For men, the climacterium is mainly psychological rather than physical, although decreases in muscle strength, endurance, and sexual performance occur.

—For women, **menopause** is the climacterium and occurs during the late 40s or early 50s.

—Menopause is characterized by the changes in and ultimate cessation of menstruation as a result of a lack of ovarian estrogen production.

—Contrary to popular belief, menopause most often occurs gradually.

—Although some women experience severe psychological symptoms such as anxiety and depression, most go through menopause with relatively few problems.

—A common problem of menopause is vasomotor instability or hot flashes, which may continue over a number of years.

III. Late Adulthood: 65 Years and Older

A. The Aging Population

Eighty percent of people reach 60 years of age in the United States.

—In 1984, 11.5% of the US population was over 65; by 2020, this will be at least 20%.

—Gerontology—the study of aging—and geriatrics—the care of aging people—have become important new disciplines.

—The life expectancy for women is 8 years longer than for men.

—Because men are often older at marriage, most women can expect 10 years of widowhood.

B. Physical and Psychological Characteristics of Aging

—In late adulthood, strength and physical health gradually decline.

—This gradual decline shows great individual variability.

—The individual recognizes that all life options are no longer open.

—The loss of friends and family in late adulthood gives the realization of one's finite life span.

—Although intelligence stays approximately the same, learning in the elderly may be impaired as a result of the effects of physical disease.

—Erikson said of late adulthood that there is either a sense of ego integrity and satisfaction and pride in one's past accomplishment or a sense of despair or worthlessness.

—Many elderly people have achieved ego integrity in old age.

C. Depression in Aging People

Psychopathology in aging people includes depression and Alzheimer's disease.

 —Depression is the most common psychiatric disorder in the elderly.

—Depression is not a natural condition of aging.

—Factors associated with depression in the elderly are loss of spouse, family members, and friends, loss of prestige, and loss of health.

—Suicide is more common in the elderly (80 per 100,000) than in the general population.

—Depression in the elderly can be treated successfully with psychotherapy, pharmacotherapy, and ECT.

D. Alzheimer's Disease

Dementia of the Alzheimer's type or Alzheimer's disease causes severe memory loss, personality changes, and cognitive deficits and results in overall apathy, cessation of normal functioning, and death.

—Alzheimer's disease may mimic depression.

—Unlike depression, Alzheimer's disease cannot be cured with psychotherapy and pharmacotherapy.

E. Other Problems Associated with Aging

—Physical illnesses characteristic of aging include hypertension, heart disease, and kidney changes.

—Changes in sleep patterns that occur in old age include decreased rapid REM eye movement and slow wave sleep (stages 3 and 4) and increased sleep latency.

—Psychoactive and other drugs have different effects in the elderly than they do in younger people.

—Anxiety related to insecurity and anxiety-producing situations can arise easily in the elderly.

F. Longevity

—Longevity has been correlated with work involving physical activity, sleeping between 6 and 9 hours per night, more years of schooling, and living in the country rather than the city.

—Longevity is also associated with being married, having strong social support systems, having a calm personality, and remaining occupationally active.

IV. Divorce

A. Occurrence

A major problem of adulthood is **divorce.**

—During 1986, there were at least 1.1 million divorces.

—The divorce rate has been rising; between 1985 and 1986, the divorce rate increased 3%.

—Approximately 33% of first marriages and 40% of second marriages end in divorce.

—In couples married for 15 to 19 years, the divorce rate has doubled since 1960.

—Factors associated with divorce include marriage at an early age and divorce in the family.

—Five of 6 divorced men and 3 of 4 divorced women remarry within 3 years.

B. Single-parent Families

Approximately 30 million families have children under 18 years of age.

—Twenty percent of these are single-parent families.

—Most single-parent families are headed by women.

—Almost 50% of black families are single-parent households headed by women.

C. Child Custody

Following divorce, types of child custody include joint, split, and sole custody.

—In joint residential custody, the child spends substantial time with both parents.

—Since 1978, more than 30 states have established joint custody as an option or a preference.

—In split custody, each parent has custody of one or more of the children.

—In sole custody, the child lives with one parent while the other has visitation rights.

—Fathers are increasingly being granted joint custody or sole custody.

D. Children in Single-parent Families

—Characteristics of children in single-parent families include failure in school and emotional problems such as depression.

—Children of divorce often suffer long-term effects such as a greater likelihood of divorce themselves.

—Children who continue to have regular contact with their fathers fare better after divorce than those who do not.

V. Death and Dying

A. Stages of Dying

According to **Elizabeth Kübler-Ross**, the process of dying occurs over time and involves five stages—**denial, anger, bargaining, depression, and acceptance.**

—*Denial stage*: the patient refuses to believe that he or she is dying.

—*Anger stage*: the patient may become angry at the physician and hospital staff.

—*Bargaining stage*: the patient may try to strike a bargain with God, eg, "I promise to go to church every day if only I can get rid of this disease."

—*Depression stage*: the patient becomes preoccupied with death and may be emotionally detached.

—*Acceptance stage*: the patient is calm and accepting of his or her fate.

—Stages similar to those of dying occur following other losses such as loss of a body part.

—Stages may be present simultaneously or may appear in any order.

B. **Characteristics of Grief**
—Initially, grief is characterized by shock.
—Physical expressions of grief include crying, weakness, decreased appetite, weight loss, difficulty concentrating, and sleep disturbances.
—In normal grief or bereavement, a sense of the deceased person's physical presence may be intense enough to be considered an illusion or hallucination.
—Normal grief generally subsides after 1 to 2 years, although some signs and symptoms may persist for much longer.
—Although similar in symptoms such as loss of appetite, diminished sexual interest, and withdrawal from normal activities, there are differences between normal grief and depression.
  —In grief, guilt and concern about not having done enough for the dead person occur; in depression, feelings of worthlessness and evilness predominate.
  —Suicide is seen more often in depressed people than in grieving persons.
—The mortality rate is high for close relatives, especially widowed men, in the first year of bereavement.

C. **The Physician and Death**
Thanatology is the study of death, dying, grief, bereavement, and mourning.
—Although the physician is responsible for classifying the cause of death, the major duty of the physician is to provide continuing support to the dying patient and the patient's family.
—Physicians often feel a sense of failure at not conquering death, which he or she perceives as the enemy.
—Emotional feelings about the patient can increase the emotional demands on the doctor.
  —Physicians often become emotionally detached in order to deal with the death of patients.
—There is a trend in hospitals to make patient and family as well as staff completely aware of the diagnosis and prognosis.
—Prescriptions of mild sedatives to help with sleep may be useful for the bereaved, but antidepressant or antianxiety drugs are rarely necessary.
  —Heavy doses of sedative drugs may interfere with the normal grieving process.

Review Test

ADULTHOOD, AGING, AND DEATH

DIRECTIONS: For each of the questions or incomplete statements below, choose the answer that is **most correct**.

5.1. All of the following are true about divorce EXCEPT:

A. Most single-parent families are headed by men.
B. Almost half of black families are single-parent families.
C. Children of divorce face a greater likelihood of divorce themselves.
D. Children who have regular contact with their fathers do better after divorce.
E. Most divorced men and women remarry within 3 years.

5.2. The statement "It is the doctor's fault that I became ill; she didn't take my blood pressure when I came for my last office visit" is most likely to be seen in which of the following stages of dying?

A. Denial
B. Anger
C. Acceptance
D. Depression
E. Bargaining

5.3. All of the following characterize early adulthood rather than previous stages of development EXCEPT:

A. peak biological development.
B. independent development of the adult self.
C. development of an intimate relationship.
D. drastic changes in work relationships in men.
E. marriage and children.

5.4. Characteristics of the families of origin of men and women likely to have a midlife crisis include all of the following EXCEPT:

A. impulsiveness.
B. withdrawal of the same-sex parent during the individual's adolescence.
C. anxiety.
D. low socioeconomic status.
E. parental discord.

5.5. Which of the following is true about menopause?

A. It occurs suddenly.
B. It is characterized by cessation of menstruation.
C. Severe psychological problems are common.
D. The hot flashes that occur have a purely psychological basis.
E. It usually occurs in the early 40s.

5.6. Which of the following is true about divorce?

A. First marriages are more likely to end in divorce than second marriages.
B. The overall divorce rate has decreased in recent years.
C. The divorce rate for couples married 15 to 19 years has doubled since 1960.
D. During 1986, about 250,000 couples divorced.
E. It is closely associated with marriage at a late age.

5.7. Which of the following is true about the elderly?

A. Suicide is rarer than in the general population.
B. Anxiety due to insecurity is rare.
C. Most of the elderly have a sense of despair or worthlessness.
D. Psychoactive drugs have different effects in the elderly than in younger people.
E. Depression is less common in the elderly than in younger people.

5.8. Longevity is associated with all of the following EXCEPT:

A. living in the country rather than the city.
B. sleeping between 9 and 12 hours per night.
C. being married.
D. physical activity.
E. a calm personality.

5.9. Which of the following is characteristic of normal bereavement?

A. Initial loss of appetite
B. Feelings of worthlessness
C. Threats of suicide
D. Grief lasting 3 to 4 years after the death
E. Feelings of evilness

5.10. All of the following are true about the physician and death EXCEPT:

A. There is a trend to make patients aware of a diagnosis of terminal illness.
B. The physician is responsible for classifying the cause of death.
C. A role of the physician is to provide strong sedation for close family members until the initial shock wears off.
D. Physicians often feel a sense of failure when a patient dies.
E. Physicians often become emotionally detached in order to deal with the death of patients.

DIRECTIONS: For each of the questions or incomplete statements below, **one** or **more** of the answers or completions given are correct. Choose answer:

A. if only **1, 2,** and **3** are correct.
B. if only **1** and **3** are correct.
C. if only **2** and **4** are correct.
D. if only **4** is correct.
E. if **all** are correct.

5.11. Which of the following is/are true about late adulthood in the United States?

1. The life expectancy for women is 8 years longer than for men.
2. Most women can expect 10 years of widowhood.
3. Eighty percent of people reach 60 years of age.
4. Approximately 5% of the population is over 65 years old.

5.12. Which of the following is/are true about the elderly?

1. Intelligence usually decreases markedly.
2. Learning may be impaired.
3. Depression is a natural condition of aging.
4. Depression may mimic Alzheimer's disease.

5.13. Which of the following is/are characteristic of sleep in old age?

1. Increased total sleep time
2. Decreased REM
3. Decreased sleep latency
4. Decreased slow wave sleep

Answers and Explanations

ADULTHOOD, AGING, AND DEATH

5.1. A. The large majority of single-parent families are headed by women.

5.2. B. During the anger stage of dying, the patient is likely to blame the doctor.

5.3. D. Drastic changes in work relationships in men characterize middle, not early, adulthood.

5.4. D. Characteristics of the families of people likely to have a midlife crisis include parental discord, anxiety, impulsiveness, and withdrawal of the same-sex parent during the individual's adolescence.

5.5. B. Most women go through menopause gradually at about age 50 years with relatively few problems.

5.6. C. Second marriages are more likely to end in divorce than first marriages. The divorce rate for couples married 15 to 19 years has doubled since 1960.

5.7. D. Suicide is more common in the elderly than in the general population. Anxiety may arise easily due to insecurity. However, many elderly people have a sense of satisfaction and pride in their past accomplishments.

5.8. B. Sleeping between 6 and 9 hours per night is associated with longevity.

5.9. A. Feelings of worthlessness, threats of suicide, and an extended period of grief characterize depression rather than normal bereavement.

5.10. C. Heavy sedation is rarely indicated because it may interfere with the grieving process.

5.11. A. In 1984, over 11% of the US population was over 65 years of age.

5.12. C. Intelligence is usually stable throughout life although a variety of physical illnesses may impair learning. Depression is not a natural condition of aging but instead may be related to loss of spouse or family members, loss of prestige, and loss of health.

5.13. C. Sleep in old age is characterized by decreased REM, decreased slow wave sleep, and increased sleep latency.

6

Psychoanalytic Theory

I. Overview

Classic psychoanalytic theory originated with **Sigmund Freud** in the late 1800s and early 1900s.

—An important concept on which psychoanalytic theory is based is that forces motivating behavior derive from **unconscious mental processes**.

—Other concepts include **psychic determinism, conflict, symbolism, repression,** and the belief that **sexual** and **aggressive drives** motivate the activities of the mind.

—The **libido** is the force by which sexual instincts are represented in the mind.

II. Topographic Theory of the Mind

In Freud's topographic theory, the mind is divided into three areas—the **unconscious**, the **preconscious,** and the **conscious**.

A. The Unconscious Mind

The unconscious contains repressed ideas and feelings that are not accessible to consciousness.

—The unconscious is associated with a type of thinking called **primary process**.

—Primary process thinking is common in young children and involves primitive drives, instincts, wish fulfillment, and pleasure.

—Logic is disregarded, and the concept of time is absent.

B. The Preconscious Mind

The preconscious develops in childhood and is accessible to both the unconscious and conscious mind.

—The preconscious functions to **repress** or censor wishes and desires.

—The preconscious uses **secondary process,** which is logical and is allied with reality.

—Secondary process is the means by which conscious thought and communication with others are carried out.

C. The Conscious Mind

The conscious operates in close association with the preconscious.

—Through the process of attention, a person gains awareness of stimuli from the external world.

—Although elements of the preconscious enter conscious awareness, the unconscious mind remains unavailable to the conscious mind.

D. Dreams

Freud believed that dreams represented gratification of unconscious instinctual impulses and wish fulfillment.

—The **manifest dream** involves the dream content, which an individual may or may not recall.

—**Latent dream** content involves the unconscious thoughts and wishes in the dream.

—**Dream work** is the means by which latent dream content is transformed into the manifest dream.

III. Structural Theory of the Mind

In Freud's **structural theory**, developed later in his career, the mind is divided into the **id, ego,** and **superego.**

A. The Id

—The id represents instinctive sexual and aggressive drives.

—The id is controlled by primary process, acts in concert with the pleasure principle, and is not influenced by reality.

B. The Ego and Superego

—The **ego** regulates the discharge of instinctual drives in order to adapt to the requirements of external reality.

 —The major function of the ego is to maintain a relationship to the external world and to be flexible to life's frustrations.

 —The ego sustains a sense of reality about one's body and about the outside world through reality testing and adaptation to reality.

 —Another important function of the ego is to maintain object relationships, ie, to sustain satisfying relationships in life.

—Id impulses are also controlled by the **superego**, which represents moral values and conscience.

—**Defense mechanisms** are used by the ego to keep conflicts out of consciousness.

IV. Defense Mechanisms

A. Definitions

Defense mechanisms are unconscious mental operations that act to decrease anxiety and maintain an individual's sense of safety, equilibrium, and self-esteem.

—**George Vaillant** classified each defense mechanism as mature or less mature according to its adaptive value (Table 6.1).

V. Psychoanalysis

A. Characteristics

Psychoanalysis is a psychotherapeutic treatment technique that is based on Freud's theories about impulses and defense mechanisms.

—The purpose of psychoanalysis is to integrate experiences repressed in the unconscious mind into the individual's personality.

Table 6.1. Defense Mechanisms

Less Mature Defense Mechanisms

Acting out: unacceptable feelings are expressed in actions.
Denial: disbelief of intolerable facts about external reality.
Displacement: emotions are transferred from an unacceptable to an acceptable idea.
Dissociation: independent functioning of some mental processes, as seen in fugue states and multiple personality.
Identification: one's behavior is patterned after that of another person.
Intellectualization: the mind is used to explain away frightening feelings or conflicts.
Isolation of affect: strong feelings are separated from the stressful events that provoked them.
Projection: unacceptable impulses are attributed to others.
Rationalization: an irrational feeling or behavior is made to appear reasonable.
Reaction formation: unconscious feelings are denied and opposite attitudes and behaviors are adopted.
Regression: childlike patterns of behavior reappear under stress such as physical illness.
Repression: unacceptable feelings are pushed out of awareness.
Splitting: people or events are seen as being totally bad or totally good.

Mature Defense Mechanisms

Altruism: an individual unselfishly assists others.
Humor: this defense mechanism serves to reduce anxiety.
Sublimation: an unacceptable instinctual drive is rerouted to a socially acceptable action.
Suppression: unwanted feelings are put aside but are not repressed.

—Treatment is usually conducted four to five times per week for 3 or 4 years.
—Interference by the therapist is limited.

B. Free Association

The major technique used in psychoanalysis is **free association**, in which the patient says whatever comes to mind.

—Inhibition of free association is called **resistance**; unconscious ideas are prevented from reaching awareness because they are unacceptable to the patient's conscious mind.

C. Transference and Countertransference

The phenomena of **transference** and **countertransference** are important in psychoanalysis.

—In transference, the patient's unconscious feelings from the past about the parent are experienced in the present relationship with the therapist.
—In countertransference, the analyst re-experiences feelings about his or her own parent with the patient.

D. Related Forms of Psychotherapy

—**Psychoanalytic psychotherapy** is another form of psychotherapy that is based theoretically on psychoanalysis.
—Rather than free association and analysis of transference reactions, **interviewing** and **discussion** are used to uncover reasons for current conflicts and behavior.
—**Cognitive therapy** is a method of short-term psychotherapy that deals specifically with depression and anxiety.
—In cognitive therapy, a patient's distorted, negative way of thinking is restructured and substituted with self-enhancing thoughts.

Review Test

PSYCHOANALYTIC THEORY

DIRECTIONS: For each of the questions or incomplete statements below, choose the answer that is **most correct.**

6.1. The major method used to investigate unconscious processes in psychoanalysis is
A. symbolism.
B. repression.
C. free association.
D. primary process.
E. examination of the preconscious.

6.2. All of the following are true about defense mechanisms of the ego EXCEPT:
A. They are used to keep conflicts out of consciousness.
B. They are unconscious mental operations.
C. They actively decrease anxiety.
D. They are always manifestations of immature functioning.
E. They help maintain an individual's sense of self-esteem.

6.3. Which of the following defense mechanisms is in action in people who exhibit multiple personality?
A. Repression
B. Displacement
C. Dissociation
D. Isolation of affect
E. Intellectualization

6.4. Which of the following defense mechanisms is in use when the mind explains away frightening feelings or conflicts?
A. Repression
B. Displacement
C. Dissociation
D. Isolation of affect
E. Intellectualization

6.5. The defense mechanism used when unacceptable feelings are pushed out of awareness is known as
A. repression.
B. regression.
C. displacement.
D. rationalization.
E. isolation of affect.

6.6. Which of the following is the most mature defense mechanism?
A. Sublimation
B. Repression
C. Rationalization
D. Projection
E. Regression

6.7. A previously toilet-trained child is hospitalized and begins wetting the bed. This is an example of
A. isolation of affect.
B. displacement.
C. projection.
D. regression.
E. denial.

6.8. All of the following are true about psychoanalysis EXCEPT:
A. The therapist plays an active role.
B. Treatment is usually conducted four times per week.
C. Interference with free association is called resistance.
D. Treatment is usually conducted for 3 or 4 years.
E. Resistance reflects unconscious ideas that are unacceptable to the conscious mind.

6.9. A patient's re-enactment of feelings about the parent with the therapist during psychoanalysis is known as
A. interference.
B. resistance.
C. association.
D. transference.
E. cognitive dissonance.

6.10. In which of the following forms of therapy is the therapist least likely to be involved in discussions with the patient?
A. Cognitive therapy
B. Psychoanalytic psychotherapy
C. Psychoanalysis
D. Behavioral therapy
E. Family therapy

6.11. Which of the following is true about primary process?

A. It disregards logic.
B. It is closely attuned to time.
C. It is allied with reality.
D. It is accessible to the conscious mind.
E. It is logical.

6.12. All of the following are true about dreams according to Freud EXCEPT:

A. They represent gratification of unconscious instinctual impulses.
B. The latent dream is made up of the unconscious thoughts and wishes in a dream.
C. They represent wish fulfillment.
D. The manifest dream cannot be recalled.
E. The latent dream is transformed into the manifest dream by dream work.

DIRECTIONS: For each of the numbered phrases below, choose the lettered defense mechanism with which it is **most closely associated.**

A. Regression
B. Acting out
C. Denial
D. Splitting
E. Projection

6.13. Unacceptable feelings are expressed in actions.

6.14. People are seen as all bad or all good.

6.15. Unacceptable feelings are attributed to others.

6.16. Intolerable facts about reality are not believed.

DIRECTIONS: For each of the questions or incomplete statements below, **one** or **more** of the answers or completions given are correct. Choose answer:

A. if only **1, 2,** and **3** are correct.
B. if only **1** and **3** are correct.
C. if only **2** and **4** are correct.
D. if only **4** is correct.
E. if **all** are correct.

6.17. Which of the following is/are concept(s) upon which psychoanalytic theory is based?

1. Behavior derives from unconscious mental processes
2. Psychic determinism
3. Conflict
4. Sexual and aggressive drives

6.18. In Freud's structural theory of the mind

1. The mind is divided into the id, ego, and superego.
2. The mind is divided into the preconscious and conscious.
3. The id is under the domination of primary process.
4. The id is closely associated with reality.

6.19. Functions of the ego include:

1. maintaining relationships to the outside world.
2. reality testing.
3. maintaining object relationships.
4. regulating instinctual drives.

Answers and Explanations

PSYCHOANALYTIC THEORY

6.1. C. The technique of free association is used to investigate unconscious processes in psychoanalysis.

6.2. D. Defense mechanisms are not always manifestations of immature functioning; they may help individuals to maintain a sense of equilibrium and self-esteem.

6.3. C. Dissociation is the defense mechanism seen in individuals with multiple personality.

6.4. E. Intellectualization is used to explain away frightening feelings or conflicts.

6.5. A. Repression is the defense mechanism in use when unacceptable feelings are pushed out of awareness.

6.6. A. Sublimation is the most mature of these defense mechanisms.

6.7. D. Regression is the defense mechanism used by the previously toilet-trained child who begins bedwetting when under stress.

6.8. A. In psychoanalysis, interference by the therapist is limited.

6.9. D. Re-enacting feelings about the parent with the therapist during psychoanalysis is known as transference.

6.10. C. In psychoanalysis, the therapist is not likely to have discussions with the patient.

6.11. A. Primary process disregards logic, has no concept of time, and is not accessible to the conscious mind. Secondary process is logical and is allied with reality.

6.12. D. The manifest dream may or may not be recalled.

6.13. B. By acting out, unacceptable feelings are expressed in actions.

6.14. D. In splitting, people are seen as all bad or all good.

6.15. E. Using projection, an individual may attribute unacceptable feelings to others.

6.16. C. By using denial, intolerable facts about reality are not believed.

6.17. E. All are correct.

6.18. B. In Freud's structural theory—in which the mind is divided into the id, ego, and superego—the id is under the domination of primary process and has no regard for reality.

6.19. E. All are correct.

7

Learning Theory and Behavioral Medicine

I. Classical Conditioning

A. Principles of Classical Conditioning

Learning is the acquisition of behavior patterns. One method of learning is through **classical conditioning**.

—The principles of classical conditioning were formulated by **Ivan Pavlov**.

—A stimulus is a cue from an internal or external event.

—A response is a behavior that occurs in association with a stimulus.

—In classical conditioning, a natural or reflex behavior is elicited in response to a learned stimulus.

B. Unconditioned and Conditioned Stimuli and Responses

—Something that naturally or automatically produces a response is an **unconditioned stimulus**, eg, salivating in response to the odor of food.

—The behavior produced (salivating) is known as the **unconditioned response** because it does not have to be learned.

—A **conditioned response** is one that is learned, eg, salivating in response to the sound of a bell that, in the past, has been rung in conjunction with the presentation of food.

C. Acquisition and Extinction of a Response

—In the **acquisition phase**, the conditioned response (eg, salivating in response to a bell) is learned.

—In the **extinction phase**, the conditioned response diminishes when the conditioned stimulus (the bell) is not followed by the unconditioned stimulus (food).

—Spontaneous recovery occurs after extinction when the conditioned response (salivating in response to a bell) reappears in the absence of a stimulus (food).

—Stimulus generalization occurs when a stimulus (eg, the noise of a buzzer) that is similar to the original conditioned stimulus (the noise of a bell) also produces the conditioned response (salivating).

D. Aversive Conditioning

Classical conditioning to an aversive stimulus, **aversive conditioning**, pairs an unwanted behavior, such as sexual interest in children (pedophilia), with a painful or aversive stimulus, such as shock.

Table 7.1. **Schedules of Reinforcement**

Schedule	Example
Continuous	Getting paid for each shirt you sew
Fixed ratio	Getting paid for every tenth shirt you sew
Fixed interval	Getting paid every Friday, no matter how many shirts you sew
Variable ratio	Getting paid, in no predictable pattern, for every second, fifth, or tenth shirt you sew (most resistant to extinction)
Variable interval	Getting paid daily, weekly, monthly, or whenever the boss can afford to pay you, no matter how many shirts you sew

—Aversive conditioning also shows phases of acquisition, extinction, and spontaneous recovery.

II. Operant Conditioning

A. Principles of Operant Conditioning

Operant conditioning is primarily associated with the work of **B.F. Skinner.**
—In operant conditioning, a nonreflex behavior is a consequent stimulus that serves as a reward or punishment.
—The focus of operant conditioning is an observable behavior; motivational state and prior historic factors are ignored.

B. Reinforcement and Punishment

Skinner's fundamental theories relate to the concept of **reinforcement**, ie, behavior is guided by its consequences for the individual.
—The consequence, or reinforcement, follows immediately after an item of behavior.
—Reinforcement establishes a connection between a stimulus and a response and can be **positive** or **negative**.
  —Reinforcement is positive if the introduction of a pleasant or positive stimulus increases the rate at which the behavior occurs.
  —Reinforcement is negative if the removal of an aversive or negative stimulus increases the rate of behavior.
  —Positive or negative reinforcement can be used to reward a desired behavior.
—**Extinction** is the disappearance of a learned behavior when reward is withheld.
—**Punishment** is an aversive stimulus aimed at reducing an unwanted behavior.

C. Patterns of Reinforcement

When and in what pattern reinforcement is presented determine the rate of the response or behavior.
—Patterns of reinforcement include **continuous, ratio,** and **interval.** Examples of schedules of reinforcement are seen in Table 7.1.
—**Continuous reinforcement** is presented after every response and is the pattern of reinforcement least resistant to extinction.
—**Fixed reinforcement** is presented after a set number of responses.
—**Variable reinforcement** occurs after a random and unpredictable number of responses and is very resistant to extinction.

—The most rapid acquisition of behavior is associated with variable reinforcement.

D. Shaping and Modeling

—**Shaping** involves rewarding closer and closer approximations of the desired behavior until the correct behavior is achieved.

—**Modeling**, like classical and operant conditioning, is a type of learning.

—Modeling is observational learning, eg, an individual adopts the behavior of someone admired or respected.

III. Applications of Behavioral Techniques to Medicine

A. Overview

Behavioral techniques have been used to eliminate unwanted habits such as smoking. They also have been used to treat medical conditions such as obesity and cardiovascular disease.

B. Systematic Desensitization

Systematic desensitization is a behavioral technique used to eliminate phobias (irrational fears).

—An individual is exposed to the frightening stimulus in increasing doses in conjunction with relaxation procedures.

—Since relaxation is incompatible with fear, the relaxed patient is less likely to be anxious or fearful when the frightening stimulus is presented.

C. Token Economy

Token economy is a behavioral technique that has been used in mental hospital wards and in the care of the mentally retarded.

—Individuals are paid for desired behavior, ie, each desired behavior is rewarded with a token reinforcer.

—Tokens are later translated into tangible objects such as candy or dessert.

D. Biofeedback

1. *Principles of Biofeedback*

Biofeedback involves learning control over physiologic activity and is an extension of operant conditioning; three fundamental principles are involved.

—First, it must be possible to determine and to measure accurately physiologic activity.

—Second, the patient must receive continuous information about the physiologic activity.

—Third, the patient must be motivated to learn, since a high degree of practice is required.

2. *Uses of Biofeedback*

Biofeedback training has been used in the voluntary control of autonomic activity and in the relaxation of striated muscle.

—Biofeedback training for control over the autonomic system has been used to treat hypertension, peptic ulcer, and asthma as well as peripheral temperature regulation in the treatment of migraine headache.

—Biofeedback training involving relaxation of the skeletal muscles has been used to treat tension headache and generalized anxiety disorders.

Review Questions

LEARNING THEORY AND BEHAVIORAL MEDICINE

DIRECTIONS: For each of the questions or incomplete statements below choose the answer that is **most correct.**

7.1. Which of the following does not have to be learned?

A. The conditioned response
B. The unconditioned response
C. The conditioned stimulus
D. The acquisition phase
E. Stimulus generalization

7.2. Which of the following schedules of reinforcement is most resistant to extinction?

A. Continuous
B. Fixed ratio
C. Fixed interval
D. Variable ratio
E. Discontinued

7.3. Adopting the behavior of someone admired or respected is an example of

A. stimulus generalization.
B. modeling.
C. shaping.
D. positive reinforcement.
E. variable reinforcement.

7.4. Relaxation of skeletal muscles through biofeedback is particularly important in the treatment of

A. hypertension.
B. peptic ulcer.
C. asthma.
D. tension headache.
E. obesity.

7.5. All of the following are true about learning EXCEPT:

A. It involves the acquisition of behavior patterns.
B. Classical conditioning is a method of learning.
C. Operant conditioning is a method of learning.
D. Past history of the organism is important in all forms of learning.
E. Stimuli may be internal or external to the organism.

7.6. Which of the following is true about spontaneous recovery in classical conditioning?

A. It diminishes when the conditioned stimulus is not followed by the unconditioned stimulus.
B. It occurs when the conditioned response reappears in the absence of a stimulus.
C. It occurs after an aversive stimulus.
D. It occurs before extinction.
E. It occurs when a related stimulus produces a conditioned response.

7.7. Which of the following is true about operant conditioning?

A. The focus is an observable behavior.
B. Motivational state is important.
C. Reflexive behaviors are elicited in response to stimuli acting as a reward.
D. Prior historical factors are significant.
E. There is no relationship between a behavior and its consequences.

7.8. All of the following are true about reinforcement in operant conditioning EXCEPT:

A. It establishes a connection between a stimulus and a response.
B. It can be positive or negative.
C. It can increase the rate at which a behavior occurs.
D. It follows a behavior.
E. It was first described by the work of Pavlov.

7.9. All of the following are true about biofeedback EXCEPT:

A. It is an extension of classical conditioning.
B. It has been used in the treatment of generalized anxiety disorder.
C. Control over physiologic activity is learned.
D. It can be used to control autonomic activity.
E. Relaxation of striated muscle can be achieved.

7.10. All of the following are important in the successful use of biofeedback EXCEPT:

A. The patient must receive continuous information about the physiologic activity.
B. The physiologic activity must be detectable and measurable.
C. The patient's motivation is important.
D. It is used to gain control over the central nervous system.
E. A large amount of practice is required.

DIRECTIONS: For each of the questions or incomplete statements below, **one** or **more** of the answers or completions given are correct. Choose answer:

  A. if only **1, 2,** and **3** are correct.
  B. if only **1** and **3** are correct.
  C. if only **2** and **4** are correct.
  D. if only **4** is correct.
  E. if **all** are correct.

7.11. Which of the following is/are true about systematic desensitization?

1. Relaxation procedures are used.
2. It is used to eliminate phobias.
3. An individual is exposed to a frightening stimulus in increasing doses.
4. It is a behavioral technique.

7.12. Which of the following conditions has/have been treated using biofeedback techniques?

1. Peptic ulcer
2. Asthma
3. Hypertension
4. Migraine headaches

7.13. A child is smacked on the hand every time she touches a stove. This is an example of

1. classical conditioning.
2. operant conditioning.
3. aversive conditioning.
4. stimulus generalization.

Answers and Explanations

LEARNING THEORY AND BEHAVIORAL MEDICINE

7.1. B. The unconditioned stimulus produces an unconditioned response that does not have to be learned.

7.2. D. Variable ratio reinforcement is most resistant to extinction.

7.3. B. Modeling involves adopting the behavior of someone admired or respected.

7.4. D. In treating tension headache with biofeedback, the patient is trained to relax skeletal muscles.

7.5. D. In learning by operant conditioning, past history of the organism is not important.

7.6. B. Spontaneous recovery occurs after extinction when the conditioned response reappears in the absence of a stimulus.

7.7. A. In operant conditioning, nonreflexive behaviors are elicited in response to rewards. The focus of operant conditioning is an observable behavior. Motivational state and prior historical factors are not important.

7.8. E. Operant conditioning is associated primarily with the work of B.F. Skinner.

7.9. A. Biofeedback is an extension of operant conditioning.

7.10. D. Biofeedback is used to gain control over the autonomic nervous system.

7.11. E. All are correct.

7.12. E. All are correct.

7.13. B. Smacking a child when he or she makes a dangerous move is an example of aversive classical conditioning.

8

Psychoactive Substance Dependence and Abuse

I. Overview

A. Definitions and Categories of Abuse

Psychoactive substances alter state of mind or consciousness.

—The DSM-III-R uses the term "psychoactive substance use disorder" to identify a pattern of pathologic use and impairment of physical, social, or occupational functioning.

—Psychoactive substance use disorder is divided into two subcategories—**psychoactive substance dependence disorder** and **psychoactive substance abuse disorder** (Table 8.1).

—An additional category—**polysubstance dependence**—also may be used.

B. Demographics

The use of illegal drugs is more common among individuals aged 18 to 25 than in other age groups.

—Drug use is more common in urban males than females by a 3:1 ratio.

C. Tolerance and Dependence

Substances of abuse can cause physical dependence or tolerance (Table 8.2).

—**Tolerance** is the need for increased amounts of the substance to achieve the desired effect.

—Cross-tolerance occurs when tolerance develops to one drug as the result of use of another drug.

—Drug dependence has biological, psychological, and social causes.

D. Withdrawal

Abstinence from substances of dependence frequently leads to withdrawal symptoms (Table 8.3).

II. Caffeine

A. Demographics

Caffeine is found in coffee, tea, cola, nonprescription stimulants, and nonprescription diet drugs.

—About 30% of adult Americans drink coffee.

Table 8.1. Categories and Characteristics of Substance Use

Category	Characteristics
Psychoactive substance dependence	Frequent intoxication, impairment in occupational or social functioning, marked tolerance, withdrawal symptoms, desire to cut down; symptoms persist for at least 1 month or repeatedly over a longer period.
Psychoactive substance abuse	A maladaptive pattern of psychoactive substance use for at least 1 month or repeatedly over a longer period associated with persistent social, occupational, or physical problems; most common in people just starting to use drugs and with use of drugs that do not have withdrawal symptoms.
Polysubstance dependence	Repeated use of at least three categories of psychoactive substances over a period of at least 6 months; no substance has predominated.

B. Physical Effects

—Caffeine use results in a more alert state as well as diuresis, CNS and cardiac stimulation, increased peristalsis, and secretion of gastric acid, and elevation of blood pressure.

—Excessive use of caffeine can result in agitation, insomnia, gastrointestinal disturbances, and cardiac arrhythmias.

C. Psychological Effects

—Psychological dependence may occur with chronic use.

—Tolerance does not occur and physical dependence has not been well-documented.

—Caffeine withdrawal may be accompanied by headache, lethargy, depression, and increased appetite.

III. Nicotine

A. Demographics

About 30% of adults in the United States smoke cigarettes.

—The proportion of teenage, black, and female smokers has increased, although the total number of smokers appears to have declined.

B. Physical Effects

Overdoses of nicotine (over 60 mg) can be fatal; an average cigarette contains 0.5 mg of nicotine.

—Nicotine causes increased peristalsis and catecholamine release, as well as vasoconstriction of peripheral blood vessels, changes in sleep patterns, and tremor.

—Cancer of the lung, pharynx, and bladder and cardiac and peripheral vascular disease have been associated with chronic tobacco use.

C. Withdrawal and Relapse

—Withdrawal from nicotine may result in irritability, headache, drowsiness, and anxiety as well as weight gain.

—Up to 80% of smokers who stop smoking relapse within the first 2 years.

—Factors associated with abstinence from smoking include encourage-

Table 8.2. Effects of Substances of Abuse

Substance	Physical Dependence	Tolerance	Adverse Effects
Alcohol	Yes	Yes	Liver problems, hallucinations, Korsakoff's and Wernicke's syndromes
Amphetamines	Yes	Yes	Cardiac problems, delusions
Barbiturates	Yes	Yes	Low safety margin
Benzodiazepines	Yes	Yes	Alcohol interactions, amnesia
Cocaine	Yes	Yes	Psychosis, nasal problems, cardiac arrhythmias, sudden death
LSD	No	Yes	Bad trips, flashbacks
Marijuana	Occasionally	No	Hallucinations, amotivational syndrome
Opioids	Yes	Yes	Overdose is life-threatening
PCP	No	Yes	Psychotic symptoms, violence

ment from a spouse or child, fear of ill effects, membership in a support group of ex-smokers, and encouragement from a nonsmoking physician.

IV. Alcohol

A. Demographics

Alcohol is used by about 65% of the adult US population, and approximately 13% of adults abuse alcohol or become alcohol dependent during their lives.

—The prevalence of alcohol use is highest in the 21- to 34-year-old age group.

—Fewer women than men use alcohol, although alcohol use is increasing in women.

  —The onset of alcoholism is later in women than in men.

  —Women may suffer more serious health effects with lower alcohol doses than men.

  —Alcohol abuse may be more difficult to detect in women because they may be more secretive about their drinking.

—In the United States, alcohol use is lowest in the southern states and highest in the northeastern states.

—Blacks in urban ghettoes, American Indians, and Eskimos have high rates of alcoholism.

—Jews, Asians, and conservative Protestants use alcohol less than liberal Protestants and Catholics.

—There is a strong genetic factor in alcoholism; sons are more susceptible than daughters.

—A childhood history of attention deficit, hyperactivity disorder, or conduct disorder correlate with a higher rate of alcoholism.

B. Effects of Alcohol Use

—Alcohol use is associated with half of all traffic fatalities and homicides and with one-quarter of suicides.

—The life expectancy of an alcoholic is reduced by 10 years.

—Family, work, and legal problems are common in the alcoholic.

Table 8.3. Withdrawal Symptoms in Substance Abuse

Substance	Withdrawal Symptoms
Alcohol	Tremor, tachycardia, hypertension, malaise, nausea, seizure, delirium tremens ("DTs")
Amphetamines	Post-use "crash," including anxiety, lethargy, headache, stomach cramps, hunger
Barbiturates	Anxiety, seizures, delirium, life-threatening cardiovascular collapse
Benzodiazepines	Long-lasting anxiety, numbness in extremities, convulsions
Cocaine	Hypersomnolence, fatigue, depression, malaise, craving, irritability
Opioids	Anxiety, insomnia, anorexia, sweating, fever, rhinorrhea, piloerection, nausea, stomach cramps

C. Intoxication

—Alcohol depresses the central nervous system.

—Legal intoxication is defined as 0.08 to 0.15% blood alcohol concentration (BAC), depending on individual state laws.

—Coma occurs at a BAC of 0.40 to 0.50% in nonalcoholics.

D. Treatment of Alcoholism

—Disulfiram occasionally helps recovery in alcoholic patients.

—The patient takes disulfiram on a regular basis, which causes a toxic reaction as a result of acetaldehyde accumulation in the blood when the patient subsequently drinks alcohol.

—In the toxic reaction, the patient experiences intense nausea, headache, and flushing.

—The anxiety accompanying alcohol withdrawal can be reduced with antianxiety drugs.

—Psychotherapy may be useful for treating alcoholic patients, particularly if the spouse is involved in therapy.

—Alcoholics anonymous (AA), a voluntary support group, is often successful in control of problem drinking.

V. Opioid Drugs

A. Demographics

The opioids include morphine, heroin, methadone, and codeine.

—Heroin is a frequently abused opioid in the United States.

—About 50% of heroin addicts in the United States live in New York City.

—The ratio of male to female addicts is 3:1.

—Most heroin addicts are in their early 30s but began using the drug in their teens or early 20s.

—Heroin crosses the blood-brain barrier more quickly, is more potent, and has a more rapid onset of action than morphine; it also has twice the euphoric action.

B. Effects of Opioid Drugs and Withdrawal

—Opioids induce euphoria and sedation, are analgesic, and decrease respiratory drive.

—The intravenous method of drug use employed by heroin addicts contributes to acquired immunodeficiency syndrome (AIDS) and hepatitis B infection through sharing of contaminated needles.

—Death from withdrawal of opioids is rare unless there is a pre-existing serious physical illness.

—Clonidine, an adrenergic agonist, can block the heroin withdrawal syndrome.

—Because of cross-dependence, other opioids such as methadone can be substituted for illegal opioids such as heroin to prevent withdrawal.

C. Methadone

Methadone is a synthetic opioid dispensed by health authorities to treat heroin addiction.

—Although methadone also causes physical dependence and tolerance, it has several advantages over heroin for the addict.

   —Methadone is legal, can be taken by mouth, suppresses withdrawal symptoms, has a longer duration of action, causes little euphoria, drowsiness, or depression.

   —Individuals taking methadone can therefore hold a job and can avoid the criminal activity necessary to maintain an expensive heroin habit.

—Opioid antagonists such as naloxone can be used to maintain abstinence in opioid abusers.

VI. Sedatives

Sedative drugs include the barbiturates and benzodiazepines.

A. Barbiturates

Barbiturates depress the respiratory system and are used as sedatives, hypnotics, tranquilizers, anticonvulsants, and anesthetics.

—Frequently used and abused barbiturates include amobarbital, pentobarbital, and secobarbital.

—Barbiturates are the drugs most commonly taken to commit suicide.

—The most severe of the drug abstinence syndromes—including seizures and cardiovascular collapse—is associated with withdrawal from barbiturates.

—Gradual reduction in dosage of the abused drug and substitution of long-acting barbituates such as phenobarbital for the more commonly abused short-acting types are used during withdrawal.

B. Benzodiazepines

Benzodiazepines are used as anxiolytics, sedatives, muscle relaxants, anticonvulsants, and anesthetics and to treat alcohol withdrawal.

—Common benzodiazepines include diazepam (Valium), flurazepam (Dalmane), oxazepam (Serax), and chlordiazepoxide (Librium).

—Unlike barbiturates, benzodiazepines produce little respiratory depression.

—Withdrawal symptoms of benzodiazepines include insomnia, tremor, and anxiety; these may last for an extended period of time.

VII. Amphetamines

A. Characteristics

Amphetamines are stimulant drugs that are frequently abused.

—Commonly used amphetamines are dextroamphetamine (Dexedrine), methamphetamine (Desoxyn), and methylphenidate (Ritalin).

—Amphetamines have a rapid onset of action, produce an increased sense of well-being, decrease fatigue, elevate the pain threshold, decrease appetite, and may increase libido.

B. Uses, Overdose, and Withdrawal

Amphetamines have been used in the past to treat attention deficit hyperactivity disorder (ADHD) in children, narcolepsy, obesity, and mild depression.

—Current indications for amphetamines include only ADHD and narcolepsy.

—Overdose can result in cardiovascular problems, fever, and psychotic symptoms.

—Withdrawal from stimulants results in fatigue and depression.

VIII. Cocaine

A. Demographics

Cocaine use has increased over the past 10 years. In a 1985 survey, 25% of young adults reported using cocaine at some time.

B. Cocaine Use, Overdose, and Withdrawal

—Cocaine produces intense euphoria that lasts for up to 1 hour; this is often followed by acute depression, "the crash."

—Cocaine intoxication is marked by aggressiveness, agitation, irritability, impaired judgment, and mania.

—Cocaine psychosis can occur with high doses.

—Propranolol may specifically antagonize cocaine's sympathomimetic effects and be useful as a treatment for overdose.

—Although no obvious physiologic signs of cocaine withdrawal may be present, severe craving often peaks 2 to 4 days after the last dose.

C. Crack

Crack is a smokable form of cocaine that is much cheaper than cocaine powder.

—Because crack is relatively inexpensive, cocaine is now available to more individuals.

IX. Marijuana

A. Physical and Psychological Effects

Of illegal drugs, marijuana is the most frequently abused in the United States.

—Tetrahydrocannabinol (THC) is the primary active compound in cannabis (marijuana).

—Physiologic effects of THC include orthostatic hypotension (low blood pressure when standing up) and tachycardia.

—Psychological effects of THC include euphoria, calmness, and drowsiness; these begin almost immediately after smoking marijuana and last for 2 to 4 hours.

—In low doses, marijuana impairs memory and complex motor function, alters sensory and time perception, causes reddening of the conjunctiva, and may increase appetite and sexual desire.

B. High Doses and Chronic Use

—With high doses, marijuana may cause delusions, hallucinations, paranoia, and anxiety and may decrease sexual functioning.

—Chronic users may experience a decrease in motivation ("the amotivational syndrome,") that is characterized by lack of desire to continue at a task and increased apathy, as well as lung problems associated with smoking.

X. Hallucinogens

A. Psychological Effects

—Hallucinogens alter perception and emotional state shortly after administration.

—In susceptible individuals, psychiatric syndromes and long-term cognitive impairment may occur.

—Lysergic acid diethylamide (LSD) is the most commonly known hallucinogen.

—The effects of LSD last from 8 to 12 hours.

B. Physical Effects

—Physical symptoms of LSD use include diaphoresis, blurring of vision, mydriasis, tachycardia, palpitations, and tremor, as well as alterations in perception, thought, and mood.

—Physical dependence and withdrawal symptoms are not often seen with the use of LSD.

XI. Phencyclidine Piperidine

A. Effects

Phencyclidine piperidine (PCP), also known as angel dust, is an illegal drug that is smoked in a marijuana or other cigarette.

—The effects of PCP are similar to those of LSD and include fantasies and euphoria and episodes of violent behavior.

—Auditory and visual hallucinations, as well as alterations of body image and distortions of time and space, may occur.

B. Dose and Long-term Effects

—A low dose of PCP is less than 5 mg; a high dose of PCP is more than 10 mg.

—Use of over 20 mg of PCP may cause convulsions, coma, and death.

—The effects of PCP may last several days, and it may remain in the blood for over a week.

—PCP psychosis may occur with use, and long-term effects include dulled thinking, loss of memory, lethargy, and difficulty in concentrating.

Review Test

PSYCHOACTIVE SUBSTANCE DEPENDENCE AND ABUSE

DIRECTIONS: For each of the questions or incomplete statements below, choose the answer that is **most correct.**

8.1. Physiologic effects of caffeine include all of the following EXCEPT:
A. blood pressure reduction.
B. central nervous system stimulation.
C. increased peristalsis.
D. increased gastric acid secretion.
E. diuresis.

8.2. All of the following are true about PCP EXCEPT:
A. Its effects may last for several days.
B. It may remain in the blood for over a week.
C. Psychosis may occur with long-term use.
D. Hallucinations may occur with use.
E. It has few long-term effects.

8.3. All of the following commonly occur following withdrawal from nicotine EXCEPT:
A. weight loss.
B. headache.
C. drowsiness.
D. anxiety.
E. irritability.

8.4. Which of the following drugs is most widely abused in the United States?
A. Marijuana
B. Cocaine
C. Speed
D. LSD
E. Heroin

8.5. All of the following are common effects of marijuana use EXCEPT:
A. impaired memory.
B. alteration in time perception.
C. decreased appetite.
D. reddening of the conjunctiva.
E. paranoia.

8.6. The amotivational syndrome is characteristic of chronic use of
A. PCP.
B. LSD.
C. marijuana.
D. cocaine.
E. heroin.

8.7. All of the following are true about LSD EXCEPT:
A. The effects commonly last from 2 to 12 hours.
B. It is a hallucinogen.
C. The effects have a rapid onset.
D. Physical dependence is uncommon.
E. Withdrawal symptoms are uncommon.

8.8. Which of the following is NOT an amphetamine?
A. Methylphenidate
B. Dextroamphetamine
C. Methamphetamine
D. Perphenazine
E. Ritalin

8.9. All of the following are effects of amphetamines EXCEPT:
A. decreased fatigue.
B. elevated pain threshold.
C. increased appetite.
D. rapid onset of action.
E. increased libido.

8.10. All of the following are uses of benzodiazepines EXCEPT:
A. as sedatives.
B. as muscle relaxants.
C. as anesthetics.
D. as antihistamines.
E. as tranquilizers.

8.11. All of the following are common results of opiate use EXCEPT:
A. sedation.
B. analgesia.
C. decreased respiratory drive.
D. euphoria.
E. hyperactivity.

8.12. All of the following are true about heroin addiction EXCEPT:

A. Most addicts are in their early 30s.
B. Addicts are more likely to be male than female.
C. Fifty percent of heroin addicts live in the United States.
D. Death from withdrawal of heroin is common.
E. Clonidine can block the heroin withdrawal syndrome.

8.13. Legal intoxication is defined by which of the following blood alcohol concentrations?

A. 0.05 to 0.09%
B. 0.08 to 0.15%
C. 0.40 to 0.50%
D. 1.5 to 2%
E. 2.5 to 3%

8.14. The age group in which illicit drug use is most common is

A. 10 to 15.
B. 15 to 18.
C. 18 to 25.
D. 25 to 35.
E. 35 to 45.

8.15. Which of the following drugs is LEAST likely to result in physical dependence?

A. Alcohol
B. Amphetamines
C. Benzodiazepines
D. PCP
E. Opiates

8.16. Withdrawal from which of the following drugs is most likely to cause life-threatening symptoms?

A. PCP
B. LSD
C. Heroin
D. Secobarbital
E. Alcohol

8.17. Flashbacks are most likely to occur following the use of

A. opiates.
B. marijuana.
C. LSD.
D. cocaine.
E. amphetamines.

8.18. Korsakoff's syndrome is associated with the use of

A. amphetamines.
B. alcohol.
C. barbiturates.
D. cocaine.
E. LSD.

8.19. In which of the following age groups is the prevalence of alcohol use highest?

A. 15 to 19
B. 21 to 34
C. 35 to 44
D. 45 to 60
E. 65 to 75

8.20. Which of the following groups has the lowest rate of alcoholism?

A. Eskimos
B. American Indians
C. Blacks in urban ghettos
D. Catholics in urban ghettos
E. Jews in urban ghettos

8.21. Which of the following is true about alcohol use in the United States?

A. It is more common in women.
B. The onset of use is later in men than in women.
C. It is used by about 25% of the adult population.
D. It is greatest in the Northeast.
E. The incidence of alcohol abuse or dependence during an individual's lifetime is approximately 2%.

8.22. All of the following are true about alcoholism EXCEPT:

A. Childhood hyperactivity disorder is associated with future alcoholism.
B. Life expectancy is reduced by approximately 10 years.
C. It is less common in Asian Americans than in white Americans.
D. Daughters are more vulnerable than sons.
E. It is associated with about 50% of traffic fatalities.

8.23. All of the following are true about heroin EXCEPT:

A. It is an opiate drug.
B. It has a slower onset of action than morphine.
C. It is more potent than morphine.
D. It has twice as much euphoric action as morphine.
E. It crosses the blood-brain barrier more quickly than morphine.

8.24. All of the following are true about methadone EXCEPT:

A. It does not cause physical dependence.
B. It shows cross-dependence with heroin.
C. Its use results in tolerance.
D. It is dispensed by health authorities.
E. It is taken orally.

8.25. All of the following symptoms occur with heroin withdrawal EXCEPT:

A. lacrimation.
B. nausea.
C. sedation.
D. sweating.
E. vomiting.

8.26. Amphetamines have been used to treat all of the following disorders EXCEPT:

A. attention deficit hyperactivity disorder.
B. narcolepsy.
C. mild depression.
D. anorexia nervosa.
E. obesity.

8.27. All of the following are true about the amphetamines EXCEPT:

A. Overdose can result in cardiovascular problems.
B. Overdose can result in subnormal body temperature.
C. Overdose can result in psychotic symptoms.
D. Withdrawal can result in depression.
E. Withdrawal can result in fatigue.

8.28. Which of the following is true about cocaine use?

A. There are usually severe physiologic signs of withdrawal.
B. Severe craving for the drug often peaks 2 to 4 days after the last dose.
C. The euphoria produced by cocaine lasts from 3 to 4 days.
D. Propranolol is useful as a treatment for withdrawal.
E. Cocaine intoxication is characterized by sedation.

8.29. Physical symptoms of LSD use include all of the following EXCEPT:

A. sedation.
B. tachycardia.
C. diaphoresis.
D. mydriasis.
E. blurred vision.

8.30. All of the following are true about PCP EXCEPT:

A. It is usually injected.
B. It is also known as angel dust.
C. Its effects are similar to those of LSD.
D. Overdose may result in coma and death.
E. It may remain in the blood for over a week.

8.31. All of the following are physical effects of nicotine EXCEPT:

A. increased catecholamine output.
B. increased peristalsis.
C. tremor.
D. sleep changes.
E. dilation of peripheral blood vessels.

8.32. All of the following are true about smoking EXCEPT:

A. About 10% of the adults in the United States smoke.
B. Nicotine is a toxic drug.
C. Overdoses of nicotine can be fatal.
D. The relapse rate for smokers who attempt to quit is up to 80% within the first 2 years.
E. Withdrawal from nicotine may result in headache.

DIRECTIONS: For each of the numbered phrases below, choose the lettered item with which it is **most closely associated.**

A. Low doses of marijuana
B. High doses of marijuana

8.33. Decreased sexual functioning

8.34. Increased sexual desire

DIRECTIONS: For each of the questions or incomplete statements below, **one** or **more** of the answers or completions given are correct. Choose answer:

    A. if only **1, 2,** and **3** are correct.
    B. if only **1** and **3** are correct.
    C. if only **2** and **4** are correct.
    D. if only **4** is correct.
    E. if **all** are correct.

8.35. Which of the following is/are medical uses of barbiturates?

1. As sedatives
2. As tranquilizers
3. To induce anesthesia
4. As anticonvulsants

8.36. Which of the following occur(s) with withdrawal from benzodiazepines?

1. Insomnia
2. Tremor
3. Anxiety
4. Respiratory depression

8.37. Chronic tobacco use is associated with which of the following?

1. Peripheral vascular disease
2. Cardiac disease
3. Cancer of pharynx
4. Cancer of bladder

8.38. Abstinence from smoking positively correlates with

1. encouragement from a nonsmoking physician.
2. membership in a support group of ex-smokers.
3. fear of the ill-effects of smoking.
4. encouragement from a spouse or child.

8.39. Which of the following is/are true about caffeine?

1. It is found in nonprescription drugs.
2. Psychological dependence may occur with chronic use.
3. Tolerance is not usually a problem.
4. Physical dependence is common.

8.40. Which of the following is/are commonly associated with caffeine withdrawal?

1. Lethargy
2. Euphoria
3. Headache
4. Decreased appetite

Answers and Explanations

PSYCHOACTIVE SUBSTANCE DEPENDENCE AND ABUSE

8.1. A. Caffeine tends to increase blood pressure.

8.2. E. Psychosis and long-term effects may occur with use of PCP.

8.3. A. Weight gain may occur following nicotine withdrawal.

8.4. A. Marijuana is the most widely abused illegal drug in the United States.

8.5. C. Appetite may increase with marijuana use.

8.6. C. The amotivational syndrome is characteristic of chronic users of marijuana.

8.7. A. The effects of LSD commonly last from 8 to 12 hours.

8.8. D. Methylphenidate (Ritalin), dextroamphetamine, and methamphetamine are amphetamines.

8.9. C. Amphetamines decrease appetite and have been used in the past as "diet pills."

8.10. D. Benzodiazepines are used as sedatives, muscle relaxants, and anesthetics as well as tranquilizers.

8.11. E. Sedation, analgesia, decreased respiratory drive, and euphoria may result from opiate use.

8.12. D. Death from withdrawal of opioids is rare unless there is a serious pre-existing physical illness.

8.13. B. Legal intoxication is defined by blood alcohol concentrations of 0.08 to 0.15%.

8.14. C. Illicit drug use is most common in the 18- to 25-year-old age group.

8.15. D. Use of PCP generally is not linked to physical dependence.

8.16. D. The most severe of the drug abstinence syndromes is associated with withdrawal from barbiturates such as secobarbital.

8.17. C. Flashbacks occur following the use of LSD.

8.18. B. Korsakoff's syndrome is associated with the use of alcohol.

8.19. B. The prevalence of alcohol use is highest in the 21- to 34-year-old age group.

8.20. E. In general, Jews have a lower rate of alcoholism than other groups.

8.21. D. In the United States, alcohol is used by more men than women, and the onset of alcohol use is later in women than in men. The incidence of alcohol abuse or dependence during an individual's lifetime is approximately 13%, it is used by about 65% of the adult population, and the highest use is in the Northeast.

8.22. D. Sons are more vulnerable than daughters to alcoholism.

8.23. B. Heroin has a faster onset of action, is more potent, has more euphoric action, and crosses the blood-brain barrier more quickly than morphine.

8.24. A. Methadone is dispensed by health authorities, is taken orally, shows cross-dependence with heroin, and causes both physical dependence and tolerance.

8.25. C. Lacrimation, nausea, sweating, and vomiting are associated with heroin withdrawal.

8.26. D. Use of amphetamines is associated with anorexia (loss of appetite).

8.27. B. Overdose of amphetamines can result in cardiovascular problems, fever, psychotic symptoms, depression, and fatigue.

8.28. B. The intense euphoria produced by cocaine lasts for only up to 1 hour. Severe craving for the drug peaks 2 to 4 days after the last dose although there may be few physiologic signs of withdrawal. Propranolol is used as a treatment for cocaine overdose. Cocaine intoxication is characterized by agitation and irritability.

8.29. A. Tachycardia, diaphoresis, mydriasis, and blurred vision are seen with LSD use.

8.30. A. PCP, or angel dust, is usually smoked. Its psychotropic effects are similar to those of LSD. PCP may remain in the blood for over a week and overdose can result in death.

8.31. E. Increased peristalsis and vasoconstriction of peripheral blood vessels are physical effects of nicotine. Tremor, sleep changes, and increased catecholamine output also occur.

8.32. A. Approximately 30% of US adults smoke cigarettes.

8.33. B. Decreased sexual functioning may occur with use of high doses of marijuana.

8.34. A. Increased sexual desire may occur with use of low doses of marijuana.

8.35. E. All are correct.

8.36. A. Withdrawal from benzodiazepines is associated with insomnia, tremor, and anxiety.

8.37. E. All are correct.

8.38. E. All are correct.

8.39. A. While psychological dependence may occur, physical dependence on caffeine has not been well-documented.

8.40. B. Caffeine withdrawal is associated with headache, lethargy and depression, and increased appetite.

9

Sleep

I. Normal Sleep

A. The Stages of Sleep

—The electroencephalograph (EEG) of an awake individual is characterized by alpha waves and low-voltage activity.

—In sleep, brain waves show distinctive changes that are classified as stages 1, 2, 3, and 4 (Table 9.1).

—Stages 1 through 4 are known as **non-rapid eye movement sleep (NREM)**, which is characterized by peacefulness, slowed pulse and respiration, decreased blood pressure, and episodic, involuntary body movement.

B. Slow Wave and Rapid Eye Movement Sleep

—**Slow wave sleep (SWS)** is the deepest part of sleep.

—SWS is relaxed, and eye movements may be absent or present.

—Brief arousals during SWS are associated with amnesia during the arousal, enuresis, somnambulism, and night terrors.

—In addition to **rapid eye movements (REM)**, REM sleep is characterized by high pulse, respiration, and blood pressure.

—REM sleep is also characterized by increased brain oxygen use, variation in temperature in relation to room temperature, penile erection, near total paralysis of skeletal muscles, and dreaming.

—The onset of REM sleep (REM latency) occurs about 90 minutes after falling asleep.

—A REM period occurs about every 95 minutes during the night; the majority of REM sleep occurs in the last third of the night.

—Reduction in SWS and REM sleep occurs in older persons.

C. Neurotransmitters Involved in Sleep

—Serotonin transmission may be involved in sleep.

—Enhancement of serotonergic transmission by ingestion of L-tryptophan has been used in the past to treat sleep disturbances, but L-tryptophan has recently been taken off the market.

—Norepinephrine is also involved in sleep.

—Drugs that increase firing of noradrenergic neurons reduce REM sleep.

—Brain acetylcholine is particularly associated with production of REM sleep.

—Sleep changes associated with major depression—shortened REM latency, a greater percentage of REM, and a shift in REM from the last to the first half of the night—are associated with central cholinergic activity.

—Patients with Alzheimer's disease have reduced SWS and REM sleep, which is likely to be due to loss of cholinergic neurons in the basal forebrain.

Table 9.1. Stages in Sleep

Sleep Stage	Cycles/Second	Characteristics	Sleep in Young Adults (% of total sleep time)
Stage 1	3–7	Alpha waves disappear; theta waves, low-voltage, regular activity, lightest stage of sleep	5
Stage 2	12–14	Sleep spindles and K-complexes	45
Stages 3 + 4	0.5–2.5	Slow wave sleep (SWS), delta waves, high voltage activity	25
REM		Low voltage, sawtooth waves	25

—Increasing brain dopamine levels with drugs results in wakefulness.
—Drugs that block dopamine increase time spent in sleep.

II. Sleep Disorders

A. Overview

Sleep disorders are common and occur in up to 30% of the population. The two major DSM-III-R categories of sleep disorders are **dyssomnias** and **parasomnias**.

—The dyssomnias include insomnia, hypersomnia, and sleep-wake schedule disorders.

—The parasomnias include sleepwalking, sleeptalking, night terrors, and dream anxiety disorder.

B. Insomnia

Insomnia is defined as a disorder of initiating or maintaining sleep that occurs three times per week for at least 1 month and leads to fatigue during the day or problems fulfilling social or occupational obligations.

—Behavioral techniques such as relaxation may be used to treat insomnia.

—Insomnia is associated with anxiety and may be the early sign of the onset of a severe depression or psychotic episode.

C. Sleep and Depression

—The insomnia common in severe **unipolar depression** is characterized by normal sleep onset, repeated nighttime awakenings, and premature morning awakenings.

  —Reduced SWS, long first REM period, and short REM latency may occur.

—Depression in **bipolar illness** may be associated with hypersomnia.

  —Manic and hypomanic patients may have trouble falling asleep and have a reduced need for sleep.

D. Physical Causes of Sleep Problems

—Frequently, medical conditions such as pain and endocrine and metabolic diseases are associated with sleep problems.

—Withdrawal of alcohol, benzodiazepines, phenothiazines, marijuana, or opiates is associated with insomnia.

—The use of CNS stimulants such as caffeine is associated with insomnia; withdrawal of CNS stimulants is associated with hypersomnolence.

E. Hypersomnia

Hypersomnia includes sleeping too much as well as feeling sleepy during the daytime (somnolence).

—Hypersomnolence is associated with sleep apnea and narcolepsy.
—Other conditions that produce hypersomnolence include Kleine-Levin syndrome (recurrent periods of hypersomnia and hyperphagia), menstrual-associated syndrome, somnolence associated with insufficient sleep, and sleep drunkenness (difficulty coming fully awake after sleep).

F. Narcolepsy

Narcolepsy occurs in about 4 of 10,000 people, most frequently is seen in adolescents or young adults, and involves sleep attacks in which the patient cannot avoid falling asleep.
—Narcolepsy includes hypnagogic hallucinations and vivid perceptual experiences and is characterized by the appearance of REM sleep within 10 minutes of falling asleep.
—Stimulant drugs and forced daytime naps are used in the treatment of narcolepsy.

G. Sleep Apnea

—In sleep apnea, air flow at the nose or mouth stops; respiratory effort may or may not cease as well.
—People with sleep apnea cannot sleep deeply because anoxia awakens them during the night; these individuals may become chronically tired.
—Sleep apnea may be the cause of sudden death during sleep in the elderly and in infants.

H. Night Terrors

Night terrors are an extreme form of fright in which an individual, usually a child, awakens in terror.
—Generally, there is no memory of the dream.
—Night terrors may develop into sleepwalking episodes.
—Night terrors may be the first sign of temporal lobe epilepsy.

Review Test

SLEEP

DIRECTIONS: For each of the questions or incomplete statements below, choose the answer that is **most correct.**

9.1. All of the following are true about narcolepsy EXCEPT:
A. The REM sleep of a narcoleptic is normal.
B. It occurs in about 4 of 10,000 people.
C. It occurs most frequently in adolescence or young adulthood.
D. It includes vivid perceptual experiences.
E. It includes hypnagogic hallucinations.

9.2. Which of the following neurotransmitters is involved particularly in the production of REM sleep?
A. Serotonin
B. Norepinephrine
C. Acetylcholine
D. Dopamine
E. Histamine

9.3. All of the following are characteristics of REM sleep EXCEPT:

A. paralysis of skeletal muscles.
B. dreaming.
C. penile erection.
D. decreased brain oxygen use.
E. increased pulse and blood pressure.

9.4. All of the following are characteristic of non-REM sleep EXCEPT:

A. involuntary body movements.
B. decreased blood pressure.
C. slowed pulse.
D. decreased respiration.
E. agitation.

9.5. All of the following are sleep changes associated with major depression EXCEPT:

A. reduced slow wave sleep.
B. shortened REM latency.
C. greater percentage of REM sleep.
D. shift in REM from last to first half of the night.
E. short first REM period.

9.6. All of the following are true about hypersomnia EXCEPT:

A. It is associated with narcolepsy.
B. It is associated with sleep apnea.
C. It is associated with withdrawal of CNS stimulants.
D. It is seen frequently in manic patients.
E. It includes complaints about somnolence.

9.7. All of the following are true about night terrors EXCEPT:

A. The dreams that occur during them are easily recalled.
B. They can develop into sleepwalking episodes.
C. They are parasomnias.
D. They may be the first sign of temporal lobe epilepsy.
E. They are more common in children.

DIRECTIONS: For each of the numbered phrases below, choose the lettered stage of sleep with which it is **most closely associated.** Answers may be used once, more than once, or not at all.

A. Stage 1
B. Stage 2
C. Stages 3 and 4
D. REM

9.8. Sleep spindles

9.9. K-complexes

9.10. Theta waves

9.11. Sawtooth waves

9.12. Slow wave sleep

9.13. Forty-five percent of sleep time

DIRECTIONS: For each of the questions or incomplete statements below, **one or more** of the answers or completions given are correct. Choose answer:

A. if only **1, 2,** and **3** are correct.
B. if only **1** and **3** are correct.
C. if only **2** and **4** are correct.
D. if only **4** is correct.
E. if **all** are correct.

9.14. Brief arousals during slow wave sleep are characterized by

1. enuresis.
2. somnambulism.
3. night terrors.
4. total recall of the arousal.

9.15. Which of the following is/are true about sleep?
1. Patients with Alzheimer's disease have reduced slow wave sleep.
2. Drugs that decrease brain dopamine produce arousal and wakefulness.
3. Patients with Alzheimer's disease have reduced REM sleep.
4. Dopamine blockers decrease sleep time.

9.16. Which of the following is/are true about insomnia?
1. It occurs in less than 5% of the population.
2. It is a disorder of initiating or maintaining sleep.
3. It is rarely associated with anxiety.
4. It may be an early sign of severe depression.

9.17. Which of the following is/are characteristic of insomnia in depression?
1. Normal sleep onset.·
2. Repeated nighttime awakenings.
3. Premature morning awakenings.
4. Repeated sudden occurrences of falling asleep during daylight hours.

9.18. Withdrawal of which of the following drugs is/are associated with insomnia?
1. Benzodiazepines
2. Phenothiazines
3. Marijuana
4. Alcohol

Answers and Explanations

SLEEP

9.1. A. Shortening of REM latency is seen in both narcolepsy and depression.

9.2. C. Acetylcholine is involved in the production of REM sleep.

9.3. D. REM sleep is characterized by increased brain oxygen use.

9.4. E. Non-REM sleep is associated with decreases in blood pressure, pulse, and respiration and with peacefulness and involuntary body movements.

9.5. E. Major depression is associated with reduced slow wave sleep, shortened REM latency, greater percentage of REM, shift in REM from the last to the first half of the night, and long first REM period.

9.6. D. Manic patients frequently have a reduced need for sleep rather than hypersomnolence.

9.7. A. The dreams that occur during night terrors are generally not recalled.

9.8. B. Sleep spindles are seen in stage 2 sleep.

9.9. B. K-complexes are also seen in stage 2 sleep.

9.10. A. Theta waves are seen in stage 1 sleep.

9.11. D. Sawtooth waves are seen in REM sleep.

9.12. C. Slow waves are characteristic of stages 3 and 4 of sleep.

9.13. B. Forty-five percent of sleep time is spent in stage 2 sleep.

9.14. A. Brief arousal during slow wave sleep is associated with enuresis, somnambulism, night terrors, and amnesia during the arousal.

9.15. B. Drugs that increase brain dopamine produce arousal and wakefulness; dopamine blockers tend to increase sleep time. Patients with Alzheimer's disease have reduced slow wave and REM sleep.

9.16. C. Insomnia occurs in up to 30% of the population, may be associated with anxiety, and may also be an early sign of severe depression.

9.17. A. Repeated sudden occurrences of falling asleep during the daytime is a symptom of hypersomnia.

9.18. E. All are correct.

10

Schizophrenia

I. Overview

A. History

—In the late 1800s, **Emil Kraepelin** categorized the seriously mentally ill by three diagnoses—**dementia praecox, manic-depressive psychosis, and paranoia**.

  —Kraepelin described dementia praecox as chronic loss of function with the presence of hallucinations and delusions.

—In the early 1900s, **Eugene Bleuler** first used the term **schizophrenia** to describe this illness.

  —Bleuler described the four "A's" that characterize schizophrenia: **autism** (self-preoccupation and lack of communication), **affect** (blunted), **associations** (loosened), and **ambivalence** (uncertainty).

B. Epidemiology

—The lifetime prevalence of schizophrenia in the United States is about 1%.

—There is no significant sex difference in prevalence of schizophrenia.

—Most male schizophrenics develop the disease between 15 and 25 years of age; women develop schizophrenia between the ages of 25 and 35.

—High population density is correlated with increased rates of schizophrenia.

—There is a higher incidence of schizophrenia in individuals who have recently immigrated to the United States.

—Schizophrenia occurs in all countries and cultures that have been studied.

  —Less developed countries may tolerate the schizophrenic individual better than more highly industrialized countries.

  ✳The season of birth is related to the incidence of schizophrenia: In the northern hemisphere, more schizophrenics are born in the winter months; in the southern hemisphere, more are born in the summer months.

C. Downward Drift

Schizophrenia is diagnosed more often in low socioeconomic populations.

—This higher incidence may be caused by **"downward drift."**

  —The downward drift hypothesis suggests that because of their handicap, people with schizophrenia move into lower socioeconomic classes.

II. Etiology

Psychological and biological theories have been proposed to explain the etiology of schizophrenia.

A. Psychological Etiology

—According to **psychoanalytic theory**, a disturbance in ego organization affects the interpretation of reality and the control of inner drives.

—Other psychodynamic factors thought to be involved in the development of schizophrenia are fixation and regression.

—In **fixation**, an individual becomes overinvested at one stage of development such that he or she cannot move on to subsequent stages.

—In **regression**, an individual reverts to earlier patterns of behavior.

—In the **stress-diathesis** model of schizophrenia, biological vulnerability (diathesis) allows the symptoms of schizophrenia to develop when the individual is stressed by internal or external environmental factors.

B. Biological Etiology

1. *Neurotransmitter Systems*

—The **dopamine hypothesis** asserts that the dopaminergic systems in the brains of schizophrenics are hyperactive.

—This is the major neurotransmitter hypothesis for schizophrenia.

—Postmortem studies conducted on the brains of schizophrenics have demonstrated increased numbers of dopamine-2 receptors in the basal ganglia and limbic systems.

—Decreased γ-aminobutyric acid (GABA) activity can also lead to increased dopaminergic neuron activity.

—Norepinephrine activity may also be increased in schizophrenia.

—Evidence of increased cerebrospinal fluid MHPG in some schizophrenic patients has supported this idea.

2. *Anatomic and Other Changes*

—Computed tomographic studies show enlargement of the lateral and third ventricles as well as cortical atrophy in schizophrenic patients.

—Damage to the frontal lobes has been implicated in the development of schizophrenia.

—The basal ganglia are also implicated because of the prevalence of movement disorders in schizophrenia.

—The hypothalamus, thalamus, brainstem, and corpus callosum have also been associated with schizophrenia.

—Viral infection, immunologic abnormalities, and psychoneuroendocrine dysregulation have been proposed as factors in the etiology of schizophrenia.

III. Clinical Signs and Symptoms

A. The Premorbid Personality

—Typically, the premorbid personality of the schizophrenic as a child is quiet, obedient, passive, and has few friends.

—As an adolescent, the premorbid personality is introverted, daydreams, has no close friends or dates, avoids social activities, and stays at home.

—Somatic complaints such as back pain, headache, digestive problems, or anxiety may coincide with the onset of illness.

—Also, at the onset of illness the patient may develop an interest in philosophy, religion, or the occult.

Table 10.1. Hallucinations, Delusions, and Illusions

Symptom	Definition	Example
Hallucination	False sensory perception	Hearing voices when alone in a room
Delusion	False belief	Feeling that the FBI is following one
Illusion	Misperception of real external stimuli	Interpreting the appearance of a coat in a dark closet as a man

—Other prodromal signs include abnormal mood changes and strange behavior and perceptual experiences.

B. Characteristics of Schizophrenia

—Most commonly, individuals with schizophrenia show flat or blunted affect; their emotions may also be extreme or inappropriate.

—The patient may report feelings of power, fear, or isolation.

—Although auditory hallucinations are most common, other types such as cenesthetic hallucinations (altered sensations of body organs) may also occur.

—The patient is usually oriented to person, time, and place.

—Memory is intact; if not, an organic brain syndrome should be suspected.

—Psychological testing may indicate strange thinking patterns.

—Tests of neuropsychological performance in schizophrenia often suggest temporal and frontal lobe dysfunction.

—Intelligence quotient scores tend to decrease over the course of the disease.

—The thought disorders of schizophrenia can be those of content, form, or process.

C. Disorders of Content of Thought

A **delusion** is an important example of a disorder of content of thought.

—Typical delusions of schizophrenia include the feeling that someone is controlling one's thoughts.

—Other delusions involve ideas of reference in which the patient believes that other people or the media are talking about him or her.

—For accurate diagnosis, a distinction must be made between **hallucinations, delusions,** and **illusions** (Table 10.1).

D. Disorders of Form and Process of Thought

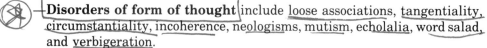—**Disorders of form of thought** include loose associations, tangentiality, circumstantiality, incoherence, neologisms, mutism, echolalia, word salad, and verbigeration.

—For example, in word salad, the patient produces an incoherent combination of words and phrases.

—Loosening of associations, in which ideas shift from one subject to another in an unrelated fashion, is also seen in mania.

—**Disorders in thought processes** include flight of ideas, illogical ideas, thought blocking, short attention span, deficiencies in thought and content of speech, impaired memory and abstraction abilities, perseveration, and clang associations.

Table 10.2. Factors Contributing to the Prognosis in Schizophrenia

Poor Prognosis	Good Prognosis
Uncommunicative and withdrawn	Depressed or manic
Young age at onset	Older age at onset
Slow onset	Rapid onset
No immediate life stressors	Immediate life stressors
Poor employment history	Good employment history
Unmarried	Married
Neurologic problems	No neurologic problems
Few or no friends	Strong relationship with friends
Family history of schizophrenia	Family history of mood disorder
Negative symptoms	Positive symptoms
Frequent relapses	Few relapses

—For example, in thought blocking, there is an abrupt halt in the train of thinking and the person cannot remember what he or she was saying.

E. Negative and Positive Symptoms

Symptoms in schizophrenia have been divided into **negative** (deficit) and **positive** (productive) symptoms.

—Negative symptoms include flattening of affect, thought blocking, deficiencies in speech or speech content, cognitive disturbances, poor grooming, lack of motivation, and social withdrawal.

—Positive symptoms include loose associations, strange behavior, hallucinations, and talkativeness.

F. Suicide in Schizophrenics

Suicide is common in schizophrenic patients; over half attempt suicide and 10% of these die by suicide.

—Risk factors that predict suicide in schizophrenia are male sex, a college education, youth, many relapses, depressed mood, high ambitions, and living alone.

G. Prognosis

Certain factors are useful in predicting the prognosis in schizophrenia (Table 10.2).

IV. Subtypes of Schizophrenia

A. Overview

—Evidence of a disorder in thinking that includes hallucinations, bizarre behavior or delusions indicate schizophrenia.

—The differential diagnoses of schizophrenia include brief reactive psychosis, manic-depressive illness, schizoaffective illness, and organic delirium.

—The DSM-III-R lists five types of schizophrenia—**disorganized (hebephrenic), catatonic, paranoid, undifferentiated,** and **residual**.

B. Disorganized (Hebephrenic) Schizophrenia

—Regression to disinhibited, unorganized behavior that usually begins before age 25 is characteristic of disorganized schizophrenia.

—An obvious thought disorder is present, personal appearance is poor, and emotional responses are inappropriate.

C. Catatonic Schizophrenia

—Catatonic schizophrenia is characterized by stupor, bizarre posturing, and excitement.

—With the introduction of the antipsychotic drugs, catatonic schizophrenia is now rare in North America and Europe.

D. Paranoid Schizophrenia

—Paranoid schizophrenia is characterized by delusions of persecution or grandeur.

—Usually, paranoid patients are older than catatonic or disorganized patients when they have their first psychotic break, which is usually in the late 20s or early 30s.

—Paranoid schizophrenics show less problems with cognitive faculties and behavior than the other subtypes and may function fairly well socially.

E. Undifferentiated Schizophrenia

Undifferentiated schizophrenia includes patients who do not fit easily into one of the preceding three categories but have characteristics of more than one subtype.

F. Residual Schizophrenia

The category of residual schizophrenia is used when one episode has occurred but no prominent psychotic symptoms are present.

—Symptoms commonly include emotional blunting, illogical thinking, odd behavior, and social withdrawal.

V. Treatment

A. Antipsychotic Drugs

Antipsychotic drugs are the major treatment for schizophrenia (see Chapter 3).

—Various antipsychotics show about equal efficacy.

—Some patients show better responses to one than to another antipsychotic.

—If adequate doses are used, the minimum trial period with an antipsychotic is 4 to 6 weeks.

—Generally, lower doses of antipsychotics produce clinical responses that are as good as higher doses.

⚹A major reason for relapse is that patients fail to comply with taking neuroleptics.

   —Adverse effects of the neuroleptics are a common reason for noncompliance.

—When antipsychotic drug treatment is stopped, about two-thirds of patients show symptoms within 18 months; most relapse within about 6 months.

—Psychosocial interventions such as behavioral, family, group, and individual therapy can boost the clinical improvement induced by neuroleptic drugs in schizophrenia.

B. Extrapyramidal Neurologic Signs

Weight gain, extrapyramidal neurologic signs (EPS), and impotence are the most common adverse effects of the neuroleptics.

—EPS include tremor, akinesia (slowing of body movements), rigidity, akathisia (motor restlessness), and acute dystonias (muscle spasms).

—EPS are seen more frequently in men than in women and in younger than in older patients.

—EPS can be treated with anticholinergic drugs.

C. Tardive Dyskinesia and Neuroleptic Malignant Syndrome

Serious side effects of neuroleptic medications are tardive dyskinesia and the neuroleptic malignant syndrome.

—**Tardive dyskinesia** involves uncontrollable writhing and jerking movements, often of the mouth and tongue, which may be irreversible.

—Tardive dyskinesia most commonly occurs in women and in older patients.

—The **neuroleptic malignant syndrome** is life-threatening and includes fever, sweating, increased pulse, increased blood pressure, muscular rigidity, dystonia, akinesia, and agitation.

Review Test

SCHIZOPHRENIA

DIRECTIONS: For each of the questions or incomplete statements below, choose the answer that is **most correct.**

10.1. Bleuler's four "A's" of schizophrenia include all of the following EXCEPT:

A. anhedonia.
B. autism.
C. affect.
D. association.
E. ambivalence.

10.2. Which of the following is thought to be the major neurotransmitter involved in the development of schizophrenia?

A. Norepinephrine
B. GABA
C. Dopamine
D. Acetylcholine
E. Enkephalin

10.3. Prodromal signs of schizophrenia commonly include all of the following EXCEPT:

A. abnormal affect.
B. peculiar behavior.
C. strange perceptual experiences.
D. excessive spending.
E. somatic complaints.

10.4. The most common type of hallucination in schizophrenia is

A. kinesthetic.
B. auditory.
C. cenesthetic.
D. visual.
E. olfactory.

10.5. All of the following are disorders of thought processes in schizophrenia EXCEPT:

A. flight of ideas.
B. neologisms.
C. poverty of thought.
D. thought blocking.
E. perseveration.

10.6. Negative symptoms of schizophrenia include all of the following EXCEPT:

A. hallucinations.
B. flattening of affect.
C. poverty of speech.
D. blocking.
E. social withdrawal.

10.7. The percentage of schizophrenic patients who attempt suicide is approximately

A. 10%.
B. 20%.
C. 35%.
D. 50%.
E. 75%.

10.8. Risk factors for suicide in schizophrenics include all of the following EXCEPT:

A. a college education.
B. female sex.
C. depression.
D. high ambitions.
E. living alone.

10.9. All of the following are true about the use of antipsychotics in schizophrenia EXCEPT:

A. Low doses generally produce clinical responses as good as high doses.
B. Most antipsychotics are equally effective.
C. Noncompliance with neuroleptics is a major reason for relapse.
D. Adverse effects of the neuroleptics are a common reason for noncompliance.
E. The minimum length of a trial with an antipsychotic is 2 to 3 weeks at adequate doses.

10.10. All of the following are true about extrapyramidal neurologic signs EXCEPT:

A. They respond to anticholinergic drugs.
B. They are more common in women than in men.
C. They are a common adverse effect of the neuroleptics.
D. They are more common in younger than in older people.
E. They include tremor.

10.11. All of the following are true about schizophrenia EXCEPT:

A. Peak age of onset is different for men than for women.
B. It is more prevalent in low socioeconomic populations.
C. Increased rates correlate with high population density.
D. More schizophrenics are born in the summer than in the winter months in the Northern hemisphere.
E. It is seen more frequently in recent immigrants.

10.12. All of the following are characteristic of the premorbid personality of the schizophrenic EXCEPT:

A. passivity.
B. obedience.
C. few friends in childhood.
D. introversion.
E. hyperactivity.

10.13. Which of the following statements is true about schizophrenia?

A. Memory is rarely intact.
B. The patient is rarely oriented as to person, time, and place.
C. The IQ stays stable over the course of the disease.
D. Tests of neuropsychological performance often suggest temporal lobe dysfunction.
E. The most common type of hallucinations are visual.

10.14. Which of the following is true about tardive dyskinesia?

A. It is more common in men than in women.
B. It is a serious side effect of the neuroleptics.
C. It is more common in younger than in older patients.
D. It is easily reversible.
E. It is characterized primarily by rigidity.

DIRECTIONS: For each of the numbered phrases below, choose the type of schizophrenia with which it is **most closely associated.**

A. Disorganized
B. Catatonic
C. Paranoid
D. Undifferentiated
E. Residual

10.15. Bizarre posturing

10.16. Delusions of persecution

10.17. No prominent psychotic symptoms

DIRECTIONS: For each of the questions or incomplete statements below, **one** or **more** of the answers or completions given are correct. Choose answer:

A. if only **1, 2,** and **3** are correct.
B. if only **1** and **3** are correct.
C. if only **2** and **4** are correct.
D. if only **4** is correct.
E. if **all** are correct.

10.18. The differential diagnoses of schizophrenia include:

1. organic delirium.
2. schizoaffective illness.
3. manic-depressive illness.
4. brief reactive psychosis.

10.19. Which of the following brain regions have been implicated in schizophrenia?

1. The basal ganglia
2. The frontal lobes
3. The hypothalamus
4. The thalamus

10.20. The feeling that someone is controlling one's thoughts is

1. a delusion.
2. a disorder of form of thought.
3. a disorder of content of thought.
4. rare in schizophrenia.

10.21. Positive symptoms of schizophrenia include:

1. hallucinations.
2. cognitive deficits.
3. increased speech.
4. poor grooming.

10.22. Which of the following psychosocial interventions can be used to increase the clinical improvement induced by neuroleptic drugs in schizophrenia?

1. Behavioral therapy
2. Family therapy
3. Group therapy
4. Individual therapy

Answers and Explanations

SCHIZOPHRENIA

10.1. A. Bleuler's four "A's" of schizophrenia are autism, affect, association, and ambivalence.

10.2. C. Dopamine is the major neurotransmitter believed to be involved in the development of schizophrenia.

10.3. D. Prodromal signs of schizophrenia include somatic complaints such as headache, as well as anxiety, abnormal affect, peculiar behavior, and strange perceptual experiences.

10.4. B. The most common type of hallucination in schizophrenia is auditory.

10.5. B. Disorders of thought processes in schizophrenia include flight of ideas, thought blocking, impaired attention, poverty of thought and content of speech, poor memory, poor abstraction abilities, perseveration, clang associations, and illogical ideas. Neologisms are disorders of form of thought.

10.6. A. Flattening of affect, poverty of speech, blocking, and social withdrawal are negative symptoms of schizophrenia; hallucinations are positive symptoms.

10.7. D. Approximately 50% of schizophrenic patients attempt suicide.

10.8. B. Risk factors for suicide in schizophrenics are male sex, college education, a large number of exacerbations, depression, high ambitions, living alone, and young age.

10.9. E. The minimum length of a trial with an antipsychotic is 4 to 6 weeks.

10.10. B. Extrapyramidal neurologic signs are a common side effect of neuroleptics, respond to anticholinergic drugs, and are more common in men than in women and in younger rather than in older people.

10.11. D. In the Northern hemisphere, more schizophrenics are born in the winter than in the summer.

10.12. E. Passivity, obedience, and few friends characterize the premorbid personality of the schizophrenic.

10.13. D. In schizophrenia, memory is intact although the IQ tends to deteriorate over the course of the disease. The patient is usually oriented as to person, time, and place. The most common type of hallucination seen in schizophrenia is auditory.

10.14. B. Tardive dyskinesia, a serious side effect of the neuroleptics, involves uncontrollable movements, is seen more commonly in women than in men, is more common in older than in younger patients, and is frequently irreversible.

10.15. B. The catatonic type of schizophrenia is characterized by stupor and bizarre posturing.

10.16. C. The paranoid type of schizophrenia is characterized by delusions of persecution and delusions of grandeur.

10.17. E. The category of residual schizophrenia is used when there has been one schizophrenic episode but no prominent psychotic symptoms. Symptoms of residual schizophrenia include emotional blunting, social withdrawal, illogical thinking, and eccentric behavior.

10.18. All are correct.

10.19. All are correct.

10.20. B. The feeling that someone is controlling one's thoughts is a delusion. A delusion is an example of a disorder of content of thought seen in schizophrenia.

10.21. B. Hallucinations, increased speech, loosening of associations, and bizarre behavior are positive symptoms of schizophrenia. Cognitive deficits and poor grooming are negative symptoms of schizophrenia.

10.22. E. All are correct.

11

Mood Disorders

I. Overview

A. Mood and Affect
—**Mood** can be defined as an individual's internal emotional state.
—**Affect** refers to how that emotional state is expressed.
—Mood disorders are pathologic conditions of mood and affect.

B. Mania and Depression
—Elevation of mood, or **mania**, is associated with flight of ideas, decreased sleep, grandiosity, and expansiveness.
—Depression of mood is associated with decreased energy and interest levels, difficulty in concentrating, guilt, reduction in appetite, and suicidal thoughts.

C. Bipolar and Unipolar Disorder
Mood disorders include **bipolar**, or manic-depressive disorder, and **unipolar** depression, or major depressive disorder.
—In unipolar depression, patients have only depression.
—Patients with bipolar disorder have both mania and depression or only mania.
—Other categories of mood disorder are **hypomania, cyclothymia,** and **dysthymia,** which are mild or attenuated forms of mania, bipolar disorder, and major depression, respectively.

II. Epidemiology

A. Occurrence
—Approximately 20% of women and 10% of men will develop unipolar depression during their lives.
—About 1% of both men and women will develop bipolar disorder.
—Only 20 to 25% of people with major depression are treated for the disorder.
—There are no racial differences in the occurrence of mood disorders.
—Mental health professionals may misdiagnose mood disorders as schizophrenia in black and Hispanic patients.
—Mood disorders are more common in single, divorced, and separated people than in married people.
—Recent immigration may be associated with depression (see Chapter 18).

Table 11.1. Comparison of Unipolar and Bipolar Disorder

Unipolar	Bipolar
Mean age of onset is 40 years	Mean age of onset is 30 years
Twice as many women as men	Equal numbers of women and men
No correlation with social class	Higher incidence in upper socioeconomic groups
Some evidence of genetic etiology	Strong evidence for genetic etiology

B. Unipolar Versus Bipolar Disorder

Demographic differences between unipolar and bipolar disorder are shown in Table 11.1.

III. Etiology

Biological and psychosocial hypotheses have been proposed to explain the etiology of mood disorders.

A. Biological Factors

1. *Neurotransmitters and Mood Disorders*

   —**Norepinephrine** and **serotonin** are the primary neurotransmitters associated with mood disorders.

   —Dopaminergic activity may be decreased in depression and increased in mania.

   —Acetylcholine may be dysregulated in mood disorders.

   —Abnormalities in 5-HIAA, HVA, and MHPG have been seen in urine, blood, and cerebrospinal fluid samples from mood disorder patients (see Chapter 17).

   —Brains of those who have committed suicide show fewer serotonin reuptake sites, as measured by the binding of 3H-imipramine, and altered levels of serotonin.

2. *The Neuroendocrine System and Mood Disorders*

   —Neuroendocrine abnormalities of the limbic-hypothalamic-pituitary-adrenal axis are seen in patients with mood disorders.

   —Some depressed patients demonstrate hypersecretion of cortisol.

   —The dexamethasone suppression test (DST) has been used in the diagnosis of depression but has limited clinical usefulness (see Chapter 17).

     —In about half of depressed patients the DST has been shown to be abnormal, but abnormal DSTs may also indicate other psychiatric and medical illnesses.

   —Depression is associated with other neuroendocrine findings:

     —Reduced release of thyroid-stimulating hormone with a challenge of thyroid-releasing hormone.

     —Decreased nighttime secretion of melatonin.

     —Decreased release of prolactin with tryptophan administration.

     —Decreased levels of gonadotropic hormones.

     —Decreased release of growth hormone with noradrenergic stimulation with clonidine.

3. *Other Biological Factors*
—Immune system function may be abnormal in persons with mood disorders.
—Sleep patterns are often abnormal in depression (see Chapter 9).
—Genetic factors are involved in the etiology of mood disorders (see Chapter 1).
—There is evidence for pathology of the basal ganglia, limbic system, and hypothalamus in mood disorders.

B. Psychosocial Factors

Life stressors are probably related to the development of depression.
—The loss of a parent prior to puberty and loss of a spouse correlate with major depression.
—Misinterpretation of life events, low self-esteem, loss of hope, and feelings of pessimism are involved in cognitive theories about the development of depression.

IV. Clinical Signs and Symptoms of Mood Disorders

A. Signs and Symptoms

—With depression, the depressed mood often is very different from sadness.
  —Unlike sad patients, depressed patients often report that they are unable to cry.
—Some patients appear unaware of or may deny depression even though symptoms are present (Table 11.2).
—Generalized psychomotor retardation is common in depression, particularly in elderly patients.
—Psychomotor agitation is also seen in depression.
—Depressed patients with delusions or hallucinations have depression with psychotic features.
—Symptoms of depression in both major depressive disorder and bipolar disorder are similar.
—Objective rating scales of depression include the **Hamilton, Raskin,** and **Zung scales**.

B. Delusions in Depression

—Delusions in depression may be mood congruent or mood incongruent.
  —**Mood congruent** delusions—those appropriate to a depressed mood—include feelings of guilt, worthlessness, failure, evilness, persecution, and terminal illness.
  —**Mood incongruent** delusions—those inappropriate to a depressed mood—may involve grandiose themes.
—Although they do occur, hallucinations are not common in major depression.
—Orientation with respect to person, place, and time is usually intact in depressed persons.
—Cognitive impairment—the impaired concentration and forgetfulness that frequently occurs in depression—is also known as **pseudodementia**.

Table 11.2. Symptoms of Mood Disorder

Symptom	Occurrence (%, if known)
Depression	
Depressed mood	*Hallmark*; may be denied in 50%
Diminished interest or pleasure in activities	Common
Reduced energy	97%
Decreased motivation	Common
Sleep problems, insomnia	80%
Suicidal ideation	66%
Suicide	10–15%
Decreased or increased appetite	Common
Weight loss	May occur
Decreased interest in sex	May occur
Diurnal variation in symptoms	50%
Inability to concentrate	84%
Impaired thinking	50–75%
Psychomotor retardation	Common (particularly in the elderly)
Delusions	May occur
Mania	
Elevated, expansive, or irritable mood	*Hallmark*
Grandiosity	Common
Disinhibition	Common
Impulsivity	Common
Distractibility	Common
Talkativeness	Common
Flight of ideas	Common
Assaultiveness	75%
Impaired judgment	Common
Delusions	75%

C. Suicide

—Frequently, severely depressed patients do not have the energy to commit suicide.

—The risk of suicide increases as depression lifts and energy returns.

D. Mania

—Mania is characterized by excitability, hyperactivity, and talkativeness.

—Although they may be euphoric, manic patients can also be irritable, angry, and hostile.

—In mania, mood congruent delusions include those of strength, exceptional abilities, and financial power.

—Disorders of form and process of thought—including loosening of associations, flight of ideas, word salad, and neologisms—may occur in a manic episode.

—As a manic episode proceeds, speech becomes difficult to follow and comprehend.

—Judgment is impaired in mania; laws are often broken.

V. Course

A. Major Depressive Disorder

—Half to three-quarters of depressed patients have a second depressive episode.

—Often the second episode occurs 4 to 6 months after the first episode.

—Periods of mental health separate periods of illness.

—Premorbid problems rarely occur in patients with depressive disorder.
—Approximately half of all patients have their first episode prior to age 40.
—First episodes after age 40 are often associated with alcoholism, no family history, and sociopathy.
—If untreated, depression lasts from half a year to a year; with treatment, an episode resolves in about 3 months.
—With age, frequency and length of episodes often increase.
—An average of five or six depressive episodes may occur over a 20-year period.

B. Bipolar Disorder

—In 75% of females and 67% of males, bipolar disorder begins with depression.
—Although patients may be originally diagnosed as having unipolar depression, 5 to 10% of them eventually (within 6 to 10 years) will experience a manic episode.
—The average age for a first manic episode is 32 years, and it often occurs after about three episodes of depression.
—The characteristics of depression in people who later have a manic episode include psychotic behavior, psychomotor retardation, depression, family history of bipolar disorder, history of hypomania following antidepressant drug treatment, and postpartum depression.
—Mania in the absence of depression is seen in only 10 to 20% of bipolar patients.
—Manic episodes usually have a rapid onset, but they may evolve slowly over weeks.
—When untreated, manic episodes usually last about 3 months.
—The time period between episodes becomes shorter as bipolar illness progresses.
 —The period between episodes in bipolar illness is generally 6 to 9 months.

VI. Prognosis

A. Major Depressive Disorder

—Indicators of recurrence include alcohol and drug abuse, anxiety, older age at onset, dysthymia (chronic low mood), and a history of multiple depressive episodes.
—Chronic impairment, which occurs in about 20% of unipolar patients, is more common in men.

B. Bipolar Illness

—The prognosis for bipolar disorder is not as favorable as that for major depressive disorder.
—Patients with only manic symptoms have a better prognosis than those with mixed symptomatology.
—Patients with psychotic symptoms do not necessarily have a poor prognosis.
—Forty percent of patients have more than 10 episodes of mania.
—Thirty percent of bipolar patients are in partial remission; chronic impairment is present in about 10%.

Table 11.3. **Nonpsychiatric Causes of Depressive Symptoms**

Medical: Pancreatic cancer and other cancers, renal and cardiopulmonary disease
Endocrine: Thyroid, adrenal, or parathyroid dysfunction
Infectious: Pneumonia, mononucleosis, AIDS
Inflammatory: Systemic lupus erythematosus, rheumatoid arthritis
Neurologic: Epilepsy, multiple sclerosis, Parkinson's disease, stroke, brain trauma
Nutritional: Nutritional deficiencies
Prescription drugs: Reserpine, propranolol, steroids, methyldopa, oral contraceptives
Drugs of abuse: Alcohol, marijuana, hallucinogens, amphetamine withdrawal

VII. Differential Diagnoses

A. Psychiatric Disorders

Psychiatric disorders that have depressive features include alcohol and drug abuse, anorexia nervosa, anxiety disorders, schizoaffective disorders, schizophrenia, and somatization disorders.

B. Nonpsychiatric Disorders

A number of medical diseases, neurologic disorders, and drugs are associated with depression (Table 11.3).

VIII. Treatment

A. Overview

Depression is a self-limiting disorder that is successfully treated in about 75% of patients. Treatment of mood disorders includes pharmacologic and psychological interventions.

B. Pharmacologic Treatment

—A 4- to 6-week trial of a heterocyclic antidepressant is usually the first treatment for major depression.
—Antidepressants often take 3 to 4 weeks to work.
—If heterocyclic antidepressants fail, atypical antidepressants such as fluoxetine (Prozac) or an MAO inhibitor can be tried.
—Combinations of heterocyclic and MAOI antidepressants and heterocyclics and lithium can be used with caution.
—Antipsychotic medication in addition to an antidepressant may be used in patients who have depression with psychotic features.
—Lithium is the drug of choice for patients with mania.
—Carbamazepine (Tegretol) may be used in manic patients if lithium is ineffective.
—Lithium is often used in a maintenance regimen in bipolar patients.

C. Psychological Treatment

—Psychotherapy in conjunction with drug treatment has been found to be more beneficial than either treatment alone.
—Psychotherapy can increase compliance with the drug regimen in mood disorders.
—Types of psychotherapy used in the treatment of mood disorders include interpersonal, family, behavior, cognitive, and psychoanalytic therapy.

Review Test

MOOD DISORDERS

DIRECTIONS: For each of the questions or incomplete statements below, choose the answer that is **most correct.**

11.1. All of the following are true about bipolar disorder EXCEPT:

A. About 1% of men and women will develop the disorder.
B. It is more common in lower socioeconomic groups.
C. It has a genetic component.
D. Differential diagnoses include schizophrenia.
E. Differential diagnoses include drug abuse.

11.2. All of the following are true about the course of major depressive disorder EXCEPT:

A. Frequency of episodes often increases with age.
B. Length of episodes often increases with age.
C. Premorbid problems are common.
D. About half of all patients have their first episode prior to the age of 40.
E. Treated episodes last for about 3 months.

11.3. All of the following are true about bipolar illness EXCEPT:

A. In most patients it begins with a depressive episode.
B. About 70% of patients experience only manic episodes.
C. Manic episodes typically have a rapid onset.
D. The period between episodes is generally 6 to 9 months.
E. The amount of time between episodes decreases as the illness progresses.

11.4. Mood congruent delusions in depression include all of the following EXCEPT:

A. guilt.
B. terminal illness.
C. failure.
D. grandiose themes.
E. persecution.

11.5. The dexamethasone suppression test

A. is used frequently in the diagnosis of schizophrenia.
B. shows abnormalities in at least 95% of depressed patients.
C. has been used in the diagnosis of depression.
D. is rarely abnormal in patients with medical illnesses.
E. is affected by decreased melatonin levels.

11.6. Neuroendocrine markers of depression include all of the following EXCEPT:

A. decreased release of growth hormone with noradrenergic stimulation with clonidine.
B. increased nocturnal secretion of melatonin.
C. decreased prolactin release following tryptophan administration.
D. decreased FSH.
E. decreased LH.

11.7. All of the following are true about depression EXCEPT:

A. It correlates with the loss of a parent before age 11.
B. The depressed mood is basically a severe form of sadness.
C. Depressed patients are often unable to cry.
D. Stressful life events have no relationship to clinical depression.
E. It is related to loss of a spouse.

11.8. All of the following are true in major depressive disorder EXCEPT:

A. Severely depressed patients often lack the energy to commit suicide.
B. As severe depression lifts, the risk of suicide decreases.
C. Orientation with respect to person, place, and time is usually intact.
D. Presence of hallucinations suggests depression with psychotic features.
E. Generalized psychomotor retardation is seen in depressed elderly patients.

11.9. All of the following occur during a manic episode EXCEPT:

A. loosening of associations.
B. flight of ideas.
C. word salad.
D. neologisms.
E. lack of energy.

11.10. Which of the following is true about bipolar illness?

A. Manic patients usually have a poor memory.
B. The judgment of manic patients is rarely impaired.
C. Manic patients are rarely assaultive.
D. The depressions in unipolar disorder and bipolar disorder have similar features.
E. Manic patients usually have poor orientation.

11.11. All of the following are characteristics of depression in people who later go on to have a manic episode EXCEPT:

A. psychomotor retardation.
B. postpartum depression.
C. psychotic symptoms.
D. family history of bipolar disorder.
E. agitated depression.

11.12. In major depressive disorder, the risk of recurrence of depression correlates with all of the following EXCEPT:

A. younger age at onset.
B. alcohol abuse.
C. divorce.
D. history of other depressive episodes.
E. anxiety.

11.13. Which of the following statements about bipolar disorder is true?

A. It has a better prognosis than major depressive disorder.
B. Patients with mixed symptomatology have better prognoses than those with only manic symptoms.
C. Chronic impairment is present in most patients.
D. Forty percent of patients have more than 10 episodes of mania in their lifetimes.
E. White patients are more likely to suffer from bipolar disorder than black patients.

11.14. Which of the following is true about the treatment of mood disorders?

A. Antidepressants usually work within 1 week.
B. Depression is treatable in approximately 20% of patients.
C. Combinations of heterocyclic and MAOI antidepressants are never used to treat depression.
D. Heterocyclic antidepressants are usually the first choice of treatment for major depression.
E. Lithium is used in manic patients only when carbamazepine is ineffective.

DIRECTIONS: For each of the following statements choose:

A. if it is associated primarily with unipolar depression.
B. if it is associated primarily with bipolar disorder.
C. if it is associated with both unipolar and bipolar disorder.
D. if it associated with neither unipolar nor bipolar disorder.

11.15. Approximately equal prevalence in men and women

11.16. Higher incidence in upper socioeconomic groups

11.17. Mean age of onset is 40 years

11.18. Evidence of a genetic etiology

11.19. Lifetime expectancy of about 1%

DIRECTIONS: For each of the following statements choose:
A. if it is associated mainly with depression.
B. if it is associated mainly with mania.
C. if it is associated with both depression and mania.
D. if it is associated with neither mania nor depression.

C **11.20.** Delusions

A **11.21.** Psychomotor retardation

B **11.22.** Flight of ideas

DIRECTIONS: For each of the questions or incomplete statements below, **one** or **more** of the answers or completions given are correct. Choose answer:
A. if only **1, 2,** and **3** are correct.
B. if only **1** and **3** are correct.
C. if only **2** and **4** are correct.
D. if only **4** is correct.
E. if **all** are correct.

B **11.23.** Which of the following has/have been found postmortem in people who have committed suicide?
1. Decreased number of serotonin reuptake sites in the brain
2. Increased dopaminergic activity in the brain
3. Altered concentration of serotonin in the brain
4. Evidence of decreased secretion of cortisol

A **11.24.** Abnormalities seen in the blood, urine, and cerebrospinal fluid of patients with mood disorders include:
1. 5-HIAA.
2. HVA.
3. MHPG.
4. dexamethasone.

E **11.25.** Cognitive theories of the etiology of major depression involve:
1. misinterpretation of a life experience.
2. negative self-evaluation.
3. pessimism.
4. hopelessness.

11.26. Which of the following is/are objective rating scales of depression?
1. The Hamilton
2. The Raskin
3. The Zung
4. The Wechsler

11.27. Which of the following psychiatric disorders can have depressive features?
1. Anxiety disorders
2. Schizoaffective disorders
3. Somatization disorders
4. Alcohol and drug abuse

E **11.28.** The use of which of the following prescription drugs is/are associated with depressive symptoms?
1. Methyldopa
2. Oral contraceptives
3. Steroids
4. Propranolol

A **11.29.** Which of the following is/are true about the treatment of mood disorders?
1. Psychotherapy in conjunction with drug treatment is more beneficial than either treatment alone.
2. Psychotherapy can increase compliance with the drug regimen in mood disorders.
3. Lithium is often used in a maintenance regimen in bipolar patients.
4. Carbamazepine is the drug of choice for patients with mania.

Answers and Explanations

MOOD DISORDERS

11.1. B. Bipolar disorder is more common in higher socioeconomic groups.

11.2. C. Patients with major depressive disorder rarely have premorbid problems.

11.3. B. About 10 to 20% of bipolar patients experience only manic episodes.

11.4. D. Mood congruent delusions are consistent with a depressed mood and include guilt, sinfulness, worthlessness, failure, persecution, and feelings that one has a terminal illness.

11.5. C. The dexamethasone suppression test has been used in the diagnosis of depression, is abnormal in about 50% of depressed patients, and may be abnormal in patients with other psychiatric and medical illnesses.

11.6. B. Decreased nocturnal secretion of melatonin, FSH, and LH hormone are neuroendocrine markers of depression.

11.7. B. In depression, the mood has a distinct quality, which distinguishes it from sadness. Although biological factors are involved, stressful life events are also related to the development of clinical depression.

11.8. B. In major depressive disorder, orientation with respect to persons, place, and time is usually normal. Although severely depressed patients may lack the energy to commit suicide, as the depression lifts the risk of suicide increases. Generalized psychomotor retardation is seen in depressed elderly patients.

11.9. E. Excessive energy and hyperactivity characterize manic episodes.

11.10. D. Manic patients usually show intact memory and orientation. Manic patients may be assaultive and show poor judgment.

11.11. E. Psychomotor retardation, postpartum depression, psychotic symptoms, and family history of bipolar disorder characterize depressed patients who later experience a manic episode.

11.12. A. The risk of recurrence of depression in major depressive disorder correlates with older age at onset, divorce, and anxiety, as well as alcohol abuse and history of other depressive episodes.

11.13. D. Bipolar disorder has a worse prognosis than major depressive disorder. There are no racial differences in the occurrence of mood disorders. Bipolar patients with only manic symptoms have a better prognosis than those with mixed symptomology. Finally, chronic impairment is present in only about 10% of bipolar patients.

11.14. D. Depression is a treatable disorder in 70 to 80% of patients. Antidepressants frequently require a 4- to 6-week trial. Heterocyclic antidepressants can be used in conjunction with MAOIs.

11.15. B. The prevalence of bipolar disorder is approximately equal in men and women.

11.16. B. There is a higher incidence of bipolar disorder in higher socioeconomic groups.

11.17. A. The mean age of onset of unipolar disorder is approximately 40 years.

11.18. C. There is evidence for a genetic etiology in both bipolar and unipolar disorder.

11.19. B. The lifetime expectancy for bipolar disorder is approximately 1%.

11.20. C. Delusions are found in both depression and in mania.

11.21. A. Psychomotor retardation is seen in depression.

11.22. B. Flight of ideas is seen in mania.

11.23. B. Decreased number of serotonin reuptake sites and altered concentration of serotonin have been found postmortem in the brains of people who have committed suicide.

11.24. A. Abnormalities in 5-HIAA, HVA, and MHPG have been seen in the blood, urine, and cerebrospinal fluid of patients with mood disorders.

11.25. E. All are correct.

11.26. A. Objective rating scales of depression include the Hamilton, the Raskin, and the Zung.

11.27. E. All are correct.

11.28. E. All are correct.

11.29. A. Lithium is the drug of choice for patients with mania; carbamazepine may be used if lithium is ineffective.

12

Anxiety Disorders

I. Overview

A. Fear and Anxiety

Fear is a normal reaction to a known external source of danger. In **anxiety,** the individual experiences apprehension or terror, but the source of the danger is unknown or unrecognized.

—Physical manifestations of anxiety include restlessness, dizziness, palpitations, syncope, tingling in the extremities, tachycardia, tremor, upset stomach, diarrhea, and urinary frequency, hesitancy, and urgency.

—The DSM-III-R classification of anxiety disorders includes panic disorder, phobias, obsessive-compulsive disorder, post-traumatic stress disorder, and generalized anxiety disorder.

B. Neurotransmitters and Anxiety

—The major neurotransmitters associated with anxiety are GABA, norepinephrine, and serotonin (see Chapter 2).

—Other neurotransmitters implicated in anxiety are histamine, acetylcholine, and endogenous opioids.

C. Anatomy

Locus Ceruleus
Raphe Nuclei

—The locus ceruleus and raphe nuclei are brain areas likely to be involved in the pathology of anxiety disorders.

—The limbic system, which receives input from the locus ceruleus and raphe nuclei, has a high concentration of benzodiazepine receptor–binding sites.

—The temporal and frontal cerebral cortex have been associated with anxiety.

—Organic causes of anxiety disorders include vitamin B_{12} deficiency, hypo- and hyperthyroidism, hypoglycemia, hypoparathyroidism, cardiac arrhythmias, and mitral valve prolapse.

II. Panic Disorder

A. Characteristics

Panic disorder is identified by episodic, intense periods of anxiety that occur suddenly and usually last about 30 minutes.

—Symptoms of panic disorder include dyspnea, palpitations, dizziness, sweating, fainting, chest pain, and trembling.

—Panic attacks commonly occur twice per week, are often associated with agoraphobia (fear of open places), and appear mainly in young adults.

B. Treatment

—Antidepressant drugs, primarily imipramine, are the principal pharmacologic treatment for panic disorder.

—The efficacy of antidepressant drugs in panic disorder may be mediated through the serotonergic system.

III. Phobias

A. Characteristics

Phobias are irrational fears of objects or social or environmental situations; because of the fear, the object or situation is avoided.

—Examples of phobic disorders are agoraphobia (fear of open areas) and claustrophobia (fear of closed areas).

—Phobias result in severe anxiety following exposure to the feared object or situation.

—In agoraphobia, an individual may feel intense anxiety accompanied by physical symptoms such as palpitations when he or she goes outdoors.

B. Treatment

—In addition to antidepressant drug therapy, treatment of phobias involves psychotherapy and treatment with β-adrenergic antagonists such as propranolol.

—Psychological treatment of panic disorders and phobias includes behavioral desensitization as well as family therapy and psychotherapy.

IV. Obsessive-Compulsive Disorder

A. Characteristics

Obsessive-compulsive disorder is characterized by obsessions (recurrent thoughts, feelings, and images) and compulsions (conscious, repetitive actions).

—Patients with obsessive-compulsive disorder show a high incidence of nonspecific electroencephalographic abnormalities.

—The cingulate gyrus has been implicated in obsessive-compulsive disorder.

B. Treatment

Clomipramine, a tricyclic antidepressant, is the most effective drug treatment for obsessive-compulsive disorder, although other tricyclics have been used.

V. Post-Traumatic Stress Disorder

A. Characteristics

People who have experienced a severe emotional trauma are at risk for **post-traumatic stress disorder.**

—Fifty to 80% of survivors of severe natural disasters may develop post-traumatic stress disorder.

B. Treatment

Psychotherapy, tricyclic antidepressants, and MAOIs are used in treating post-traumatic stress disorder.

VI. Generalized Anxiety Disorder

A. Characteristics

Generalized anxiety disorder is characterized by chronic (over 6 months) persistent anxiety with tension, sympathetic and parasympathetic symptoms, and insomnia.

—Generalized anxiety disorder develops more frequently in women than in men and commonly occurs in the 20s.

—Symptoms of anxiety cannot be related to a specific person or situation.

B. Treatment

Treatment of generalized anxiety disorder includes relaxation therapy and antianxiety agents.

Review Test

ANXIETY DISORDERS

DIRECTIONS: For each of the questions or incomplete statements below, choose the answer that is **most correct.**

12.1. All of the following are physical manifestations of anxiety EXCEPT:

A. palpitations.
B. syncope.
C. tingling in the extremities.
D. ideas of reference.
E. gastrointestinal problems.

12.2. All of the following are true about panic attacks EXCEPT:

A. Symptoms include dizziness, sweating, and fainting.
B. Panic attacks commonly occur once per month.
C. The intense periods of anxiety usually last 3 to 4 hours.
D. Panic attacks commonly first appear in young adulthood.
E. Imipramine is the primary pharmacologic treatment.

12.3. All of the following are true about obsessive-compulsive disorder EXCEPT:

A. EEG abnormalities are rare.
B. It is characterized by recurrent thoughts or feelings.
C. The most effective drug treatment is clomipramine.
D. Tricyclic antidepressants are used in its treatment.
E. Standardized patterns of recurrent behavior commonly occur.

12.4. All of the following are true about generalized anxiety disorder EXCEPT:

A. It occurs more frequently in women.
B. It is characterized by chronic persistent anxiety.
C. Sympathetic and parasympathetic symptoms occur.
D. The symptoms cannot be related to a single cause.
E. It commonly develops at around age 50.

12.5. All of the following brain regions have been implicated in the anxiety disorders EXCEPT:

A. the cerebellum.
B. the locus ceruleus.
C. the raphe nuclei.
D. the cingulate gyrus.
E. the temporal cerebral cortex.

12.6. Treatments for phobias include all of the following EXCEPT:

A. β-adrenergic antagonists.
B. electroconvulsive therapy.
C. antidepressant drugs.
D. psychotherapy.
E. behavioral desensitization.

12.7. Which of the following is/are true about post-traumatic stress disorder?

A. Psychotherapy is used in treatment.
B. Tricyclic antidepressants are used in treatment.
C. Fifty to 85% of survivors of severe disasters develop the disorder.
D. It occurs following a severe emotional trauma.
E. All of the above.

Answers and Explanations

ANXIETY DISORDERS

12.1. D. Physical manifestations of anxiety include syncope, palpitations, gastrointestinal problems, tingling in the extremities, dizziness, tremor, urinary frequency, hesitancy, urgency, and tachycardia. Ideas of reference are seen in schizophrenia.

12.2. B. Panic attacks commonly occur twice per week.

12.3. A. There is a high incidence of nonspecific EEG abnormalities in patients with obsessive-compulsive disorder.

12.4. E. Generalized anxiety disorder commonly develops in the 20s.

12.5. A. The locus ceruleus, raphe nuclei, limbic system, and temporal cerebral cortex are brain areas involved in the anxiety disorders.

12.6. B. Common treatments for phobias include antidepressant drugs such as imipramine and β-adrenergic antagonists as well as psychotherapy and behavioral desensitization.

12.7. E. All are correct.

13

Organic Mental Syndromes

I. Overview

A. Etiology

—Organic mental syndromes are caused by abnormalities in brain chemistry, structure, or physiology.

—The underlying problem may originate in the brain or may be secondary to systemic disease.

B. Characteristics

—The hallmarks of organic mental disease are **cognitive problems,** ie, deficits in memory, orientation, judgment, or mental functions.

  —Cognitive loss in organic mental syndromes may be associated with anxiety, irritability, depression, euphoria, paranoia, apathy, and loosening of control of sexual and aggressive impulses.

—Organic mental disease can result in psychosis that is difficult to distinguish from that of mental illness.

—The major organic mental syndromes are **delirium** and **dementia**.

II. Delirium

A. Characteristics

Delirium is impaired cognitive functioning caused by central nervous system dysfunction; it is characterized by clouding of consciousness.

—Cognitive impairment shows diurnal variability and is worse at night and in the early morning.

—In delirium, orientation to time and place is impaired; orientation to person is usually intact.

—Illusions and hallucinations, often visual in nature, occur.

  —The hallucinations associated with delirium are less organized than those in schizophrenia.

—The patient is often either hypoactive or hyperactive.

—Autonomic dysfunction, fear, and anxiety occur.

B. Occurrence

—Delirium is the most common psychiatric syndrome seen in patients on medical and surgical hospital wards.

Table 13.1. Causes of Delirium

Cerebral	Somatic	External or Pharmacologic
Brain trauma	Hepatic encephalopathy	Hypnotics
Encephalitis	Uremic encephalopathy	Sedatives
Epilepsy	Endocrine dysfunctions	Tranquilizers
Meningitis	Hypoxia	Alcohol
Subarachnoid hemorrhage	Carbon dioxide narcosis	Anticholinergics
	Cardiac failure	Anticonvulsants
	Arrhythmias	Antihypertensives
	Hypotension	Antiparkinson drugs
	Systemic infections	Cardiac glycosides
	Thiamine deficiency	Cimetidine
	Electrolyte imbalance	Disulfiram
	Postoperative states	Insulin
	Normal pressure hydrocephalus	Opiates
		Phencyclidine
		Salicylates
		Steroids
		Carbon monoxide
		Poisons

—Delirium has many causes and may occur in up to 30% of patients in surgical and coronary intensive care units (Table 13.1).

—Delirium is more common in the elderly and in children.

—A history of prior delirium increases the risk of developing it again.

C. Treatment of Delirium

—If the underlying cause is treated and removed, the delirium will resolve.

—Untreated delirium can advance to dementia or to another more severe organic brain syndrome.

III. Dementia

A. Characteristics

Dementia involves a general loss of intellectual abilities and impaired functioning.

—Memory loss is an early symptom of dementia; in contrast to delirium, level of consciousness remains normal.

—Inability to control impulses and lack of judgment are often found, particularly with involvement of the frontal lobes.

—Paranoid ideation may occur.

B. Occurrence

Dementia occurs mostly in the elderly.

—Approximately 1,000,000 Americans over age 65 have dementia that impairs functioning; 2,000,000 more have mild dementia.

—Because the incidence of dementia increases with age, as people live longer, it is seen more frequently.

—In about 65% of cases, the disorder is primary degenerative dementia of the Alzheimer's type.

—Alzheimer's disease is mainly associated with severe memory loss.

Table 13.2. Causes of Dementia

Nervous System	Somatic	Infections
Alzheimer's disease	Endocrine disorders	Creutzfeldt-Jakob disease
Brain trauma	Folic acid deficiency	Viral encephalitis
Cerebral hypoxia	Cyanocobalamin deficiency	HIV infection
Huntington's disease	Urinary tract disease	Neurosyphilis
Intracranial tumors	Respiratory encephalopathy	Fungal meningitis
Multi-infarct dementia	Sarcoidosis	Tuberculosis
Multiple sclerosis	Normal pressure hydrocephalus	Cryptococcal meningitis
Pick's disease	Cardiovascular disease	
	Liver disease	

C. Causes of Dementia

—Although the etiology is unknown, genetic factors, reduction in brain choline acetyltransferase (needed to synthesize acetylcholine), and aluminum toxicity have been implicated in Alzheimer's disease.

—Multi-infarct dementia accounts for 10% of cases of dementia.

—Increasing numbers of patients have dementia related to AIDS.

—Although normal aging is associated with reduction in memory and general slowing down of mental processes, in contrast to dementia, these changes do not interfere with normal life.

—A variety of factors, including exposure to drugs and toxins, can result in dementia (Table 13.2).

D. Pseudodementia

—Pseudodementia, which occurs in elderly patients, may mimic dementia.

—Pseudodementia is characterized by cognitive dysfunction that results from depression.

—The distinction between dementia and both delirium and pseudodementia is important because the latter two conditions are highly treatable (Table 13.3).

E. Treatment of Dementia

—Dementia is treatable in some cases; in other cases, treatment of dementia is symptomatic.

　—In about 15% of patients, dementia is reversible.

　—Pharmacotherapy is used for the associated symptoms of anxiety, depression, and psychosis.

—In the psychosocial treatment of dementia, support is given to patient and family.

　—The lives of individuals with dementia can be improved by providing a structured environment, nutritious diet, exercise, and recreational therapy.

IV. Acquired Immunodeficiency Syndrome (AIDS) Dementia Complex

A. Incidence and Causes

—About 60% of AIDS patients eventually have some level of dementia.

—In over 95% of patients with AIDS dementia, the multinucleated giant cells of the brain are involved.

Table 13.3. Comparison Between Dementia and Delirium

Dementia	Delirium
Hallmark: memory loss	*Hallmark*: impaired consciousness
Consciousness not impaired	Consciousness impaired
Normal level of arousal	Stupor or agitation
Develops slowly and insidiously	Develops rapidly
Often irreversible	Often reversible

—On CT scan, ventricular enlargement and cerebral atrophy are seen.

—Cerebral lymphomas, small nodules of inflammatory cells in the gray matter, and vacuolar myelopathy of the spinal cord are also seen in AIDS.

B. Symptoms

—Early symptoms of AIDS dementia include memory loss, difficulty concentrating, mild confusion, agitation, and depression.

—Later symptoms include frank dementia, confusion, and psychosis progressing to coma.

C. AIDS-Related Complex

—AIDS-related complex (ARC) is often associated with psychiatric problems that result from the physical symptoms of fatigue and general malaise characteristic of the disease.

—Fear, anxiety, and depression are common in patients with ARC.

—Antidepressants and antipsychotics are used to treat the psychiatric symptoms of AIDS and ARC.

Review Test

ORGANIC MENTAL SYNDROMES

DIRECTIONS: For each of the questions or incomplete statements below, choose the answer that is **most correct.**

13.1. All of the following are common causes of delirium EXCEPT:

A. brain trauma.
B. encephalitis.
C. meningitis.
D. epilepsy.
E. all of the above.

13.2. All of the following are true about dementia EXCEPT:

A. At least 1 million Americans over age 65 have significant dementia.
B. The incidence of dementia increases with age.
C. The most common cause of dementia is primary degenerative dementia of the Alzheimer's type.
D. The quality of life of a patient with dementia can be improved by providing a structured environment.
E. Dementia is reversible in the majority of patients.

13.3. All of the following are true about AIDS dementia EXCEPT:

A. AIDS dementia complex is seen in about 60% of patients with AIDS.
B. Psychiatric symptoms include psychosis.
C. Antidepressants are of no value in treating the depression associated with AIDS and AIDS dementia.
D. Ventricular enlargement is often seen on CT scan.
E. In most patients with AIDS dementia, the multinucleated giant cells of the brain are involved.

13.4. Which of the following is true about delirium?

A. It is the most common psychiatric syndrome seen in patients on medical hospital wards.
B. It is rare in the elderly.
C. A history of prior delirium is not related to the risk of developing it again.
D. It rarely occurs in children.
E. Orientation to person is usually affected.

13.5. Which of the following drugs is/are associated with the development of delirium?

A. Anticholinergic agents
B. Anticonvulsants
C. Steroids
D. Sedatives
E. All of the above

13.6. All of the following are true about delirium EXCEPT:

A. Cognitive impairment is worse at night than during the day.
B. If left untreated, delirium usually resolves on its own.
C. The patient may be hyperactive.
D. Autonomic dysfunction may occur.
E. Illusions may occur.

DIRECTIONS: For each of the following statements choose:
   A. if it is associated primarily with delirium.
   B. if it is associated primarily with dementia.
   C. if it is associated with both delirium and dementia.
   D. if it is associated with neither delirium nor dementia.

13.7. Impaired consciousness

13.8. Acute onset

13.9. Normal level of arousal

13.10. Frequently irreversible

13.11. Associated with normal aging

13.12. Caused by exposure to drugs and toxins

DIRECTIONS: For each of the questions below, **one** or **more** of the answers or completions given are correct. Choose answer:
   A. if only **1, 2,** and **3** are correct.
   B. if only **1** and **3** are correct.
   C. if only **2** and **4** are correct.
   D. if only **4** is correct.
   E. if **all** are correct.

13.13. Which of the following is/are associated with both delirium and dementia?
1. Endocrine dysfunctions
2. Cardiovascular disease
3. Normal pressure hydrocephalus
4. Brain trauma

13.14. Which of the following is/are true about pseudodementia?
1. It is highly treatable.
2. It is characterized by depression.
3. There is cognitive dysfunction.
4. It is common in young adults.

Answers and Explanations

ORGANIC MENTAL SYNDROMES

13.1. E. All are correct.

13.2. E. Dementia is reversible in only about 15% of patients.

13.3. C. Antidepressants may be useful in treating depression associated with AIDS and AIDS dementia.

13.4. A. Delirium is commonly seen on medical hospital wards, is more common in children and the elderly than in the rest of the population, and is related to a history of prior delirium. Although orientation to time and place may be impaired, orientation to person in delirium is usually intact.

13.5. E. All are correct.

13.6. B. If the underlying cause of delirium is treated and removed, the condition will usually resolve. If untreated, delirium can progress to dementia or other organic brain syndrome.

13.7. A. Impaired consciousness is seen in delirium.

13.8. A. Acute onset is characteristic of delirium.

13.9. B. There is usually a normal level of arousal in people with dementia.

13.10. B. Dementia is frequently irreversible.

13.11. D. Neither delirium nor dementia is associated with normal aging.

13.12. C. Both delirium and dementia can result from exposure to drugs and toxins.

13.13. E. Endocrine dysfunctions, cardiovascular disease, normal pressure hydrocephalus, and brain trauma are associated with both delirium and dementia.

13.14. A. Pseudodementia occurs in elderly patients and may mimic dementia. It is characterized by depression and is treatable.

14

Other Psychiatric Disorders in Adults and in Children

I. Somatoform Disorders

   A. **Definition and Categories**

      —**Somatoform disorders** consist of physical symptoms without organic pathology.

      —The six DSM-III-R categories of somatoform disorders are somatization disorder, conversion disorder, somatoform pain disorder, hypochondriasis, body dysmorphic disorder, and undifferentiated somatoform disorder.

   B. **Somatization Disorder**

      —Somatization disorder involves multiple physical complaints with no physical disease and is associated with medical help-seeking.

      —Somatization disorder is more common in women and low socioeconomic groups, runs in families, and has higher concordance rates in monozygotic than in dizygotic twins.

   C. **Conversion Disorder**

      —Conversion disorder involves serious change in body function, including loss of sensory or motor function with no medical cause.

      —Conversion disorder is more common in women, young adults, and adolescents and in lower socioeconomic groups.

   D. **Somatoform Pain Disorder and Hypochondriasis**

      —**Somatoform pain disorder** is characterized by severe and prolonged pain without physical disease.

      —**Hypochondriasis** is extreme concern about illness and exaggerated attention to one's own health.

      —Hypochondriasis is found equally in men and women and in all age groups.

   E. **Body Dysmorphic Disorder and Undifferentiated Somatoform Disorder**

      —In **body dysmorphic disorder**, a normal-appearing patient believes he or she is physically abnormal or defective.

Table 14.1. Personality Disorders

Type	Characteristics
Cluster A	*Hallmarks*: eccentric, strange, fear of social relationships
Paranoid	Suspiciousness, mistrust, responsibility for problems attributed to others; seen more in males, minorities, and the deaf
Schizoid	Lifelong pattern of social withdrawal without psychosis; seen more in males
Schizotypal	Peculiar appearance, odd thought patterns, and behavior without psychosis
Cluster B	*Hallmarks*: emotional, dramatic, erratic
Histrionic	Dramatic, extroverted behavior; cannot maintain intimate relationships; seen more in females; associated with somatization and alcoholism
Narcissistic	Grandiosity, sense of entitlement, lack of empathy, envy
Antisocial	Inability to conform to social norms, criminality; seen more in males
Borderline	Unstable affect, mood and behavior, impulsiveness; seen more in females
Cluster C	*Hallmarks*: fearful, anxious
Avoidant	Sensitive to rejection, socially withdrawn, shy; inferiority complex; may be related to timidity in infancy
Obsessive-compulsive	Orderliness, emotional constriction, stubborn, indecisive; above average intelligence; EEG abnormalities
Passive-aggressive	Procrastination, stubborn, inefficient
Dependent	Lack of self-confidence; lets others assume responsibilities

—Six months of multiple physical symptoms without adequate physical or medical cause is classified as **undifferentiated somatoform disorder**.

F. **Treatment**

—Treatment of somatoform disorders includes individual and group psychotherapy.

—Anxiolytic drugs, hypnosis, and behavioral relaxation therapy may also be used, particularly in the treatment of conversion disorder.

II. Personality Disorders

A. **Characteristics**

—Individuals with **personality disorders** often show long-standing, rigid, unsuitable patterns of relating to others and to the world around them.

—People with personality disorders generally are not aware of their problems and do not have empathy with others.

B. **Classification**

—Personality disorders are categorized by the DSM-III-R into three Clusters—A, B, and C (Table 14.1).

C. **Treatment of Personality Disorders**

—Treatment of personality disorders involves individual and group psychotherapy as well as self-help groups.

—Pharmacotherapy can also be used to treat symptoms such as depression and anxiety that may be associated with the personality disorders.

III. Dissociative Disorders

A. **Characteristics**

The **dissociative disorders** are rare, dramatic disorders characterized by sudden but tempory loss of memory or identity.

Table 14.2. Dissociative Disorders

Category	Definition
Psychogenic amnesia	Failure to remember important information about oneself
Psychogenic fugue	Amnesia combined with sudden unexpected wandering away from home
Multiple personality disorder	Two or more distinct personalities in an individual
Depersonalization disorder	Feelings of detachment from one's own reality

B. Classification

The five DSM-III-R categories of dissociative disorders are psychogenic amnesia, psychogenic fugue, multiple personality, depersonalization disorder, and dissociative disorder not otherwise specified (Table 14.2).

C. Amnesia

Besides psychogenic amnesia, other causes of amnesia include head injury, electroconvulsive therapy, or anesthesia.

—In psychogenic amnesia, the amnesia is usually retrograde (for past memories).

—In head trauma, the amnesia is usually anterograde (for current events).

D. Treatment

Treatment of the dissociative disorders includes hypnosis and amytal interviews as well as long-term psychotherapy.

IV. Eating Disorders

The eating disorders include anorexia nervosa and bulimia.

A. Anorexia Nervosa

1. *Overview*

Anorexia nervosa is characterized by dieting and weight loss, as well as abnormal patterns of dealing with food, disturbance of body image, and intense fear of becoming obese.

—The average incidence is 0.37 per 1000 population.

—Anorexia is more common in women, during late adolescence, and in higher socioeconomic groups.

—Anorexia is one of the few psychiatric illnesses that can lead to death.

—Amenorrhea may occur.

—Early age of onset and few or no previous hospitalizations are predictors of a positive outcome.

2. *Treatment of Anorexia Nervosa*

—Treatment is aimed at first restoring the nutritional state of the patient.

—Psychoactive drugs such as amitriptyline and cyproheptadine (Periactin) have been used in the treatment of anorexia.

—Family therapy has proved useful.

B. Bulimia

1. *Overview*

Bulimia is characterized by binge eating followed by purging with vomiting, laxatives, and diuretics.

Table 14.3. Infantile Autism vs. Childhood Schizophrenic Disorder

Infantile Autism	Childhood Schizophrenic Disorder
Onset before 3 years	Onset after 3 years
More males affected	Approximately equal sex ratio
No family history of schizophrenia	Family history of schizophrenia
Cerebral dysfunction	Cerebral dysfunction less common
Subnormal intelligence common	Intelligence usually in the normal range
Grand mal seizures	Seizures absent or rare
Severe problems with language	Hallucinations and delusions

　　　—Like anorexia, bulimia usually begins in adolescence and is more common in women.

　　　—In contrast to anorexics, most bulimics are at or near their normal weight.

　　　—Also in contrast to anorexics, most bulimics are sexually active.

　　2. *Treatment of Bulimia*

　　　—Treatment of bulimia includes psychotherapy and behavioral therapy.

　　　—Some studies suggest that imipramine may be useful.

V.　Infantile Autism and Childhood Schizophrenia

A. Characteristics

Autistic disorder or **infantile autism**, as well as childhood schizophrenia, are severe pervasive developmental disorders of childhood.

　　—Autistic disorder becomes apparent in infancy or childhood and is characterized by deficits in the ability to interact and communicate with others.

　　—A very limited repertoire of physical activities and interests is seen.

　　—Some autistic children show unusual abilities, for example, idiot-savants who have unusual memories or can calculate square roots of large numbers in seconds.

　　—Factors that distinguish infantile autism from childhood schizophrenic disorder are listed in Table 14.3.

B. Occurrence

　　—Autistic disorder occurs in 4 to 5 children per 10,000, usually begins before 36 months of age, and is much more common in boys than in girls.

　　—When present in girls, autistic disorder is more severe and is associated with a family history of other cognitive disorders.

C. Etiology

　　—Recent studies suggest that physiologic abnormalities are associated with autistic disorder.

　　　—Perinatal complications are found frequently in the history of autistic children.

　　—As in some children with severe mental retardation, elevated serum serotonin levels are present in about 33% of autistic children.

　　—A concordance rate for autism in monozygotic twins of 35% and a lack of concordance in dizygotic twins suggest a genetic influence.

D. Treatment

Treatment of autistic children involves intensive work with the child with aims of increasing social and communicative skills, decreasing behavioral

Table 14.4. DSM-III-R Criteria for Attention Deficit Hyperactivity Disorder

before age 7yrs
last at least 6 months
at least 8 of the 14

1. Fidgeting
2. Difficulty remaining seated
3. Easily distracted
4. Difficulty awaiting his or her turn
5. Blurts out answers
6. Difficulty following through on instructions
7. Difficulty sustaining attention
8. Shifts uncompleted activities
9. Difficulty playing quietly
10. Excessive talking
11. Interrupts others
12. Does not listen
13. Loses things
14. Engages in physically dangerous activities

symptoms, improving self-care skills, and providing parental support and counseling.

VI. Attention Deficit Hyperactivity Disorder (ADHD)

A. Characteristics

—Major characteristics of children with ADHD include hyperactivity, limited attention span, and impulsiveness.

—Although some children with ADHD were placid as infants, more commonly, children with ADHD cried excessively, showed high sensitivity to stimuli, and did not sleep well.

—ADHD children are often emotionally labile, irritable, impulsive, and accident prone.

—Emotional problems are common in ADHD children.

—For a diagnosis of ADHD, the behavioral disturbances must appear before age 7, last for a minimum of 6 months, and at least eight of the DSM-III-R criteria must be present (Table 14.4).

—Other terms previously used for ADHD were hyperactive child syndrome, hyperkinetic reaction of childhood, minimal brain dysfunction, minor cerebral dysfunction, and minimal brain damage.

—Differential diagnoses of ADHD include depression, anxiety states, an early form of manic-depressive disorder, and conduct disturbances.

B. Occurrence

—In the United States, the incidence of ADHD is about 3 to 5% of prepubertal grade school children.

—The sex ratio of boys to girls is 5 to 1, and ADHD is more common in firstborn boys.

C. Etiology

—Genetic factors may be involved in the etiology of ADHD.

—Parents of children with ADHD have a higher incidence of hyperkinesis, sociopathy, and alcoholism.

—Siblings of children with ADHD have a higher incidence of the disorder than children in the general population.

—Although evidence of gross structural problems in the brain is not present, children with ADHD may have minimal or subtle brain damage.

D. Treatment of ADHD

Pharmacologic treatment for ADHD consists of the amphetamines, including methylphenidate (Ritalin), dextroamphetamine sulfate (Dexedrine), and pemoline (Cylert).

—CNS stimulants may lower activity level and increase attention span and the ability to concentrate in children with ADHD.

—Drawbacks of CNS stimulants include inhibition of growth and weight gain, although these usually return to normal after the medication is stopped.

Review Test

OTHER PSYCHIATRIC DISORDERS IN ADULTS AND IN CHILDREN

DIRECTIONS: For each of the questions or incomplete statements below, choose the answer that is **most correct**.

14.1. Which of the following somatoform disorders is characterized by loss of sensory function?

A. Hypochondriasis
B. Body dysmorphic disorder
C. Conversion disorder
D. Undifferentiated somatoform disorder
E. Somatoform pain disorder

14.2. All of the following are true about children with attention deficit hyperactivity disorder (ADHD) EXCEPT:

A. Genetic factors are not involved.
B. They are often accident prone.
C. They are often emotionally labile.
D. They are often irritable.
E. Emotional difficulties are common.

14.3. Which of the following is true about the somatization disorders?

A. They are more common in men.
B. They are more common in high socioeconomic groups.
C. They involve multiple physical complaints with no physical disease.
D. They have similar concordance rates in monozygotic and dizygotic twins.
E. Patients rarely seek medical help.

14.4. Which of the following is true about anorexia nervosa?

A. It is most common in early adolescence.
B. It is more common in lower socioeconomic groups.
C. It is associated with amenorrhea.
D. It has few serious medical consequences.
E. All of the above.

14.5. Treatment of anorexia nervosa includes all of the following EXCEPT:

A. Periactin.
B. amitriptyline.
C. cyproheptadine.
D. β-adrenergic blockers.
E. family therapy.

DIRECTIONS: For each of the following statements choose:

  A. if it is associated with infantile autism.
  B. if it is associated with childhood schizophrenic disorder.
  C. if it is associated with both infantile autism and childhood schizophrenic disorder.
  D. if it is associated with neither infantile autism nor childhood schizophrenic disorder.

14.6. Onset after 5 years of age

14.7. More males affected

14.8. Family history of schizophrenia

 14.9. Pervasive developmental disorder of childhood

 14.10. Grand mal seizures

DIRECTIONS: For each of the numbered statements below, choose the lettered personality disorder with which it is **most closely associated.**

  A. Antisocial
  B. Avoidant
  C. Paranoid
  D. Schizotypal
  E. Schizoid

 14.11. Lifelong pattern of social withdrawal

14.12. Peculiar appearance

14.13. Suspiciousness

14.14. Inferiority complex

14.15. Criminality

DIRECTIONS: For each of the questions or incomplete statements below, **one** or **more** of the answers or completions given are correct. Choose answer:

  A. if only **1, 2,** and **3** are correct.
  B. if only **1** and **3** are correct.
  C. if only **2** and **4** are correct.
  D. if only **4** is correct.
  E. if **all** are correct.

14.16. Synonyms for ADHD are:
1. schizophreniform disorder.
2. hyperactive child syndrome.
3. conduct disorder of childhood.
4. minimal brain dysfunction.

14.17. Which of the following is/are true about ADHD?
1. Central nervous system stimulants are used in treatment.
2. The differential diagnosis includes depression.
3. The differential diagnosis includes anxiety states.
4. As infants, children with ADHD showed high sensitivity to stimuli.

Answers and Explanations

OTHER PSYCHIATRIC DISORDERS IN ADULTS AND IN CHILDREN

14.1. C. Conversion disorder involves changes in body functions including loss of motor or sensory function with no medical cause.

14.2. A. There is evidence that genetic factors may be involved in the etiology of attention deficit hyperactivity disorder.

14.3. C. Somatization disorders are more common in women, are more common in low socioeconomic groups, and have different concordance rates in monozygotic and dizygotic twins. Although there is no physical disease, patients frequently seek medical help.

14.4. C. Anorexia nervosa is seen more in females, is more common in late adolescence in higher socioeconomic groups, and may have very serious medical consequences.

14.5. D. Drugs used in the treatment of anorexia nervosa include heterocyclic antidepressants. Family therapy has also been found useful.

14.6. B. Childhood schizophrenia commonly begins after 5 years of age.

14.7. A. Infantile autism affects more males than females.

14.8. B. A family history of schizophrenia is seen in patients with childhood schizophrenic disorder.

14.9. C. Both childhood schizophrenia and infantile autism are pervasive developmental disorders of childhood.

14.10. A. Grand mal seizures are seen in 4 to 32% of children with infantile autism; they are not commonly seen in children with childhood schizophrenic disorder.

14.11. E. A life-long pattern of social withdrawal is seen in the schizoid personality disorder.

14.12. D. Peculiar appearance, thinking, and behavior are seen in schizotypal personality disorder.

14.13. C. Individuals with paranoid personality disorders show suspiciousness and mistrust.

14.14. B. The avoidant personality is sensitive to rejection, socially withdrawn, and shy and may have an inferiority complex.

14.15. A. The inability to conform to social norms, as well as criminality, is seen in individuals with antisocial personality disorder.

14.16. C. Other terms for attention deficit hyperactivity disorder are hyperkinetic reaction of childhood, hyperactive child syndrome, minimal brain dysfunction, minimal brain damage, and minor cerebral dysfunction.

14.17. E. All are correct.

15

Suicide

I. Suicide Rates

A. Suicide in the United States

—Suicide is the eighth leading cause of death in the United States; only heart disease, cancer, stroke, accidents, pneumonia, diabetes, and cirrhosis are more common.

—The suicide rate in the United States is about 12 per 100,000.

—New Jersey has the lowest suicide rate among men and women aged 15 to 44.

—Suicide rates in immigrants are higher than in native-born Americans.

B. Suicide in Other Countries

—The highest suicide rates are found in the Eastern European countries, Scandinavia, Austria, Switzerland, West Germany, and Japan.

—The lowest suicide rates are found in Ireland, Spain, Italy, Egypt, and Israel.

II. Risk Factors

A. Sex Differences

—Three times more men than women commit suicide even though more women attempt suicide.

—Men are more successful at suicide in part because they use violent means such as guns, jumping from high places, or hanging; women are more likely to take drugs.

—In men, suicides increase after age 45; in women, most suicides occur after 55 years of age.

—The suicide rate in males 14 to 24 years old is increasing significantly; in females it is increasing only slightly.

B. Age-related Factors

—The elderly constitute approximately 25% of suicides, although they make up a much smaller percentage of the population.

—Suicide is rare in children under the age of 12.

—About 13% of normal children have thought about committing suicide.

—Suicide is the third leading cause of death in 15 to 24 year olds after accidents and homicide.

—Suicides among adolescents may run in clusters within communities.

Table 15.1. Marital Status and Suicide Risk

Marital Status	Approximate Suicide Rate (per 100,000)
Married	11
Single, never married	22
Widowed	24
Divorced women	18
Divorced men	69

C. Family Factors

—Suicide is more common in adolescents from broken homes.

✱Children who lose parents before age 13 are at higher risk for depression and suicide.

—Marriage is associated with reduced risk of suicide (Table 15.1).

D. Socioeconomic Factors

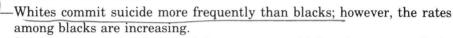

—Whites commit suicide more frequently than blacks; however, the rates among blacks are increasing.

—Suicide rates among Jews and Protestants are higher than among Catholics.

—Suicide rates are higher during economic recessions and economic depressions.

E. Profession and Suicide

—Physicians may be especially at risk for suicide.

   —Among physicians, psychiatrists appear to be at greatest risk; ophthalmologists and anesthesiologists are also at risk.

—Other professionals at high risk for suicide are dentists, law enforcement officers, lawyers, musicians, and insurance agents.

F. Physical and Psychological Factors

—Serious medical problems are associated with increased risk for suicide.

—Highly significant factors associated with suicide include alcoholism, drug abuse, and mental illnesses such as depression and schizophrenia (Table 15.2).

G. Attempted Suicide

—There are about nine times more suicide attempts than successful suicides.

—Thirty percent of attempted suicides will make another attempt.

—Individuals are at highest risk for committing suicide during the 3 months after the first attempt.

III. Who Will Commit Suicide

A. Ideation, Intent, and Plan

—Clinicians should assess suicide risk during every mental status examination and should give particular attention to depressed patients.

✱The vast majority of patients who eventually kill themselves give warnings of their intent; about half tell the clinician that they want to die.

—Patients who have a plan of action to commit suicide are at high risk.

—Other factors that can help identify patients likely to commit suicide include a family history of suicide, available means of suicide, preparation

Table 15.2. Risk Factors Associated with Suicide

Single, divorced, or widowed
Unemployed or retired
Loss of physical health
Depression
Recent divorce or death of spouse
Prior treatment as a psychiatric inpatient
Refusal to accept help
Male sex
Prior suicide attempts
Rage
Alcoholism and drug abuse
Age over 45

of a will, and verbalization of worry about how suicide may affect family members.

IV. Management of Suicidal Patients

A. Hospitalization

—Indications for hospitalization of a suicidal patient include impulsiveness, lack of social support, and presence of a specific plan for suicide.
—Patients may commit suicide even when hospitalized.

B. Recovery

—As patients recover from suicidal depression, they are at increased risk since they have the energy to put suicidal plans into action.
—Acutely suicidal patients have a better prognosis than chronically suicidal patients.

Review Test

SUICIDE

DIRECTIONS: For each of the questions or incomplete statements below, choose the answer that is **most correct.**

15.1. Which of the following countries has the highest suicide rate?

A. Spain
B. Italy
C. Israel
D. Japan
E. Ireland

15.2. The state with the lowest suicide rate of people 15 to 44 years old is:

A. New York.
B. New Jersey.
C. New Mexico.
D. Texas.
E. California.

15.3. All of the following are risk factors for suicide EXCEPT:

A. alcoholism.
B. male sex.
C. depression.
D. loss of physical health.
E. Catholic religion.

15.4. Which of the following specialties appears to be at the highest risk for suicide?

A. Pediatrician
B. Obstetrician
C. Psychiatrist
D. Radiologist
E. Urologist

15.5. Which of the following groups is at the highest risk for suicide?

A. Married men
B. Widowed women
C. Single women
D. Divorced men
E. Divorced women

DIRECTIONS: For each of the questions or incomplete statements below, **one** or **more** of the answers or completions given are correct. Choose answer:

        A. if only **1, 2,** and **3** are correct.
        B. if only **1** and **3** are correct.
        C. if only **2** and **4** are correct.
        D. if only **4** is correct.
        E. if **all** are correct.

15.6. Which of the following professions are at high risk for suicide?

1. Musicians
2. Law enforcement officers
3. Lawyers
4. Dentists

15.7. Increased risk of suicide is associated with

1. male sex.
2. old age.
3. loss of parents before age 13.
4. family history of suicide.

Answers and Explanations

SUICIDE

15.1. D. The highest suicide rates are found in Scandinavia, Switzerland, West Germany, Austria, the Eastern European countries, and Japan. The lowest suicide rates are found in Spain, Italy, Ireland, Egypt, and Israel.

15.2. B. New Jersey has the lowest suicide rate in the United States among people in the 15- to 44-year-old age group.

15.3. E. Catholics have a lower suicide rate than Protestants or Jews.

15.4. C. Psychiatrists appear to be at highest risk for suicide, followed by ophthalmologists and anesthesiologists.

15.5. D. Both divorce and male sex put an individual at higher risk for suicide.

15.6. E. All are correct.

15.7. E. All are correct.

16

Psychological Assessment of Intelligence, Personality, and Achievement

I. Overview

A. Uses of Psychological Tests

—Intelligence and personality can be assessed with psychological tests.

—Psychological tests can also help a clinician to diagnose a variety of psychological problems and suggest treatment approaches.

B. Validity and Reliability

Methods of assessment, such as tests of validity and reliability, have been developed to evaluate psychological tests.

—Test **validity** refers to whether the test actually measures what it is supposed to measure.

—Test **reliability** refers to how consistent, accurate, and reproducible the results of the test are.

C. Objective and Projective Tests

Tests can be classified by what functional area is addressed or by whether information gathering is achieved objectively or projectively.

—An **objective test** is based on specific items or questions that can be easily scored and statistically analyzed.

—A **projective test** requires the subject to give answers based on his or her interpretation of the item or question.

—In a projective test, the subject's responses are assumed to be based on his or her own needs, motivational state, abilities, and defense mechanisms.

D. Individual and Group Testing

Both individual and group testing have been used for evaluation.

—**Individual tests** allow careful observation and evaluation of a particular person.

—**Group tests** have the advantage of easy administration and scoring.

—**Battery tests** are composed of individual tests that together can give a picture of a person's functioning in a number of different areas.

Table 16.1. Types of Commonly Used Assessment Instruments

Test Type	Examples
Objective	Minnesota Multiphasic Personality Inventory (MMPI)
Projective	Rorschach Test
	Thematic Apperception Test (TAT)
	Sentence Completion Test
	Draw-A-Person Test
Individual	Wechsler Adult Intelligence Scale
	Bender Gestalt Test
Group	California Achievement Test
Battery	Luria-Nebraska Neuropsychological Battery
	Halstead-Reitan Test Battery

—Tests commonly used clinically to evaluate patients are listed in Table 16.1.

II. Major Intelligence Tests

A. Intelligence and Mental Age

—**Intelligence** is an individual's ability to reason logically, manipulate abstract concepts, assimilate facts, recall what she or he had learned, analyze and organize information, and deal with the special problems of a new situation.

—**Mental age**, as defined by **Alfred Binet**, is the average intellectual level with respect to the individual's chronological age.

—The **Stanford-Binet Scale** is used to test general intellectual ability in individuals 2 to 18 years old.

B. Intelligence Quotient

—On the Stanford-Binet Scale, an individual's **intelligence quotient (IQ)** is the ratio of mental age over chronological age multiplied by 100.

　—When mental and chronological ages are the same, the person's IQ is 100 (Table 16.2).

　—Because IQ is relatively stable throughout life, the highest chronological age used in the IQ formula is 15 years.

—IQ test results are influenced by an individual's culture and early learning; intelligence tests cannot be totally free of cultural influences.

C. Wechsler Intelligence Tests

—The **Wechsler Adult Intelligence Scale-Revised (WAIS-R)** is the most commonly used intelligence test.

　—Different tables are used to score seven age groups from 16 to 64 years.

　—The WAIS-R consists of 11 subtests, 6 verbal and 5 performance.

　—The subtests of the WAIS-R are information, comprehension, similarities, arithmetic, vocabulary, picture assembly, picture completion, block design, object assembly, digit span, and digit symbol.

　—In addition to heredity, performance on the subtests of the WAIS-R is influenced by anxiety (arithmetic, digit span), educational background (information and vocabulary), neuropsychiatric problems (large disparity between verbal and performance tests), and psychopathology.

Table 16.2. Intelligence Quotient (IQ) and Classification of Intelligence According to the DSM-III-R and WAIS-R

IQ	Classification
<20–25	Profound mental retardation
20–25 to 35–40	Severe mental retardation
35–40 to 50–55	Moderate mental retardation
50–55 to 70	Mild mental retardation
70–79	Borderline
80–89	Low average/dull normal
90–109	Average/normal
110–119	High average/bright normal
120–129	Superior
>130	Very superior

—The **Wechsler Intelligence Scale for Children-Revised (WISC-R)** is used for children 6 to 17 years old.

—The **Wechsler Preschool and Primary Scale of Intelligence (WPPSI)** is used for children 4 to 6 years old.

III. Achievement Tests

A. Uses

Achievement tests evaluate knowledge of information and skills on which an individual has been specifically instructed.

—Achievement tests are used in the educational system for career counseling and in industry.

B. Specific Achievement Tests

—The **Wide-Range Achievement Test (WRAT)** evaluates achievement in arithmetic, reading, and spelling.

    —The WRAT is available for children under 12 (level 1) and for ages 12 to 75 (level 2).

—Other achievement tests include the California Achievement Tests, the Iowa Test, and the Stanford Achievement Test.

IV. Personality Tests

A. The Minnesota Multiphasic Personality Inventory

The most widely used objective personality test is the Minnesota Multiphasic Personality Inventory (MMPI).

—The MMPI has 10 clinical scales: hypochondriasis, depression, hysteria, psychopathology, masculinity/femininity, paranoia, psychasthenia (a general measure of anxiety), schizophrenia, hypomania, and social distance.

—The lie scale, frequency scale, and correction scale of the MMPI increase the validity of the test.

—A number of additional scales have been developed and are available for interpretation.

B. The Rorschach Test

The Rorschach test is the major projective test of personality.

—The Rorschach is used as a diagnostic aid, ie, to determine whether a

Table 16.3. Brain Dysfunction and Localization

Dysfunction	Suggested Brain Location
Immediate recall	Temporal lobes/frontal lobes (hippocampus)
Recent memory	Temporal lobes (hippocampus, thalamus, fornix, mamillothalamic tract)
Long-term memory	Temporal lobes (hippocampus)
Concentration	Frontal lobes
Global disorientation	Frontal lobes
Expressive language	Dominant frontal lobe
Anomia (cannot name common objects)	Dominant temporal lobe, angular gyrus
Conversation	Dominant temporal lobe
Dyspraxia (patient copies examiner's movements)	Contralateral parietal lobe
Finger agnosia (errors in naming fingers)	Dominant parietal lobe
Dyscalculia (errors in calculating)	Dominant parietal lobe
Dysgraphia (errors in writing)	Dominant parietal lobe
Right/left disorientation	Dominant parietal lobe
Construction apraxia (difficulties outlining simple objects)	Nondominant parietal lobe
Identification of camouflaged object	Occipital lobes
Inability to copy sentence, read it, and follow instructions	Dominant temporoparietal lobe

Adapted from Taylor MA et al: Cognitive tasks in the mental status examination. *J Nerv Ment Dis* 1980;**168**:168. © 1980, The Williams & Wilkins Co., Baltimore.

   thought disorder exists in an individual and the nature and integrity of a person's defenses.
   —The Rorschach test consists of 10 cards, 5 in black and white and 5 in color, each containing a bilaterally symmetrical inkblot design.
   —The cards are shown to the patient in a particular order and a record is kept of the patient's initial reaction time, responses to the card, and total time spent looking at each card.

C. **The Thematic Apperception Test** ⇒ PROJECTIVE

   The Thematic Apperception Test (TAT) requires a patient to construct a story based on the picture presented. The story is then used to evaluate emotions and conflicts that may be out of the individual's awareness.
   —The TAT consists of 30 cards depicting persons engaging in activities that are ambiguous and must be interpreted by the patient.
   —The TAT is useful for determining what motivates an individual and possible interpersonal conflicts; it is less useful for making diagnoses.

D. **Sentence Completion Tests**

   Sentence completion tests are used to identify a patient's conscious associations in areas of interest to the therapist.

V. Neuropsychiatric Tests

A. **Uses**

   Neuropsychiatric and psychological tests are designed to assess general intelligence, memory, reasoning and problem solving, orientation, and perceptuomotor performance.
   —Neuropsychiatric tests are also used to assess language function, attention, and concentration in patients with neurologic problems such as dementia and brain damage.

B. Specific Tests

1. *The Halstead-Reitan Neuropsychological Test Battery*

The Halstead-Reitan Neuropsychological Test Battery (HRB) is used to detect the presence of and to localize and determine the effects of brain lesions.

—The HRB consists of approximately 10 tests: category, tactual performance, rhythm, speech-sounds perception, finger-oscillation, critical flicker frequency, trail-making, time sense, aphasia, and sensory-perceptual.

2. *The Luria-Nebraska Neuropsychological Battery*

The Luria-Nebraska Neuropsychological Battery is used to evaluate cognitive functioning.

—The Luria-Nebraska is particularly useful for determining left or right cerebral dominance, localizing areas of the cortex involved in specific dysfunctions, and for identifying specific types of brain dysfunction, such as dyslexia.

C. Performance

—Other than neuropathology, deviation from normal on neuropsychiatric tests may be due to anxiety, depression, confusion about the directions, language problems, or uncooperativeness.

—Performance of a variety of tasks on the mental status examination cognitive tasks section is associated with problems in specific brain areas (Table 16.3).

Review Test

PSYCHOLOGICAL ASSESSMENT OF INTELLIGENCE, PERSONALITY, AND ACHIEVEMENT

DIRECTIONS: For each of the questions or incomplete statements below, choose the answer that is **most correct.**

16.1. Test validity refers to
A. how reproducible the results of the test are.
B. whether the test actually measures what it is supposed to measure.
C. whether the test is objective.
D. whether the test measures an individual's defense mechanisms.
E. whether the individual has a thought disorder.

16.2. An individual with a mental age of 8 and a chronological age of 10 has an IQ of
A. 180.
B. 80.
C. 60.
D. 40.
E. 100.

16.3. An individual with an IQ of 75 would be classified as
A. severely retarded.
B. borderline.
C. dull normal/low average.
D. normal.
E. mildly retarded.

16.4. If there is a large disparity between the verbal and performance tests on the Wechsler Adult Intelligence Scale-Revised (WAIS-R), it is most likely related to the individual's
A. educational background.
B. anxiety level.
C. cultural background.
D. early learning.
E. neuropsychiatric problems.

16.5. Which of the following is the most widely used objective personality test?

A. Thematic Apperception Test (TAT)
B. Sentence Completion Test
C. Iowa Test
D. Minnesota Multiphasic Personality Inventory (MMPI)
E. Luria-Nebraska Test

16.6. All of the following are projective tests EXCEPT:

A. the TAT.
B. the Sentence Completion Test.
C. the MMPI.
D. the Rorschach Test.
E. the Draw-A-Person Test.

16.7. Which of the following is true about the IQ?

A. It is usually stable throughout adult life.
B. It is rarely influenced by an individual's culture.
C. It is rarely influenced by an individual's early learning.
D. It is easily increased by formal training in specific subject areas.
E. The highest chronological age used in the IQ formula is 25 years.

16.8. All of the following are primarily achievement tests EXCEPT:

A. the Iowa.
B. the Stanford.
C. the California.
D. the Luria-Nebraska.
E. the WRAT.

16.9. Clinical scales of the MMPI include all of the following EXCEPT:

A. depression.
B. hysteria.
C. masculinity/femininity.
D. schizophrenia.
E. intelligence.

DIRECTIONS: For each of the numbered phrases below, choose the part of the brain with which it is **most closely associated.**

A. Dominant temporal lobe
B. Dominant frontal lobe
C. Dominant parietal lobe
D. Occipital lobe
E. Nondominant parietal lobe

16.10. Expressive language

16.11. Anomia

16.12. Identification of camouflaged object

16.13. Construction apraxia

16.14. Errors in calculation

DIRECTIONS: For each of the questions or incomplete statements below, **one** or **more** of the answers or completions given are correct. Choose answer:

A. if only **1, 2,** and **3** are correct.
B. if only **1** and **3** are correct.
C. if only **2** and **4** are correct.
D. if only **4** is correct.
E. if **all** are correct.

16.15. Which of the following is/are associated with intelligence?

1. The ability to reason logically
2. The ability to manipulate concepts
3. The ability to recall events
4. The ability to assimilate factual knowledge

16.16. Which of the following is/are used for testing intelligence in children?

1. WAIS-R
2. WPPSI
3. MMPI
4. WISC-R

16.17. Which of the following increase the validity of the MMPI?

1. The lie scale
2. The frequency scale
3. The correction scale
4. The psychopathology scale

16.18. Neuropsychiatric tests are designed to assess

1. memory.
2. orientation.
3. problem solving.
4. emotional tone.

Answers and Explanations

PSYCHOLOGICAL ASSESSMENT OF INTELLIGENCE, PERSONALITY, AND ACHIEVEMENT

16.1. B. Test validity refers to whether a test actually measures what it is intended to measure.

16.2. B. The IQ of this individual is 80.

16.3. B. With an IQ of 75, an individual would be classified as borderline.

16.4. E. A large disparity between the verbal and performance test on the WAIS-R may be an indication of neuropsychiatric problems or psychopathology.

16.5. D. The Minnesota Multiphasic Personality Inventory is the most widely used objective test of personality.

16.6. C. The MMPI is an example of an objective test.

16.7. A. The results of an intelligence test can be influenced by an individual's culture and early learning. IQ is relatively stable throughout adult life, despite increased educational level.

16.8. D. The Luria-Nebraska is a test of neuropsychological functioning.

16.9. E. Clinical scales of the MMPI include hypochondriasis, depression, hysteria, psychopathology, masculinity/femininity, paranoia, psychasthenia, schizophrenia, hypomania, and social distance.

16.10. B. Expressive language is associated with the dominant frontal lobe.

16.11. A. Anomia may result from dysfunction of the dominant temporal lobe or angular gyrus.

16.12. D. Inability to identify camouflaged objects may be associated with dysfunction of the occipital lobes.

16.13. E. Inability to outline simple objects (construction apraxia) may be associated with dysfunction of the nondominant parietal lobe.

16.14. C. Dyscalculia (errors in calculation) may be associated with dysfunction of the dominant parietal lobe.

16.15. E. All are correct.

16.16. C. The Wechsler Intelligence Scale for Children-Revised (WISC-R) and the Wechsler Preschool and Primary Scale of Intelligence (WPPSI) are used to test intelligence in children aged 5 to 15 years and 4 to 6 1/2 years, respectively.

16.17. A. The lie, frequency, and correction scales increase the validity of the MMPI.

16.18. A. Neuropsychiatric tests are designed to assess general intelligence, reasoning and problem solving, memory, orientation, and perceptuomotor performance.

17

History, Current Functioning, and Biological Status of the Patient

I. The Medical History

A. Uses

The purpose of taking the medical history is to obtain basic identifying information about the patient, to determine how reliable the patient is, to identify the patient's chief complaint, and to establish rapport with the patient.

—The medical history is also used to obtain the history of the present illness, the past medical history, and the family medical history.

—During the medical history, a complete inventory of each symptom is obtained including onset, location, quality and severity, possible precipitating factors, what increases or decreases the symptoms, changes over time, and previous treatment.

—Because stress can have a serious impact on health, it is important to identify the major stressors in the patient's life by obtaining information on family, home, sexual history, diet, activities, and social life.

B. The Psychiatric History

As part of the medical history, the patient's psychiatric history is taken.

—The psychiatric history includes careful questioning concerning the causes, complications, and effects of previous illnesses.

—The patient is asked about his or her past and present drug and alcohol use.

—The psychiatric history addresses the patient's current living situation in terms of other people, financial hardship, and source of family income.

—Questions are also asked concerning past psychiatric illness, hospitalization, and psychiatric treatment of members of the patient's immediate family.

—The psychiatric history addresses the relationship between events in the patient's life and current emotional problems.

—Questions about events in the patient's history are usually divided into developmental periods: prenatal, infancy, early childhood, latency, adolescence, and adulthood (Table 17.1).

Table 17.1. The Developmental Psychiatric History

Prenatal
Was the child wanted, problems in pregnancy and delivery?

Early Childhood (0–3 years)
Earliest recollections and recurrent dreams?
Early problems with feeding, with sleep, with toilet training?
Sibling relationships?
Caretakers other than mother?
Personality as a child, eg, hyperactive, shy, outgoing?
Preference for active or passive role during games?

Childhood (3–11 years)
Response to first separation from mother?
Personality patterns, eg, assertive, aggressive (a bully), anxious?
Development of reading skills, motor skills?
History of learning problems?
Peer relationships in school, eg, follower or leader, popularity?
Presence of fears, setting fires, cruelty to animals, nightmares, bed wetting?
Punishment methods employed in the home?

Puberty Through Adolescence
First appearance of emotional problems, eg, weight, drug use, running away?
Idealized role models?
Relationships with classmates and teachers?
Participation in sports?
Family attitudes toward religion?
Sexuality, eg, masturbation, petting, crushes? Sexual abuse?

Adulthood
Social life and quality of human relationships?
Employment history, relationship, and sexual interaction?
Interaction with children?

II. The Mental Examination

A. Uses

The **mental status examination** is used to evaluate an individual's current state of mental functioning (Table 17.2).

B. Psychophysiologic Terms

Terms used to describe psychophysiologic symptoms and mood in psychiatric illness are listed in Table 17.3.

III. Laboratory Tests of Neuroendocrine Function

A. Evaluation

—Laboratory tests are used in psychiatry to detect medical conditions, to determine blood levels of psychoactive drugs, and to increase the accuracy of diagnoses.
—The neuroendocrine system is evaluated by the dexamethasone suppression test, thyroid function tests, and tests to measure levels of catecholamines, growth hormone, and prolactin.

B. The Dexamethasone Suppression Test

—Dexamethasone is a synthetic glucocorticoid that, when given to a normal patient with a normal hypothalamic-adrenal-pituitary axis, suppresses the secretion of cortisol.

Table 17.2. Variables Evaluated on the Mental Status Examination

Category	Examples
Appearance	Dress, grooming, facial expression, appearance for age
Behavior	Posture, gait, eye contact, motor activity, mannerisms
Speech	Rate, clarity, vocabulary abnormalities, volume
Emotions	Mood, affect (blunted, labile, appropriate)
Thought process	Preoccupations, disturbances (delusions, ideas of reference)
Perception	Depersonalization, derealization, illusions, hallucinations
Sensorium	Level of consciousness, concentration, memory, orientation
Intellectual functions	Intelligence, judgment, insight, reliability
Attitude toward interviewer	Cooperative, interested, seductive, defensive

—In depressed patients, this suppression may be absent and the **dexamethasone suppression test (DST)** may be used as a tool to gather further evidence of mental depression.

—Evidence indicates that patients with a positive DST (reduced suppression of cortisol) will respond well to treatment with antidepressants or to electroconvulsive therapy.

C. Thyroid Function

Thyroid function tests are used to screen for hypothyroidism, which can mimic depression.

—Patients taking lithium can develop hypothyroidism and, occasionally, hyperthyroidism.

—A blunted response to a challenge with thyrotropin-releasing hormone (TRH) may occur concurrently with depression.

—Secretion of prolactin in response to TRH and opiates may be blunted in depressed patients.

D. Growth Hormone and Melatonin

—Depressed patients may have abnormal growth hormone regulation and lowered melatonin levels.

—The response of growth hormone secretion to challenge by clonidine (responsiveness of α_2-adrenergic receptors) is blunted in some depressed patients.

IV. Measurement of Biogenic Amines and Psychotropic Drugs

A. Biogenic Amines

—Abnormalities in catecholamine levels and levels of catecholamine metabolites are found in some psychiatric syndromes (Table 17.4).

—A metabolite of norepinephrine measured in urine and plasma is 3-methoxy-4-hydroxyphenylglycol (MHPG).

—The metabolite of serotonin commonly measured is 5-hydroxyindoleacetic acid (5-HIAA).

B. Psychoactive Drugs

—Measurement of plasma levels of psychotropic drugs may be appropriate for some patients taking certain drugs.

—Plasma levels of antipsychotic drugs do not correlate well with clinical effects but may be used to detect noncompliance or nonabsorption.

Table 17.3. Psychophysiologic States and Affects

Consciousness and Attention

Distractibility: attention diverted to irrelevant external stimuli; cannot concentrate
Clouding of consciousness: loss of ability to respond normally to external events
Somnolence: abnormal sleepiness
Delirium: confusion, restlessness, and disorientation associated with anxiety and hallucinations
Stupor: little or no response to environmental stimuli
Coma: total unconsciousness

Affect

Inappropriate affect: discordance between mood and behavior
Blunted affect: severely decreased display of emotional responses
Restricted affect: less severely decreased display of emotional responses
Flat affect: lack of signs of emotional responsiveness
Labile affect: sudden alterations in emotional responsiveness that do not appear related to environmental
  events

Mood

Euphoria: strong feelings of elation
Expansive mood: feelings of self-importance
Irritable mood: easily bothered and quick to anger
Euthymic mood: normal mood; no significant depression or elevation of mood
Dysphoric mood: a subjectively unpleasant feeling
Grief: sadness due to a real loss
Depression: sadness not due to a specific loss
Anhedonia: Lack of ability to feel pleasure
Mood swings: alternations between euphoric and depressive moods

Other Emotions

Anxiety: apprehension to an imagined danger
Free-floating anxiety: anxiety not connected to a specific cause
Fear: anxiety from a real threat or danger

—Lithium levels should be monitored regularly because of the narrow therapeutic range of this drug.
—Measurement of blood levels of heterocyclic antidepressants may be useful in patients who have not responded to normal doses of the drug, in high-risk patients, and to ascertain whether therapeutic blood levels of the drug have been attained.

V. Other Laboratory Measurements

A. Evoked Potentials

Evoked potentials, the response of brain to repetitive sensory stimuli as measured by electrical activity, may be used in psychiatric evaluation.
—Evoked potentials can be used to evaluate the physiology of sensory nerves and can help localize brain lesions.
—Evoked potentials may differ between schizophrenic and normal patients.
—Auditory evoked potentials are useful because they are not affected by sleep or coma and can also be used to evaluate loss of vision and hearing in infants.

B. Radioisotope Brain Scans

Radioisotope brain scans—positron emission tomography (PET), computed tomography (CT), and nuclear magnetic resonance imaging (NMR or MRI)—can be used to identify brain abnormalities.

Table 17.4. Psychiatric Conditions Associated with Altered Levels of Catecholamines and Metabolites

Substance	Condition
Norepinephrine and epinephrine	Elevated in urine with post-traumatic stress disorder; lower ratio of norepinephrine to epinephrine in depression
MHPG	Decreased with severe depression and attempted suicide
5-HIAA	Elevated in urine in carcinoid syndrome and when taking phenothiazines; decreased in CSF with anxiety, severe depression, aggressive, antisocial, or impulsive personality characteristics

—PET and CT scans can aid in the diagnosis of organic mental syndromes and may show abnormalities (enlargement of lateral cerebral ventricles) in patients with schizophrenia.
—MRI shows the biochemical state of tissue as well as anatomy and is particularly useful in identifying demyelinating diseases such as multiple sclerosis.

Review Test

HISTORY, CURRENT FUNCTIONING, AND BIOLOGICAL STATUS OF THE PATIENT

DIRECTIONS: For each of the questions or incomplete statements below, choose the answer that is **most correct.**

17.1. A patient who is confused, disoriented, fearful, and restless is manifesting

A. stupor.
B. delirium.
C. somnolence.
D. clouding of consciousness.
E. distractibility.

17.2. A patient shows abrupt changes in emotional responses that appear to be unrelated to external events. The affect displayed by this patient is:

A. blunted.
B. restricted.
C. flat.
D. labile.
E. inappropriate.

17.3. The inability to experience pleasure is:

A. grief.
B. anhedonia.
C. depression.
D. dysphoria.
E. euthymia.

17.4. A man reacts when the engine on the plane on which he is riding catches fire. The emotion that he is feeling is:

A. free-floating anxiety.
B. anxiety.
C. fear.
D. mood swings.
E. dysthymia.

17.5. Which of the following techniques shows the biochemical state of tissue as well as its anatomy?

A. PET scan
B. CT scan
C. MRI
D. Evoked potentials
E. Auditory evoked potentials

17.6. Which of the following is/are appropriate questions to ask in taking the developmental psychiatric history?

A. How did you get along with your brother?
B. What is the earliest dream you can remember?
C. What was your family's attitude toward religion?
D. A and B only.
E. A, B, and C.

17.7. All of the following are true about the mental status examination EXCEPT:

A. It is rarely used to evaluate intellectual functioning.
B. Mood is evaluated.
C. Appearance and dress are evaluated.
D. The patient's attitude toward the interviewer is evaluated.
E. Speech is evaluated.

17.8. All of the following are true about studies of 5-HIAA EXCEPT:

A. It is decreased in CSF in antisocial personality disorder.
B. It is decreased in CSF in suicidal depression.
C. It is elevated in urine in carcinoid syndrome.
D. It is decreased in individuals taking phenothiazines.
E. It is decreased in individuals with aggressive or impulsive personality traits.

DIRECTIONS: For each of the questions or incomplete statements below, **one** or **more** of the answers or completions given are correct. Choose answer:

A. if only **1, 2,** and **3** are correct.
B. if only **1** and **3** are correct.
C. if only **2** and **4** are correct.
D. if only **4** is correct.
E. if **all** are correct.

17.9. Which of the following is/are taken during the medical history?

1. An inventory of symptoms
2. Information on diet
3. Sexual history
4. Information on the individual's social life

17.10. Which of the following is/are laboratory findings in individuals with depression?

1. Abnormal growth hormone regulation
2. Negative dexamethasone suppression test
3. Blunted prolactin response to thyrotropin-releasing hormone
4. Increased melatonin levels

17.11. Which of the following has/have been shown to be elevated in urine in patients with post-traumatic stress disorder?

1. Norepinephrine
2. Dexamethasone
3. Epinephrine
4. TRH

17.12. Which of the following can be used in the psychiatric evaluation of patients?

1. Evoked potentials
2. Auditory evoked potentials
3. PET scans
4. CT scans

Answers and Explanations

HISTORY, CURRENT FUNCTIONING, AND BIOLOGICAL STATUS OF THE PATIENT

17.1. B. An individual who is confused, fearful, restless, and disoriented is exhibiting delirium.

17.2. D. Abrupt changes in emotionality unrelated to external events is an example of a labile affect.

17.3. B. The inability to experience pleasure is known as anhedonia.

17.4. C. Anxiety caused by a consciously recognized and realistic danger such as a fire is likely to elicit the normal reaction of fear.

17.5. C. The MRI shows the biochemical as well as the anatomic state of tissue.

17.6. E. Family relationships and attitudes as well as dream content are appropriate areas to examine when taking a developmental psychiatric history.

17.7. A. Variables evaluated on the mental status examination include appearance and dress, behavior, speech, emotions, thought processes, thought content, perception, intellectual functioning, and attitude toward the interviewer.

17.8. D. 5-HIAA, a metabolite of serotonin, may be increased in individuals taking phenothiazines.

17.9. E. All are correct.

17.10. B. Depressed individuals may show abnormal growth hormone regulation, blunted prolactin response to thyrotropin-releasing hormone, a positive dexamethasone depression test, and lowered melatonin levels.

17.11. B. Norepinephrine and epinephrine have been found to be elevated in the urine of individuals with post-traumatic stress disorder.

17.12. E. All are correct.

18

The Family, Culture, and Illness

I. Overview of the Family

A. The Family and Health

—A group of people related by blood, adoption, or marriage is a **family.**

—Intense interpersonal relationships are found in families, and these relationships play an important role in the health of family members.

B. Nuclear and Extended Families

—The **nuclear family** includes mother, father, and offspring living together under one roof.

—The **extended family** includes family members such as grandparents, aunts, uncles, and cousins who live outside of the household.

C. Phases in the Life of the Family

The span of family life can be categorized into phases.

—In the first phase, the family is formed at marriage and continues until the first child is born.

—The second phase involves the raising of children.

—The third phase begins when the children leave home and the parents must re-establish their marital relationship, careers, or interests as well as deal with their own aging and ill parents.

—The final phase of the family consists of the physical decline of the parents and the final distribution of the goods and money that the family has acquired over the years.

II. Demographics

A. Marriage and Children

—Approximately 95% of the people in the United States marry during their lifetimes.

—Eighty to 90% of people in the United States between the ages of 35 and 45 are married.

—Ten to 15% of couples are childless; 50% of these by choice.

—Approximately 40% of children live in families with two working parents.

133

B. Divorce
—Almost half of new marriages will end in divorce.
—Factors that predict risk for divorce include poor social support, marriage during teenage years, premarital pregnancy, short courtship period, and differences in religion or socioeconomic background.
—Approximately 20% of families are single-parent families; most are headed by women.
  —Frequently, single-parent families have lower incomes and less social support and thus are likely to be at risk for health problems.

III. Family Systems

A. Family Systems Theory
Family systems theory uses an ecological approach to explain human behavior.
—Individual behavior is explained in terms of interactions between individuals in a family rather than in terms of motivational forces within an individual in a family.
—All causality is regarded as circular, not linear; members of the family influence each other in a reciprocal fashion.
—In systems theory, symptoms such as anxiety or depression are not signs of individual pathology; rather, they indicate dysfunction within the family.

B. Interactions in Family Systems
The following terms are used to describe interactions in family systems.
—Family systems exhibit **homeostasis**, ie, deviations from typical family patterns are kept within a restricted range.
  —Homeostasis maintains equilibrium in the family.
—Family systems are comprised of **subsystems** on which the vitality of the family depends.
  —One example is the executive subsystem, which is composed of the two parents.
—**Boundaries** determine who is allowed to participate in the functioning of a particular subsystem and how an individual may participate.
—**Flexibility** allows family members to adapt to changes within and outside of the family.
—**Mutual accommodation** is the process by which two family members get to know one another's needs and act to meet those needs.
—Breakdowns in communications and in mutual accommodation within a **dyad** (relationship between two family members) result in **emotional cutoffs** or **triangles**.
  —A triangle is a rigid coalition between two family members against a third.
  —Triangles in a family stabilize the system at an immature level.
—The **multigenerational transmission process** is the method by which patterns of adaptation in relationships are passed from generation to generation.

IV. Family Therapy

A. Theory and Uses

—Family therapy is based on the assumption that even if only one person in the family has been identified as having a psychological or social problem, it is important to involve all members of the family system in the remediation of the difficulty.

—Family therapy sessions are usually held once per week for 1 ½ to 2 hours.

—Parents' concerns about family therapy include fear of blame for their child's difficulties and that therapy involving the entire family will have a negative effect on the other children.

—Family therapy includes identification of the dysfunctional behavior, followed by communication training and problem-solving training.

B. Models of Family Therapy

Major models of family therapy include structural, psychodynamic-experiential, family systems, and general systems.

—In the **structural model**, associated mainly with Minuchin, the family is considered to be a single interconnected system in which alliances exist among family members and a hierarchy of power and boundaries form between one generation and another.

  —Malfunctioning of boundary and hierarchical structures is associated with family dysfunction.

—In **psychodynamic-experiential models**, associated mainly with Ackerman and Whitaker, individual growth within the family system is stressed.

—In the **family systems model**, associated mainly with Bowen, the ability of an individual to differentiate the self from the family of origin is important.

—In the **general systems model of family therapy**, which overlaps with the Bowen and structural models, changes in behavior within the family produce reactions in one or another of the family members.

V. United States Culture

A. Characteristics

—The United States is made up of a variety of minority subcultures as well as the large white middle class.

—Although many subcultures both in the past and present have made up US culture, some feel that the culture itself has developed certain characteristics.

  —Characteristics of US culture include the nuclear family with few children.

  —Emphasis is placed on personal hygiene and cleanliness.

  —Independence is valued at all ages but especially in old age.

  —Goals in US culture include financial independence at a young age, home ownership, and upward social mobility.

B. Culture and Illness

—Recognized **minority subcultures** in the United States include black Americans, Hispanics (including Mexican Americans, Puerto Rican Americans, Cuban Americans), Asian Americans (including Chinese, Japanese, Koreans, Pacific Islanders), and Native Americans (American Indians and Eskimos).

—Although stereotyping of ethnic groups can be problematic, these groups often have characteristic ways of dealing with illness.

—Although the same major mental disorders—like schizophrenia and depression—are seen cross-culturally, what is considered abnormal behavior may differ greatly by culture.

—Culture also influences the reporting of symptoms.

    —Differences in presentation of symptoms may stem from the individual psychology of a patient or from adherence to the customs of a certain ethnic group.

C. Culture Shock

Culture shock may occur when individuals relocate to a foreign culture.

—Culture shock can be minimized by prior preparation, the presence of an intact family unit, and a geographical clustering of immigrants.

—Immigrants to the United States have a higher rate of psychiatric hospitalization than do native-born Americans.

—Young immigrant men appear to be at greater risk for psychiatric problems than other sex and age groups.

—In particular, immigrants are more likely to show paranoid symptoms.

—Paranoid symptomology in immigrant groups is often recurrent, is associated with obvious environmental events, and generally has a good prognosis.

VI. Minority Subcultures

A. Black Americans

—There are approximately 26 million black Americans, making them the largest ethnic group in America.

＊The median income of black families is only about half that of whites.

    —This lower socioeconomic status is associated with increased health risks and decreased access to health care services.

—When compared with white Americans, young black American men have a shorter life expectancy, a higher rate of hypertension, and higher suicide and homicide rates.

—Religion plays a major role in social and personal support among many black Americans.

—Strong kinship networks are characteristic of many black families.

B. Mexican Americans

—As a group, Hispanics place great value on the nuclear family.

—There are 10 million Mexican Americans in the United States, making them the largest group of Hispanics.

—Mexican Americans are called Chicanos, especially in the Southwest where most live.

—Mexican Americans often seek health care from folk healers known as *curanderos*.

    —Treatment provided by *curanderos* includes magic, herbal medicine, or specific dietary changes.

C. Puerto Rican Americans

—The second largest group of Hispanics in the United States are Puerto Rican Americans.

—Most Puerto Rican Americans live in the Northeast.

—Puerto Rican American adults may visit folk healers, or *espiritismos.*

—In the small neighborhood centers, or *centros,* where spiritism is performed, a medium uses magical techniques to release spirits that have entered the patient.

—The process used to release the evil spirits is known as *trabajando la causa,* or working the cause.

D. Asian Americans

—The largest groups of Asian Americans are the Chinese and Japanese; there are over 800,000 Chinese and 700,000 Japanese people in the United States.

—Although acculturated to a large extent, ethnic differences may still result in different responses to illness in Asian Americans.

—Chinese children are expected to care for parents in their old age.

—Chinese patients may respond by smiling when they are unhappy or embarrassed.

E. Native Americans

—There are 1.4 million Native Americans including American Indians and Eskimos.

—American Indians have a separate medical care program administered by the Indian Health Service of the federal government.

—In American Indian culture, the distinction between mental and physical illness is blurred; problems in one's environment—as well as witchcraft—are thought to result in illness.

—Both American Indians and Eskimos have high rates of alcoholism and suicide.

Review Test

THE FAMILY, CULTURE, AND ILLNESS

DIRECTIONS: For each of the questions or incomplete statements below, choose the answer that is **most correct.**

18.1. Individual maturation in the context of the family system is most closely associated with

A. Ackerman.
B. Bowen.
C. Minuchin.
D. Erikson.
E. Piaget.

18.2. All of the following are true about the Hispanic subculture in the United States EXCEPT:

A. The largest group of Hispanics are the Mexican Americans.
B. Folk healers are used in the Hispanic culture.
C. Warding off of evil spirits is one of the techniques used by folk healers in the Puerto Rican American culture.
D. There are approximately 6 million Hispanics in the United States.
E. *Trabajando la causa* is a process used to draw off evil spirits in the Puerto Rican culture.

18.3. Which of the following is true about the family in the United States?

A. Approximately 30% of couples are childless.
B. Approximately 65% of the population marries at some time.
C. Approximately 10% of children live in families in which both parents work.
D. Almost half of new marriages will end in divorce.
E. The nuclear family commonly includes parents, grandparents, uncles, aunts, and children.

18.4. Risk factors for divorce include all of the following EXCEPT:

A. Marriage during teenage years.
B. A long courtship period.
C. Premarital pregnancy.
D. Differences in socioeconomic background.
E. Differences in religion.

18.5. All of the following are true about single-parent families EXCEPT:

A. They have more limited finances than two-parent families.
B. They have less social support than two-parent families.
C. They are likely to be at risk for health problems.
D. Most are headed by men.
E. Approximately 20% of families are headed by a single parent.

18.6. All of the following are true about family therapy EXCEPT:

A. It includes problem-solving training.
B. It includes identification of the dysfunctional behavior patterns.
C. Therapy sessions are usually held once per month.
D. It includes communication training.
E. All family members should be involved.

18.7. Which of the following is NOT a major model of family therapy?

A. Instructionist
B. Psychodynamic-experiential
C. Family systems
D. Structural
E. General systems

18.8. Which of the following is/are associated with the structural model of family therapy?

A. Salvatore Minuchin
B. Alliances among family members
C. Boundaries between one generation and another
D. Emphasis on individual maturation
E. A, B, and C

18.9. All of the following are true about native American Indian and Eskimo subcultures EXCEPT:

A. There is a high rate of alcoholism.
B. The suicide rate is lower than in the general population.
C. The federal government administers a separate medical care program for American Indians.
D. The distinction between mental and physical illness may be blurred.
E. They number about 1.4 million individuals.

DIRECTIONS: For each of the numbered phrases below, choose the lettered item with which it is **most closely associated.** Letters may be used once, more than once, or not at all.

A. Subsystems
B. Triangles
C. Emotional cutoff
D. Mutual accommodation
E. Multigenerational transmission process

18.10. The process by which two family members act to meet each other's needs

18.11. Results from a breakdown in communication

18.12. Coalition of two family members against another family member

18.13. How patterns of adaptation are passed from generation to generation in a family

DIRECTIONS: For each of the questions or incomplete statements below, **one** or **more** of the answers or completions given are correct. Choose answer:

A. if only **1, 2,** and **3** are correct.
B. if only **1** and **3** are correct.
C. if **2** and **4** are correct.
D. if only **4** is correct.
E. if **all** are correct.

18.14. Which of the following is/are true about the United States culture?

1. It includes a variety of minority subcultures.
2. It is characterized by the nuclear family with few children.
3. There is an emphasis on personal hygiene.
4. Independence in children is discouraged.

18.15. Which of the following is/are true about Asian American subculture?

1. There are over 700,000 Japanese Americans in the United States.
2. Chinese children are expected to care for their parents in old age.
3. Inappropriate smiling may occur in Chinese patients when they are sad.
4. Asian Americans are acculturated to the United States culture to a large extent.

18.16. Which of the following is/are true about black Americans?

1. They have a shorter life expectancy than white Americans.
2. They have a higher suicide rate than white Americans.
3. They have a higher incidence of hypertension than white Americans.
4. The median income of black families is about 90% that of whites.

Answers and Explanations

THE FAMILY, CULTURE, AND ILLNESS

18.1. A. In the psychodynamic-experiential model of family therapy associated mainly with Ackerman and Whitaker, individual maturation within the family system is stressed.

18.2. D. There are at least 10 million Mexican Americans in the United States.

18.3. D. Approximately 95% of the population marry, and approximately half of these marriages will end in divorce. Only 10 to 15% of couples are childless in the United States. Approximately 40% of children live in families in which both parents work.

18.4. B. Risk factors for divorce include less social support, marriage during teen years, premarital pregnancy, short courtship period, and differences in religious or socioeconomic background.

18.5. D. Most single-parent families are headed by women.

18.6. C. Family therapist sessions are usually held once per week for 1½ to 2 hours.

18.7. A. Models of family therapy include structural, psychodynamic-experiential, family systems, and general systems.

18.8. E. Individual maturation is stressed in the psychodynamic-experiential model of family therapy.

18.9. B. There are high rates of suicide and alcoholism in Native American subcultures.

18.10. D. Mutual accommodation is the process by which family members get to know one another's needs and act to meet those needs.

18.11. C. Emotional cutoff results from a breakdown in communication.

18.12. B. A triangle is a coalition of two family members against a third.

18.13. E. Multigenerational transmission process is how patterns of adaptation are passed from one generation to another.

18.14. A. In the United States culture, independence in both children and old people is encouraged.

18.15. E. All are correct.

18.16. A. The median income of black families in the United States is about one-half that of white families.

19

Human Sexuality and Human Aggression

I. Biology

A. Sex Determination

—An individual's sex is determined by the genetic sex, sex of the gonads, sex of the internal and external genitalia, brain sex, and sex of assignment and rearing.

—Differentiation of the gonads is dependent on the presence or absence of the **Y chromosome** and the **H-Y antigen**.

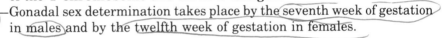—Gonadal sex determination takes place by the seventh week of gestation in males and by the twelfth week of gestation in females.

B. Sexual Differentiation of the Body

—The hormonal secretions of the **testes** direct the differentiation of the male internal and external genitalia.

—In the absence of testicular hormones during prenatal life, the internal and external genitalia will be feminine.

—In addition to their action on the genitalia, sex hormones during prenatal life may cause the brains of males and females to be different.

II. Gender Identity

A. Definition

—**Gender identity** is an individual's sense of himself or herself as male or female.

—A child's gender identity is based on genital sex as well as on sex of assignment and rearing.

B. Transsexualism

—If genital sex does not match gender identity, the individual is a **transsexual**.

—Transsexuals believe since early childhood that they belong to the opposite sex in spite of their physical form.

—Transsexuals have sexual interest in individuals of the same biological sex.

C. Homosexuality and Transvestism

—In contrast, **homosexual** individuals accept their actual physical sex but have sexual and love interest in same-sex individuals.

—**Transvestites** dress in clothes of the opposite sex for sexual pleasure, are almost exclusively male, and may be either heterosexual or homosexual.

III. Gonadal Hormones and Behavior

A. Hormones and Behavior in Women

—**Gonadal hormones** in adulthood affect the display of sexual behavior to a lesser extent in humans than in animals.

—In some studies, sexual interest and behavior in women has been correlated with phase of the menstrual cycle.

  ＊Peaks in sexual interest and behavior have been seen in women at around the time of ovulation, just prior to menstruation, and just following menstruation.

—These peaks may correlate with high estrogen and/or low progesterone levels.

B. Hormones and Behavior in Men

—In men, testosterone levels are generally higher than necessary to maintain normal sexual functioning.

—Testosterone levels in men show seasonal and daily peaks that may correlate with increased sexual interest and behavior.

—Stress may result in reduction in testosterone levels.

—Treatment with estrogen or progesterone reduces sexual interest and behavior in men.

—Homosexual men generally have normal testosterone levels in adulthood.

  —Recent evidence may indicate a prenatally based difference in hypothalamic responsiveness to estrogen between heterosexual and transsexual or homosexual men.

IV. Abnormalities of Sexual Development

A. Chromosomal Abnormalities

Genetic abnormalities of sexual development include Turner's and Klinefelter's syndromes.

XO ——In **Turner's syndrome**, the individual is a phenotypic female, has only one X chromosome, does not mature at puberty, and has only "streak" ovaries.

  —Other physical defects such as short stature and webbed neck may also be present.

  —Adult gender identity and sexual orientation in Turner's syndrome are like those of normal females.

XXY ——In **Klinefelter's syndrome**, the individual is a phenotypic male, has a Y chromosome and more than one X chromosome, has small testes, and may have breast development in adulthood.

  —Gender identity in men with Klinefelter's syndrome is generally male.

B. Androgen Insensitivity Syndrome

Androgen insensitivity syndrome is caused by a genetic defect in which the body's cells do not respond to androgen produced by the testes; although

Table 19.1. The Sexual Response Cycle

Stage	Male	Both Sexes	Female
Excitement	Penile erection	Nipple erection	Clitoral erection, vaginal lubrication; uterus rises in pelvic cavity (tenting effect)
Plateau	50% increase in testes size; testes move upward	Heart rate, blood pressure, respiration increase	Contraction of the outer ⅓ of the vagina (orgasmic platform); tenting effect continues
Orgasm	Testes, prostate, seminal vesicles and urethra contract; seminal fluid forcibly expelled	Heart rate, blood pressure, respiration increase	Vagina and uterus contract
Resolution	Refractory period	Return of sexual organs to prestimulation state over 10–15 minutes; heart rate, blood pressure, respiration decrease	Little if any refractory period

the individual is a genetic male with internal testes, feminine external genitalia are present.
—Adult gender identity and sexual orientation in individuals with androgen insensitivity syndrome are like those of normal females.

C. Congenital Adrenal Hyperplasia
Individuals with adrenogenital syndrome or congenital adrenal hyperplasia (CAH) are genetic females.
—In CAH, there is a defect in the adrenal gland's production of cortisone during fetal development, causing the adrenal glands to work harder.
—In working harder, the adrenal glands produce excessive amounts of androgens and the external genitalia are masculinized prior to birth.
⚹Girls with CAH are more likely to be homosexual than girls without this condition.

V. The Sexual Response Cycle
A. The Four Stage Model
Masters and Johnson devised a four stage model for sexual response—the excitement, plateau, orgasm, and resolution stages (Table 19.1).
—Both males and females experience all four stages of the sexual response cycle.

B. Excitement Phase
—Sexual excitement may occur by psychological or physical stimulation.
—In the excitement phase, erection in the male and vaginal lubrication in the female begin.
—Vaginal lubrication is the result of production of a watery exudate due to increased pelvic blood flow.
—Excitement can last from minutes to hours and may start within minutes of stimulation.
—In the female, the tenting effect—characterized by a lifting of the uterus and increase in length of the vagina—begins.

C. Plateau Phase

—In the plateau phase, the outer third of the vagina shrinks, creating the orgasmic platform.

—During the plateau phase in men, the testes increase up to 50% in size and move upward toward the body as the scrotal skin thickens and local smooth muscle fibers contract.

—A few drops of fluid, which may contain sperm, are secreted during the plateau phase.

D. Orgasm

—During orgasm, which occurs in two stages, intense muscular contractions and dramatic increases in pulse, blood pressure, and respiration occur.

—The first stage of orgasm is **ejaculatory inevitability**, in which the man can no longer prevent ejaculation from occurring.

—The second stage of ejaculation is **emission,** in which the semen is ejected forcibly from the urethra.

E. Resolution Phase

—For both men and women, the sex organs return to the nonstimulated condition when blood leaves the genitals in the resolution phase.

—Resolution takes 10 to 15 minutes if orgasm has occurred.

—If orgasm has not occurred, resolution can take considerably longer.

—During resolution, restimulation is possible for females but not for males.

—The **refractory period** after orgasm can be from minutes to hours, depending on the age and physical condition of the man.

—In women, the physiologic responses that characterize orgasm are the same whether the sexual stimulation has been vaginal or clitoral.

VI. Sexual Dysfunction

A. Characteristics

—**Sexual dysfunctions** can result from biological, psychological, or interpersonal causes or a combination of causes.

—Dysfunctions may have been present throughout life or may occur after an interval of normal functioning.

—Sexual dysfunctions can occur in all situations or only with a specific partner or in a specific location.

—Individuals may be completely or only partially dysfunctional.

B. Categories of Sexual Dysfunctions

Sexual dysfunctions as defined by the DSM-III-R include sexual desire disorders, sexual arousal disorders, inhibited female orgasm, inhibited male orgasm, premature ejaculation, and the sexual pain disorders, including dyspareunia and vaginismus.

C. Sexual Desire Disorders

—The two classes of sexual desire disorders are deficiency of desire for sexual activity and aversion to sexual activity.

—Absence of desire for sexual activity is a common complaint among married couples.

—Lack of sexual desire is not a dysfunction no matter how infrequently sexual activity occurs unless it disturbs one or both partners.

D. Sexual Arousal Disorders in Men

Sexual arousal disorders involve failure to maintain erection (in the male) or lubrication (in the female) until the sex act is completed.

—In men, sexual arousal disorder is commonly called **impotence**.

    —In **primary impotence**, the man has never had an erection sufficient for penetration of the vagina to occur.

        —Primary impotence is rare, occurring in only about 1% of men under 35 years of age.

    —In **secondary impotence**, which occurs in about 10 to 20% of men, the man has at some time achieved vaginal penetration.

        —Organic diseases implicated in erectile problems include infection and cardiovascular, pulmonary, renal, hepatic, neurologic, and endocrine diseases.

    —In **selective impotence**, the man can gain vaginal intromission under some conditions, such as during an extramarital affair, but not others, eg, with his wife.

—Because men normally have erections at regular intervals during sleep, nocturnal erections may be monitored to distinguish psychogenic from physical impotence.

—A common cause of occasional impotence in men is overuse of alcohol.

E. Sexual Arousal Disorders in Women

—In women, sexual arousal disorder is commonly called frigidity.

—Sexual arousal disorder in women is underestimated and may occur in one-third of relatively happily married couples.

—Hormonal causes may be involved in sexual arousal disorder in women.

F. Inhibited Orgasm

—**Inhibited male orgasm**, or retarded ejaculation, is much less common than premature ejaculation or impotence and has a prevalence of about 5%.

—**Inhibited female orgasm** refers to inability to achieve orgasm by masturbation or coitus following a normal sexual excitement phase during sexual activity.

    —Inhibited female orgasm is found in primary form in about 10% of women.

    —Kinsey found that first orgasm in 50% of women occurs during adolescence.

    —The overall prevalence of inhibited female orgasm from all causes is about 30%.

    —Psychological causes of inhibited female orgasm include guilt, fears of loss of control, pregnancy, rejection by the sex partner, and vaginal damage, and hostility toward men.

G. Premature Ejaculation

—Premature ejaculation occurs when the man achieves climax too soon, ie, before or immediately following vaginal entry.

—In premature ejaculation, the man passes from the excitement to orgasm with little or no plateau phase.

—Important factors in the diagnosis of premature ejaculation include age of the man, frequency of sexual intercourse, and characteristics of the sex partner.

—Anxiety is frequently present in premature ejaculation.

—Thirty-five to 40% of men treated for sexual dysfunction report premature ejaculation.

—Behavioral techniques such as the squeeze technique (see later discussion) can help patients increase control over the duration of any phase of the sexual response cycle.

H. Functional Dyspareunia

Functional dyspareunia is persistent or recurrent pain before, during, or after intercourse with no organic cause.

—Although much more common in women, dyspareunia can occur in either sex.

—Dyspareunia is often associated with vaginismus.

I. Functional Vaginismus

Functional vaginismus is a spasm of the outer third of the vagina that prevents intercourse.

—The penis cannot be damaged nor is the removal of the penis affected by the vaginal spasm in vaginismus.

—Vaginismus can also occur during a gynecologic examination and may prevent vaginal entry of the speculum.

—Vaginismus may be associated with pain at the first coital experience, a strict religious upbringing, or a sexual crime such as rape or incest.

VII. Homosexuality

A. Occurrence

—In **Alfred Kinsey's** study, 4% of men were reported to be exclusively homosexual and 13% of men were mainly homosexual for at least 3 of their adult years.

—Current estimates of the occurrence of homosexuality are 3 to 6% in men and 1 to 3% in women.

—There are no significant ethnic differences in the occurrence of homosexuality.

—About 50% of all men have had some prepubertal homosexual experience.

—Most homosexuals have experienced heterosexual sex and one-half to three-fourths have had children.

B. Etiology

—Both biological and psychosocial factors have been proposed in the etiology of homosexuality.

—Alterations in prenatal hormones, ie, high levels of androgens in females and decreased androgens in males, may contribute to the development of homosexuality.

—A higher incidence of concordance among monozygotic than among dizygotic twins suggests that genetic factors may be involved in homosexuality.

—Cross-gender behavior during childhood may be predictive of later homosexual orientation, more so in boys than in girls.

C. Intervention

—Although homosexuality is not considered a dysfunction in the DSM-III-R, persistent distress about one's sexual orientation is listed as a sexual disorder.

—Psychological intervention in homosexuality generally involves helping the person who is distressed about his or her sexual orientation to become comfortable with that orientation.

VIII. Sex Therapy

A. Treatment Modalities

—Prior to the work of **Masters and Johnson**, the primary modality for treating sexual problems was individual psychotherapy.

—Modalities for treating sexual problems now include dual-sex therapy, hypnotherapy, behavior therapy, and group therapy.

B. Dual-Sex Therapy

—Dual-sex therapy, in which the couple participates with both a male and a female therapist, was developed by Masters and Johnson.

—Dual-sex therapy is a short-term, behavioral approach.

—Specific exercises such as sensate focus and the squeeze technique are used.

　—In **sensate focus exercises**, sensory awareness to touch, sight, smell, and sound are heightened.

　—In the **squeeze technique**, the threshold of penile excitability is raised to the sensation of ejaculatory inevitability and the man is taught to identify that time point.

　　—With identification of the moment of ejaculatory inevitability, the man can slow his sexual response.

　　—At the recognized time point, the partner exerts pressure on both sides of the penis until the erection subsides.

　　—Some reports of penile damage have decreased the use of the squeeze technique.

—Dual-sex therapy integrated with psychotherapy is a very successful treatment modality for sexual problems.

C. Hypnotherapy

—Hypnotherapy aims at reducing the stresses around sexual activity that produce anxiety.

—Relaxation techniques are also used before sexual activity begins.

D. Behavioral Approaches

—Behavioral approaches to sex therapy are based on the idea that sexual problems are **maladaptive patterns of behavior** that have been learned.

—In behavior therapy, the patient reduces the anxiety associated with sex through **systematic desensitization**.

Assertiveness training, in which the patient is taught to talk about sexual feelings and desires, is also a behavioral sex therapy technique.

E. Group Therapy

—Group therapy provides support for patients who are anxious or guilty about specific sexual activities or dysfunctions.

—Techniques used in group therapy for sexual problems include **psychodrama** and **role playing.**

F. Outcome of Sex Therapy

—If the couple is young, follows instructions about specific exercises, and has a flexible attitude, the likelihood of a successful treatment outcome is much greater.

—There is a growing tendency not to refer patients with sexual problems to specialists but for the physician to treat the sexual problems of patients.

IX. Common Illnesses and Sexuality

A. Overview

Heart disease and **diabetes** affect at least 14 million Americans. Fear of sexual activity can hamper full recovery of these patients.

B. Myocardial Infarction

—**Impotence** and **decreased libido** are common following myocardial infarction.

—Sexual problems after a heart attack frequently have a psychogenic cause.

—Many heart patients fear that the exertion or excitement of sexual activity will lead to another heart attack or to sudden death.

—Some researchers have compared the sexual activity of middle aged men with familiar partners as equivalent to climbing a flight of stairs or engaging in ordinary occupational tasks.

—Generally, if exercise that raises the heart rate to 110 to 120 beats per minute can be tolerated without severe shortness of breath or chest pain, sexual activity can be resumed.

C. Diabetes

1. *Impotence*

—Twenty-seven to 55% of diabetic men become impotent.

—Impotence generally occurs several years after the diabetes is diagnosed.

—Occasionally, impotence is the first symptom of diabetes.

—The major cause of impotence in diabetic men is diabetic neuropathy, which involves microscopic damage to nerve tissue as a result of hyperglycemia.

—Poor metabolic control of diabetes is related to increased incidence of sexual problems.

—In some diabetic men, impotence may be caused by vascular changes that affect the blood vessels in the penis.

—Although physiologic causes may be present, psychological factors influence impotence associated with diabetes.

Table 19.2. Sexuality and Spinal Cord Injury in Men

Type of Lesion	Percent Achieving Erection	Percent Able to Ejaculate
Complete upper motor neuron	93 (R)	4
Incomplete upper motor neuron	99 (R)	33
Complete lower motor neuron	26 (P)	18
Incomplete lower motor neuron	90 (P & R)	70

R = reflexogenic erections: caused by tactile stimulation of the genitalia or surrounding area, are brief in duration, and do not produce pleasurable genital sensations. P = psychogenic erections: caused by psychological stimuli and, while not necessarily complete, last longer than reflexogenic erections.

2. *Treatment*
   —Treatment of impotence in diabetic men includes identifying both interpersonal problems and evidence of physiologic damage.
   —Surgical approaches, including penile implants, may be used to treat impotence associated with diabetes.
   —Although penile implants may be used, diabetic men often have greater difficulties in wound healing and greater susceptibility to infection.

X. Spinal Cord Injuries and Sexuality

A. Spinal Cord Injuries in Men
   —Spinal cord injuries are becoming more common as individuals in the society become more mobile.
   —Although sexual functioning in men is frequently affected by spinal cord injury, the sexual prognosis is better for men with incomplete rather than complete lesions.

   —Men with upper motor neuron lesions have more erections but ejaculate less frequently than those with lower motor neuron lesions.
   —The prognosis is also better for men with lesions of the lower rather than upper motor neurons (Table 19.2).
   —When ejaculation does occur, it may be retrograde in spinal cord–injured men.
   —Testosterone levels after spinal cord injury may be reduced.

B. Spinal Cord Injuries in Women
   —The effects of spinal cord injury in women have not been well studied.
   —Studies indicate reduced incidence of orgasm, decrease in vaginal lubrication, and lowered levels of pelvic vasocongestion following spinal cord injury in women.
   —Even if they can ejaculate, fertility is reduced in spinal cord–injured men; in women, fertility does not appear to be reduced.

XI. Aging and Sexuality

A. Physical Changes
   Aging persons normally show alterations in sexual functioning.
   —In men, these changes include slower erection, diminished intensity of ejaculation, and longer refractory period.
   —In women, these changes include vaginal thinning, shortening of vaginal length, and vaginal dryness.

Table 19.3. Aging and Sexuality

	Age (years)	Percent Reporting	
		Men	Women
Coitus:			
	61–65	37	39
	66–71	28	27
Sexual interest:			
	61–65	93	67
	66–71	90	50

B. Sexual Interest and Activity

—In spite of the physical changes and in spite of negative societal attitudes, studies show that many older people are interested and do continue to engage in sexual activity (Table 19.3).

—In women, menopause and aging do not result in decreased libido if general health is good.

—Prolonged abstention from sex may lead more quickly to physical atrophy of the genital organs in old age.

—Decreasing sexual activity with increasing age is related to death of the spouse, divorce, illness and impotence as well as to decreased interest.

XII. Drugs of Use and Abuse and Sexuality

A. Prescription Drugs

A number of commonly used prescription drugs have negative effects on sexuality (Table 19.4).

B. Alcohol

—Alcohol use decreases erection and vaginal lubrication.

—The negative physiologic effects are counteracted by alcohol's disinhibiting properties, which may increase sexuality.

—Over long-term use, alcohol may cause liver dysfunction, resulting in increased estrogen availability and decreased potency in men.

C. Marijuana

—Marijuana appears to enhance the enjoyment of sex by psychological, not physiologic, means.

—Testosterone levels may be reduced with chronic marijuana use.

—Marijuana may lower pituitary gonadotropin levels in women.

D. Heroin and Methadone

—Heroin and methadone use are associated with suppressed libido, retarded ejaculation, and failure to ejaculate.

—Methadone is associated with fewer sexual problems than heroin.

E. Amphetamines and Cocaine

—**Amphetamine** use often results in increased libido.

—Although **cocaine** use is sexually stimulating for some people, such use is associated also with loss of erection and priapism (constant erection).

Table 19.4. The Effects of Prescription Drugs on Sexuality

Type of Drug		Drug Effect	Approximate Percent Affected
Antihypertensives:			
Thiazide diuretics		I	5
Nonthiazide diuretics		I	5
Spironolactone		I, L	22
Antiadrenergic drugs:			
α-methyldopa	(1 g/day)	I	10–15
	(1-1.5 g/day)	I	20–25
	(2 g/day)	I	50
guanethidine	(>25 mg/day)	EJ, I, L	50–60
hydralazine	low doses	R	
	(>200 mg/day)	L	5–10
Clonidine		I, L	10–20
Prazosin		L	15
		I	rare
β-Adrenergic blockers:			
propranolol		R	
metoprolol		P	rare
Tranquilizers and sedatives:			
Benzodiazepines		R	
Barbiturates		I, L	rare
Antipsychotics:			
Chlorpromazine	low doses	R	
	(>400 mg/day)	I, L	10–20
Haloperidol		I	10–20
Antidepressants:			
Tricyclics		I	5
		EJ	
MAO inhibitors		I	10–15
		EJ	25–30
Lithium carbonate		I	
Anticholinergics		I, VD	
Clofibrate (anticholesterol)		I, L	
Cimetidine (histamine antagonist)		I	
Digitalis		I	
Antihistamines		L, VD	
L-dopa		increased libido	

I = impotence; EJ = inhibited ejaculation; L = inhibited libido; VD = vaginal dryness; R = relatively few problems; P = Peyronie's disease (sclerotic plaques on the penis that cause curvature).

F. Amyl Nitrate

—Amyl nitrate is a vasodilator that is used as an aphrodisiac to enhance the sensation of orgasm.

—Although amyl nitrate may increase sensation, cardiovascular accidents may result from its use.

G. Gonadal Hormones

Gonadal hormones and related substances are used clinically for treatment of a number of medical conditions.

—Drugs with **androgenic activity** may increase sex drive in women, primarily by causing clitoral hypertrophy.

—Androgenic drugs have little effect in men with normal androgen levels.

—Drugs with **estrogenic activity** may decrease sex drive in men but have no known direct effect on sexuality in premenopausal women.

—In postmenopausal women, estrogens may reduce vaginal dryness and thus may decrease physical discomfort associated with coitus.

XIII. Rape

A. Definitions

—Rape is an act of aggression demonstrated through sexual activity.
—By legal definition, rape requires penetration of the outer vulva by the penis; erection and ejaculation are not necessary.
—Sodomy includes fellatio (oral-penile contact) and anal penetration.
—In most states, male rape is legally defined as sodomy.

B. Characteristics of the Rapist

—Rape often occurs in the context of other criminal activity and is frequently associated with use of weapons.
—Fifty-one percent of rapists are white; 47% are black.
—Rapists tend to rape women of the same race.
—Alcohol is associated with 34% of rapes.
—The majority of rapists are under 25 years of age.

C. Characteristics of the Rape Victim

—Females 10 to 29 years old are most likely to be raped.
—Most commonly, rape occurs inside a woman's own home.
—Fifty percent of rapists are known by the victims; 7% are close relatives.

D. The Emotional Results of Rape

—Women often suffer the emotional results of a rape for a year or longer.
—Factors associated with recovery from the effects of rape include immediate support from people in her environment, the opportunity to talk about her intense anger, and the arrest of the rapist.
—Group therapy with other rape victims is also effective.

E. Legal Aspects of Rape

—Only 1 in 10 rapes is reported; 60,000 rapes were reported in 1986.
—In the courtroom, a woman does not have to prove that she fought or resisted the rapist.
—In some states, the victim's previous sexual activities are inadmissible as evidence in trials of rape.
—In some states, husbands can be prosecuted for the rape of their wives.

XIV. Overview of Aggression

A. Theories of Aggression

—**Freud** considered aggression to be a redirection of the **death instinct**.
—**Konrad Lorenz** believed that, as in animals, aggression in humans is a result of a fighting instinct.
—In the **drive theory**, aggression results from frustration caused by thwarted drives.
—Some researchers, eg, **Albert Bandura**, maintain that aggression is **learned behavior**.

B. Social and Environmental Determinants of Aggression

—**Social determinants** of aggression include frustration, provocation by others, and exposure to aggression in the media, eg, television.

—Violence on television correlates directly with increased aggression in children.

—Possible **environmental determinants** of aggression include overcrowding, noise, and air pollution.

—Other determinants of aggression include pain and sexual arousal.

XV. Biological Determinants of Aggression

A. Hormones

—Testosterone is closely associated with aggression in animals.

—In humans, males are more aggressive than females in all societies observed to date; homicide is committed mainly by men.

—Other hormones linked to aggression include progesterone, luteinizing hormone, and prolactin.

B. Drugs and Alcohol

—Drugs linked to aggression include **alcohol** and **barbiturates**.

—Low doses of these drugs inhibit and high doses facilitate aggression.

—Other drugs linked to increased aggression are **cocaine, amphetamines, hallucinogens,** and extremely high doses of **marijuana**.

C. The Brain and Aggression

—**Neurotransmitters** linked to aggression include dopamine, norepinephrine, acetylcholine, serotonin, and β-endorphin.

—**Brain abnormalities** associated with increased aggression include abnormal activity in the medial amygdala and mesencephalic tegmentum and temporal lobe and psychomotor epilepsy.

—**Brain lesions** associated with increased aggression include temporal lobe tumors and anterior hypothalamic and frontal lobe lesions.

XVI. Control of Aggression

A. Social Control of Aggression

—Punishment may temporarily control aggression in an individual, but often it can elicit a desire for revenge and increased aggression.

—Training aggressive individuals in social skills has brought about reduction in aggression.

B. Pharmacologic Control of Aggression

Drugs used to treat aggression include lithium (especially in adolescent boys), antipsychotics, antidepressants, anticonvulsants, minor tranquilizers, antiandrogens, and β-blockers and stimulants (in children).

Review Test

HUMAN SEXUALITY AND HUMAN AGGRESSION

DIRECTIONS: For each of the questions or incomplete statements below, choose the answer that is **most correct.**

19.1. All of the following are true about premature ejaculation EXCEPT:
A. Premature ejaculation is the rarest sexual dysfunction.
B. In premature ejaculation, the plateau phase is usually absent.
C. An important factor in the diagnosis of premature ejaculation is the age of the man.
D. Anxiety is a characteristic of premature ejaculation.
E. Forty percent of men treated for sexual dysfunction report premature ejaculation.

19.2. The current estimate of the occurrence of homosexuality in men is:
A. 0.5 to 2%.
B. 3 to 6%.
C. 12 to 14%.
D. 14 to 16%.
E. 17 to 20%.

19.3. The major technique used in conjunction with hypnotherapy during sex therapy is:
A. the squeeze technique.
B. sensate focus.
C. relaxation.
D. psychotherapy.
E. behavior modification.

19.4. All of the following are true about sexuality in spinal cord–injured men EXCEPT:
A. Sexual prognosis is better for men with incomplete lesions.
B. Sexual prognosis is better for men with lesions of the lower motor neurons.
C. Reflexogenic erections are often brief in duration.
D. Retrograde ejaculation may occur.
E. Hormone levels are not affected after spinal cord injury.

19.5. All of the following are true about sexuality in normally aging patients EXCEPT:
A. Erection is slower.
B. Vaginal dryness occurs.
C. Decrease in estrogen with menopause commonly results in reduced libido in women.
D. Aging men have a longer refractory period following ejaculation.
E. Prolonged abstention from sex leads more quickly to atrophy of the genital organs.

19.6. Which of the following drugs is LEAST likely to cause impotence?
A. Guanethidine
B. Spironolactone
C. Propranolol
D. α-Methyldopa
E. Clonidine

19.7. All of the following are true about the sexual effects of prescription drugs EXCEPT:
A. Use of tricyclic antidepressants result in impotence in about 5% of individuals.
B. The incidence of impotence with MAO inhibitors is higher than with tricyclic antidepressants.
C. Lithium carbonate has been associated with the occurrence of impotence.
D. Ejaculatory problems occur in approximately 25% of users of MAO inhibitors.
E. Impotence occurs in approximately 80% of patients treated with high doses of chlorpromazine.

19.8. All of the following are true about rape EXCEPT:
A. The emotional effects of rape commonly last for approximately 1 month.
B. Fifty-one percent of rapists are white.
C. Forty-seven percent of rapists are black.
D. Fifty percent of rapists are known by their victims.
E. Rapists tend to rape women of the same race.

19.9. All of the following are true about rape EXCEPT:

A. It often occurs in the context of another crime.
B. Alcohol is frequently involved.
C. It commonly occurs inside a woman's own home.
D. Most rapes are not reported to the authorities.
E. For the court to convict a rapist, the female victim must prove that she actively fought against the rapist.

19.10. All of the following are true about sex determination EXCEPT:

A. In the absence of ovarian hormones during prenatal life, the internal and external genitalia of the developing fetus will be masculine.
B. Differentiation of the gonads takes place about the twelfth week of gestation in females.
C. Chromosomes direct the early differentiation of the gonads.
D. The brains of males and females are affected by gonadal hormones during early development.
E. Differentiation of the gonads takes place about the seventh week of gestation in males.

19.11. Individuals who dress in clothes of the opposite sex for sexual pleasure

A. are known as transsexuals.
B. are almost always homosexual.
C. are almost exclusively males.
D. usually have a defect in gender identity.
E. believe that they were born the wrong sex.

19.12. All of the following are true about sexual behavior in adult women EXCEPT:

A. Peaks in sexual interest are seen around the time of ovulation.
B. Peaks in sexual interest and behavior are seen just prior to menstruation.
C. Peaks in sexual interest in behavior may correlate with low progesterone levels.
D. Peaks in sexual behavior correlate with low estrogen levels.
E. Gonadal hormones have more of an effect on behavior in female animals than in women.

19.13. Which of the following is true about the hormonal control of male sexuality?

A. There is no temporal pattern of testosterone release.
B. Stress results in an increase in testosterone levels.
C. Treatment with progesterone increases sexual interest and behavior in men.
D. Homosexual men generally have normal testosterone levels.
E. None of the above.

19.14. Which of the following is true about human sexual response?

A. If orgasm has not occurred, resolution takes approximately 5 minutes.
B. Restimulation immediately following orgasm is not possible for females.
C. Restimulation immediately following orgasm is usually possible for males.
D. The refractory period after orgasm is often variable.
E. Vaginal and clitoral orgasm are different physiologically.

19.15. All of the following are true about the sexual dysfunctions EXCEPT:

A. They can develop after a period of normal functioning.
B. They occur with all partners.
C. They may be total or partial.
D. They can have a combination of causes.
E. They include functional sexual pain disorders.

19.16. Which of the following is true?

A. Lack of sexual desire is not considered a sexual dysfunction.
B. Primary impotence is common.
C. Sexual arousal disorder in men involves failure to maintain erection.
D. Secondary impotence occurs in 1 to 2% of men.
E. Absence of nocturnal erections during sleep indicates a psychological cause for a patient's impotence.

19.17. All of the following are true about the etiology of male homosexuality EXCEPT:

A. Alterations in prenatal hormones may be involved.
B. There is a higher concordance among monozygotic than among dizygotic twins.
C. Cross-gender behavior during childhood commonly occurs.
D. Most homosexual men have female rather than male siblings.
E. Homosexuality is not considered a sexual dysfunction in the DSM-III-R.

19.18. Which of the following is/are modalities for treating sexual problems?

A. Dual sex therapy
B. Hypnotherapy
C. Behavior therapy
D. Group therapy
E. All of the above

19.19. All of the following are true about sexual activity in heart patients EXCEPT:

A. Sexual problems after a heart attack frequently have a psychogenic component.
B. Fear of sexual activity can hamper full recovery.
C. If exercise that raises the heart rate to 110 beats per minute can be tolerated, sexual activity can generally be resumed.
D. Decreased libido is relatively rare following a heart attack.
E. There is a high occurrence of impotence following a heart attack.

19.20. All of the following are true about impotence associated with diabetes EXCEPT:

A. Impotence occurs in approximately 40% of diabetic men.
B. Occasionally, impotence is the first symptom of diabetes.
C. The major causes of impotence in diabetic men are psychogenic.
D. Metabolic control of diabetes is related to decreased incidence of sexual problems.
E. Penile implants may be used.

19.21. All of the following are true about the sexual effects of spinal cord injury in women EXCEPT:

A. There is a reduced incidence of orgasm.
B. There are decreased levels of pelvic vasocongestion.
C. There is a decrease in vaginal lubrication.
D. Fertility is usually reduced.
E. Few studies have addressed sexual effects of spinal cord injury in women.

19.22. Which of the following statements is/are true?

A. Benzodiazepines are likely to cause ejaculatory problems.
B. Haloperidol is associated with impotence.
C. Barbiturate use frequently results in ejaculatory problems.
D. Chlorpromazine in high doses is likely to result in problems with impotence and libido.
E. Both B and D.

19.23. Which of the following drugs is/are associated with the occurrence of impotence?

A. Clofibrate
B. Cimetidine
C. Digitalis
D. Thiazide diuretics
E. All of the above

19.24. Drugs used in treating aggression include all of the following EXCEPT:

A. stimulants (in children).
B. lithium.
C. antidepressants.
D. calcium channel blockers.
E. antiandrogens.

19.25. All of the following are true about sexual dysfunctions EXCEPT:

A. Nocturnal erections can help to distinguish psychogenic from physical impotence.
B. Sexual arousal disorder in women may occur in relatively happily married couples.
C. Hormonal causes may be involved in sexual arousal disorder in women.
D. Inhibited female orgasm in its primary form is found in about 50% of women.
E. Causes of inhibited female orgasm include fear of pregnancy.

19.26. Determinants of aggression include all of the following EXCEPT:

A. overcrowding.
B. sexual arousal.
C. estrogen.
D. alcohol.
E. pain.

DIRECTIONS: For each of the numbered phrases below, choose the lettered stage of the sexual response cycle with which it is **most closely associated.**

A. Excitement
B. Plateau
C. Orgasm
D. Resolution

19.27. Erection begins.

19.28. The tenting effect begins.

19.29. Sex organs return to nonstimulated condition.

19.30. Emission of semen occurs.

19.31. A few drops of sperm-containing fluid are secreted.

19.32. Formation of the orgasmic platform occurs.

DIRECTIONS: For each of the numbered phrases below, choose the drug with which it is **most closely associated.**

A. Alcohol
B. Marijuana
C. Heroin
D. Amphetamine
E. Amyl nitrate

19.33. A vasodilator used as an aphrodisiac

19.34. Lowered pituitary gonadotropin levels in women

19.35. Increased estrogen availability in men

DIRECTIONS: For each of the questions or incomplete statements below, **one** or **more** of the answers or completions given are correct. Choose answer:

A. if only **1, 2,** and **3** are correct.
B. if only **1** and **3** are correct.
C. if **2** and **4** are correct.
D. if only **4** is correct.
E. if **all** are correct.

19.36. Which of the following is/are true?
1. Behavioral techniques are used in sex therapy.
2. Dyspareunia can occur in either sex but is more common in women.
3. Dyspareunia is often associated with vaginismus.
4. Vaginismus can make intercourse impossible.

19.37. Which of the following is/are true about homosexuality?
1. There are significant ethnic differences in its occurrence.
2. Occurrence is estimated at 1 to 3% in women.
3. Approximately 10% of all men have had some prepubertal homosexual experience.
4. Most homosexuals have had children.

19.38. Which of the following factors is/are associated with a successful outcome in sex therapy?
1. Practicing the assigned exercises
2. Older age of the couple
3. Flexibility of attitude
4. Intervention of a physician

19.39. Which of the following is/are associated with decreased sexual behavior in older people?
1. Illness
2. Divorce
3. Impotence
4. Death of a spouse

19.40. Factors associated with recovery from the effects of rape include:
1. immediate support.
2. opportunity to ventilate rage.
3. a socially acceptable means of recourse.
4. group therapy with other rape victims.

19.41. Brain abnormalities associated with increased aggression include:
1. temporal lobe tumors.
2. frontal lobe lesions.
3. anterior hypothalamic lesions.
4. cerebellar atrophy.

Answers and Explanations

HUMAN SEXUALITY AND HUMAN AGGRESSION

19.1. A. Premature ejaculation is a relatively common sexual dysfunction.

19.2. B. The current estimate of homosexuality in men is 3 to 6%.

19.3. C. Hypnotherapy patients are taught relaxation techniques to use before sexual activity begins.

19.4. E. Testosterone levels after spinal cord injury may be reduced.

19.5. C. Despite decreased estrogen production, menopause is not generally associated with reduced libido in women.

19.6. C. Sexual problems in patients taking propranolol are relatively rare.

19.7. E. Doses of chlorpromazine of more than 400 mg per day are associated with impotence and inhibited libido in 10 to 20% of patients.

19.8. A. The emotional effects of rape may continue for a year or longer.

19.9. E. Women no longer have to prove in court that they actively fought against the rapist.

19.10. A. In the absence of testicular or ovarian hormones during prenatal life, the external genitalia of the fetus will be feminine.

19.11. C. Transvestites, individuals who dress in clothes of the opposite sex for sexual pleasure, are almost always male, may be homosexual or heterosexual, and do not generally have a defect in gender identity.

19.12. D. The connection between estrogen levels and female sexual behavior is unclear. If anything, high estrogen levels may be associated with peaks in sexual behavior.

19.13. D. Testosterone is released in a cyclic pattern, stress results in decreased testosterone levels, and treatment with progesterone decreases sexual interest and behavior in men.

19.14. D. If orgasm has occurred, resolution takes approximately 15 minutes. Length of the refractory period depends on the age and physical condition of the individual. Restimulation immediately following orgasm is not usually possible for men but is possible for women. Vaginal and clitoral orgasm are associated with similar physiologic responses.

19.15. B. Sexual dysfunction may occur only with specific partners.

19.16. C. In sexual arousal disorder, the man cannot maintain erection until completion of the sexual act. Although primary impotence is rare, secondary impotence occurs in 10 to 20% of men. Lack of sexual desire may be considered a sexual dysfunction if it disturbs the individual or partner.

19.17. D. The sex of siblings is not commonly associated with the occurrence of homosexuality.

19.18. E. All are correct.

19.19. D. Decreased libido is relatively common following a heart attack.

19.20. C. Twenty-seven to 55% of diabetic men eventually become impotent. The major cause of this impotence is thought to be physiologic.

19.21. D. Pelvic vasocongestion and vaginal lubrication may be lower in spinal cord–injured women; fertility is not usually affected.

19.22. E. Benzodiazepines rarely cause sexual problems; barbiturate use is not generally associated with ejaculatory problems. Antipsychotics may cause sexual problems.

19.23. E. All are correct.

19.24. D. Drugs used in the treatment of aggression include lithium, antidepressants, stimulants (in children), anticonvulsants, antipsychotics, minor tranquilizers, antiandrogens, and β-blockers.

19.25. D. Inhibited female orgasm in its primary form is rare.

19.26. C. Determinants of aggression include pain, sexual arousal, alcohol, overcrowding, and testosterone.

19.27. A. Erection begins in the excitement phase.

19.28. A. The tenting effect begins in the excitement phase.

19.29. D. The sex organs return to the non-stimulated condition during resolution.

19.30. C. Emission of semen occurs during ejaculation and orgasm.

19.31. B. A few drops of sperm-containing fluid are secreted during the plateau phase.

19.32. B. Formation of the orgasmic platform occurs during the plateau phase in women.

19.33. E. Amyl nitrate is a vasodilator used as an aphrodisiac.

19.34. B. Lowered pituitary gonadotropin levels are associated with use of marijuana in women.

19.35. A. Increased estrogen availability in men may result from chronic alcohol use.

19.36. E. All are correct.

19.37. C. There are no significant ethnic differences in the occurrence of homosexuality. Approximately 50% of men have had prepubertal homosexual experiences.

19.38. B. The younger the couple and the more flexible their attitudes about sex, the more successful the outcome of sex therapy.

19.39. E. All are correct.

19.40. E. All are correct.

19.41. A. Brain abnormalities associated with increased aggression include temporal lobe and psychomotor epilepsy, abnormal activity in the amygdala, temporal lobe tumors, and anterior hypothalamic and frontal lobe lesions.

20

Doctor-Patient Communication and Roles

I. Communication

A. Expectations of Patients

Patients have a variety of expectations of doctors.

—Expectations of the doctor include that he or she will be helpful, has knowledge about the problem, and will allow the patient to participate in diagnosis and treatment of the illness.

—Patient expectations about the doctor-patient relationship are influenced by the patient's cultural background, previous experience with illness and doctors, physical and emotional state, childhood developmental experiences, and personality style.

B. Transference Reactions

—Patients have unconscious transference reactions to their doctors.

—Transference reactions are rooted in childhood parent-child relationships.

—In **positive transference**, the patient feels very positively about the doctor and has a high level of confidence in his or her abilities.

—Overidealization of the physician can lead to disillusionment and negative transference.

—Idealization of the physician can also result in sexual feelings by the patient toward the physician.

—In **negative transference**, patients may develop resentment or anger toward the doctor if their desires and expectations are not realized.

—Unconscious hostility toward the doctor can result in misuse of medication and generally oppositional behavior.

C. Countertransference Reactions

—Countertransference reactions of doctors toward patients also occur such that doctors may have guilt feelings when they are unable to help a patient or may have particular feelings toward patients who remind them of a close relative or friend.

—Countertransference reactions of the physician can also result in the tendency of physicians to minimize the severity of a colleague's illness.

D. Characteristics of the Physician

—The characteristics of the doctor have important influences on the doctor-patient relationship.

—The doctor's ethnic background, sex, and age affect the patient's reaction to him or her.

—Although young physicians may initially be viewed as childlike by patients, the power of the role of the physician usually overrides this initial view.

E. Medical Practice

—Only about one-third of individuals with symptoms visit physicians.

—Most people manage illness at home with over-the-counter medications and home treatment.

—The occurrence of a stressful life event increases the probability by 50% that medical attention will be sought when symptoms are present.

—Although chronically ill patients express the most skepticism about medical care, they seek help most frequently.

—There is a strong correlation between psychological illness and physical illness; morbidity and mortality are much higher in psychiatric populations.

II. The Clinical Interview

A. Skills and Communication

Communication between the physician and the patient significantly impacts on patient health.

—Patient compliance with medical advice, detection of both physical and psychological problems, and patient satisfaction with the physician are improved by good physician-patient communication.

—One of the most important skills that a physician must learn is how to interview patients.

   —In an interview, the physician must first establish trust and confidence in the patient.

   —The physician must then gather physical, psychological, and social information to identify the patient's problem.

B. The Open-ended Question

Although direct questioning can elicit information, the **open-ended** type of question and interview is most likely to produce a good clinical relationship and aid in acquisition of information about the patient.

—Open-ended questions do not close off potential areas of pertinent information.

—The open-ended question is one in which the interviewer gives little structure to the patient and elicits a great deal of information, eg, "Tell me about your fall."

   —In contrast, **direct questions** ask the patient for specific information, eg, "Did you fall on your hip?"

C. Basic Interviewing Techniques

Basic interviewing techniques include facilitation, silence, direct questions, confrontation, and support and empathy.

—**Facilitation** is used by the interviewer to encourage the patient to elaborate on an answer, eg, "And then what happened?"

—**Reflection** is a variation of facilitation in which the physician repeats the response of the patient, eg, "You said that your pain increased after you washed the floor."

—The physician can use the technique of **silence** to increase the patient's responsiveness.

—Silence is the least controlling interview technique.

—**Direct questions** are used to elicit specific information, eg, "Where on your side do you feel the most pain?"

—The physician can also use **confrontation** during an interview.

—In confrontation, the patient's attention is called to inconsistencies in his or her own responses or body language, eg, "You seem really upset about the circumstances under which the fall took place."

—**Support** is used to express the physician's interest and concern for the patient, eg, "That must have been a frightening experience for you."

—**Empathy** is used to express the physician's understanding of the patient's problem, eg, "I understand that you are worried about the financial consequences of this injury."

III. Compliance

A. Definition and Examples

—The extent to which a patient follows the clinical recommendations and instructions of the physician with whom he or she is in treatment is known as **compliance**.

—Examples of compliance include taking medications on schedule, keeping appointments, and following directions for changes in behavior or diet.

B. Patient Characteristics Associated with Compliance

—Approximately one-third of patients are compliant with treatment, one-third comply some of the time, and one-third do not comply with treatment at all.

—Fifty-four percent of patients can be expected to comply with treatment at a particular point in time.

—In hypertensive patients, about half fail to comply with treatment; of these, half leave treatment within 1 year.

—The relationship between compliance and patient's sex, religion, socioeconomic or marital status, race, intelligence, or educational level is not apparent.

—Factors associated with compliance are listed in Table 20.1.

IV. The Psychobiology of Chronic Pain

A. Psychosocial Factors

—**Chronic pain** is one of the most frequent complaints of patients.

—Pain can be caused by physical or psychological factors.

—Particular psychological factors associated with chronic pain include depression, alcohol and drug abuse, childhood neglect and physical and sexual abuse, and life stress.

Table 20.1.   Factors Associated with Patient Compliance with Medical Advice

Decrease Compliance

Perception of the physician as rejecting and unfriendly
Physician failure to explain the diagnosis or causes of symptoms
Increased complexity of treatment regimen, ie, more than three types of medication taken more than four times a day
Increased number of required behavioral changes
Verbal instructions for taking medication
Visual problems reading prescription labels (particularly in the elderly)

Increase Compliance

Good doctor-patient relationship
Written instructions for taking medication
Patient's subjective feelings of distress or illness
Doctor's awareness of and sensitivity to the patient's belief system
Physician enthusiasm, permissiveness, time spent talking with the patient
Physician experience and older physician age
Short waiting room time
Patient knowledge of the expected positive treatment outcome
Patient knowledge of the names and effects of prescribed drugs

—Patients with borderline or narcissistic personality disorders or those with hypochondriasis are at risk for developing chronic pain syndrome.

—Religious, cultural, and ethnic factors may influence the patient's expression of pain and the responses of the patient's support systems to the pain.

—Psychological "uses" of chronic pain include personal, social, or financial gain and justification of failure to establish social relationships.

B. **The Perception of Pain**

—The neural center for psychogenic pain may be different than that of purely physical pain.

—Most people have similar thresholds for pain perception, which may be altered by biofeedback, physical therapy or activity, optimistic emotional state, relaxation exercises, meditation, guided imagery, electrical stimulation of pain transmission pathways, suggestion, hypnosis, placebos, and analgesics.

—Extreme sensitivity to pain is associated with depression, anxiety, and hypochondriasis.

C. **Depression and Chronic Pain**

—Depression and chronic pain are linked.

—Depression may predispose a person to develop chronic pain.

—Chronic pain also frequently leads to depression.

—Pain relief in chronic pain patients can be achieved by use of antidepressant drugs and phenothiazines.

D. **Treatment**

—If the chronic pain is caused by cancer or other chronic medical disease, pain relief is best achieved by **analgesics** or **nerve block**.

—Although medicine offers the first line of treatment, **behavior modification** and **deconditioning** also have use in pain caused by cancer or chronic disease.

—In chronic diseases, a medication schedule that disassociates the experience of pain from the receipt of medication through the scheduled administration of medication rather than medication on demand can help control pain.

—For effective pain management, patients should receive positive reinforcement for healthy, active behavior and minimal attention should be given to passive, pain-related behavior.

—Patients with chronic pain benefit from psychotherapy and behavior therapy by needing less pain medication, becoming more active, and showing increased attempts to return to a normal lifestyle.

Review Test

DOCTOR-PATIENT COMMUNICATION AND ROLES

DIRECTIONS: For each of the questions or incomplete statements below, choose the answer that is **most correct.**

20.1. Which of the following is the most open-ended question or statement?

A. "Point to the area of pain in your chest."
B. "Tell me about the pain."
C. "Tell me about the pain in your chest."
D. "Have you been to a physician within the past 6 months?"
E. "Is there a history of heart disease in your family?"

20.2. Which of the following is an example of the interviewing technique known as facilitation?

A. "Please go on."
B. "How much liquor do you drink?"
C. "Do you drink?"
D. "Why did you wait so long to come in?"
E. "I see that the situation upsets you."

20.3. Which of the following is an example of the interviewing technique known as confrontation?

A. "Tell me again about the pain in your chest."
B. "What happened then?"
C. "I'll be here to help you."
D. "You look terrified."
E. "How do you feel about giving up your job?"

20.4. All of the following are common reasons for noncompliance EXCEPT:

A. an asymptomatic illness.
B. deliberate misuse of medication.
C. misunderstanding of the instructions for taking the medication.
D. denial of the severity of the illness.
E. fear of the severity of the illness.

20.5. All of the following are true about transference in the doctor-patient relationship EXCEPT:

A. In positive transference, the patient may develop an unshakable confidence in the doctor.
B. Overidealization of the physician can lead to negative transference.
C. Transference reactions are rooted in the parent-child relationship.
D. Patients are consciously aware of their transference reactions toward the doctor.
E. In a negative transference reaction, the patient may become resentful if his or her expectations of the doctor are not met.

20.6. Which of the following is true?

A. Most people with symptoms of illness visit physicians.
B. Chronically ill patients are the least skeptical about medical care.
C. Over-the-counter medications are rarely used by people with serious illnesses.
D. Morbidity is high in psychiatric populations.
E. Mortality is equivalent in psychiatric and nonpsychiatric populations.

20.7. Which of the following characteristics of the patient is commonly associated with compliance?

A. Race
B. Socioeconomic status
C. Attitude toward the physician
D. Intelligence
E. Gender

20.8. All of the following are associated with increased compliance EXCEPT:

A. verbal instructions for taking medications.
B. older age of the physician.
C. simple treatment regimen.
D. severe symptoms of the disease.
E. decreased waiting room time.

20.9. All of the following are true about psychogenic pain EXCEPT:

A. Its neural control may be different than for that of physical pain.
B. It may be used to justify an individual's failure to establish social relationships.
C. It may involve social gain.
D. It is rarely influenced by cultural factors.
E. Financial gain may be involved.

20.10. All of the following are true about chronic pain EXCEPT:

A. It is a relatively rare complaint of patients.
B. It is commonly associated with depression.
C. It frequently results in depression.
D. It can be treated with phenothiazines.
E. It can be treated with antidepressant drugs.

20.11. All of the following are true about pain relief in chronic pain EXCEPT:

A. If benign, pain can be treated with behavior modification.
B. Pain medication should be given only when the patient is experiencing severe distress.
C. Medication is the first line of treatment in pain caused by cancer or chronic disease.
D. Behavior modification is useful for pain caused by cancer.
E. The patient should receive attention for his or her healthy, active behavior.

20.12. All of the following are true about patients with chronic pain who receive psychotherapy and behavior therapy EXCEPT:

A. They need less pain medication.
B. They become overly dependent on the therapist.
C. They become more active.
D. They show increased attempts to get back to their pre-illness lifestyle.
E. Behavioral therapy and psychotherapy are generally beneficial to chronic pain patients.

DIRECTIONS: For each of the questions or incomplete statements below, **one** or **more** answers or completions given are correct. Choose answer:

A. if only **1, 2,** and **3** are correct.
B. if only **1** and **3** are correct.
C. if only **2** and **4** are correct.
D. if only **4** is correct.
E. if **all** are correct.

20.13. The patient's reactions to the doctor are influenced by the doctor's

1. ethnic background.
2. sex.
3. age.
4. behavior toward the patient.

20.14. Psychological factors associated with chronic pain include:

1. drug abuse.
2. childhood neglect.
3. childhood sexual abuse.
4. depression.

20.15. Which of the following psychological problems are associated with the chronic pain syndrome?
1. Hypochondriasis
2. Borderline personality disorder
3. Narcissistic personality disorder
4. Paranoid personality disorder

Answers and Explanations

DOCTOR-PATIENT COMMUNICATION AND ROLES

20.1. B. The most open-ended of these questions, "Tell me about the pain," gives little structure to the patient and can therefore elicit the most information.

20.2. A. Facilitation is used by the interviewer to encourage the patient to elaborate on an answer. The phrase "Please go on" is such a facilitative statement.

20.3. D. The statement "You look terrified" calls the patient's attention to his or her own response or body language.

20.4. B. Deliberate misuse of medication is rarely the reason for noncompliance with medical advice.

20.5. D. Transference reactions are unconscious.

20.6. D. Only about one-third of people who have symptoms visit physicians. Most people manage their illnesses at home with over-the-counter medication and home treatment. Although chronically ill people are skeptical about medicine, they seek medical help more frequently than other groups. Both morbidity and mortality are high in psychiatric populations.

20.7. C. Although a patient's attitude toward the physician is very important, there is no clear association between compliance and a patient's sex, marital status, race, religion, socioeconomic status, intelligence, or educational level.

20.8. A. Compliance is associated with older physician age, written instructions for taking medications, simple treatment regimen, decreased waiting room time, and how ill the patient feels.

20.9. D. Cultural, religious, and ethnic factors can influence a patient's expression of pain and the responses of the support system of the patient to the pain.

20.10. A. Chronic pain is one of the most frequent complaints of patients.

20.11. B. Behavior modification and deconditioning have been used in pain caused by cancer or chronic diseases. For pain relief in chronic diseases, the medication schedule should be disassociated from the experience of pain, ie, medication should be scheduled at regular intervals rather than received on demand. Pain patients should also receive attention for the healthy, active behavior that they show.

20.12. B. Patients with chronic pain benefit from psychotherapy and behavior therapy by needing less pain medication, becoming more mobile, and showing increased attempts to get back to their pre-illness lifestyles.

20.13. E. All are correct.

20.14. E. All are correct.

20.15. A. Patients with narcissistic or borderline personality disorders and patients with hypochondriasis are at risk for developing the chronic pain syndrome.

21

Psychological Reactions to Illness

I. Emotional Responses

A. Coping with Illness

—**Denial**—ie, refusing to accept or minimizing the severity of an illness—is common in the initial stages of illness.

—**Regression**—ie, returning to immature ways of dealing with psychological stress by crying or tantrums—frequently occurs with physical illness.

—**Depression** due to illness may result in overt expressions of sadness such as crying or withdrawal.

B. Fear, Anxiety, and Anger in Illness

—Illness nearly always results in fear and anxiety since it is perceived as a dangerous situation.

—Fears associated with illness include fear of loss or injury to parts of the body, fear of loss of function, fear of separation from loved ones, fear of loss of love and approval by loved ones, and fear of strangers.

—Patients often express anger when they are fearful about their illness.

—Some patients displace fear about one body part to another.

II. Patient Personality and Illness

A. Personality Types

A patient's psychological reactions to illness are dependent on his or her psychological resources, social resources, and personality style.

—The **dependent personality** type is afraid of being helpless and has a need to be cared for resulting in demands for attention during an illness.

—The **passive-aggressive personality** type may ask for help from the physician and then not comply with his or her advice.

—The **compulsive personality** type fears loss of control and may respond by becoming overcontrolling during illness.

—The **histrionic personality** type fears loss of attractiveness and may become dramatic and emotionally changeable during illness.

—For the **narcissistic personality** type, the perfect self-image is threatened by illness.

—Narcissistic patients are often grandiose and may request that only the most eminent physicians be involved in their treatment.

—The **masochistic personality** type may view illness as a punishment for real or imagined misdeeds and may prolong illnesses to receive love and attention.

—The **paranoid personality** type often blames others (particularly doctors) for their illness and is supersensitive to a perceived lack of attention or caring.

—The **schizoid personality** type becomes anxious and even more withdrawn with illness.

III. The Hospitalized Patient

A. Consultation-Liaison Psychiatry

—The most common problems seen in medical inpatients are depression, anxiety, and disorientation.

—Consultation-liaison (CL) psychiatrists deal with the psychological problems of hospitalized medical patients.

—Common problems dealt with by CL psychiatrists are depression, agitation, suicide attempts or threats, disorientation, hallucinations, sleep disorders, noncompliance, and refusal to consent to medical procedures.

—Techniques used by the CL psychiatrist include support, devising methods for dealing with real problems, and informing and organizing the patient's social support system.

—If psychotherapy is used in the hospitalized medical patient, it is usually of the brief, short-term, dynamic type.

—Behavioral therapy or hypnosis may also be used.

B. Patients at Risk

Certain patients are at greater risk for developing psychological reactions in response to illness, hospitalization, or surgery.

—Those at risk for psychological problems include patients with a prior history of psychotic decompensation or other psychiatric illness and patients whose relationships with their families or with the medical staff become strained during the illness.

C. The Intensive Care Unit

Special psychological problems are associated with being in intensive care units (ICUs).

—Because of the serious nature of patients' illnesses on ICUs, psychological problems can be life-threatening or influence the likelihood of recovery.

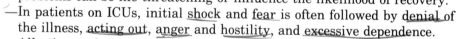

—In patients on ICUs, initial shock and fear is often followed by denial of the illness, acting out, anger and hostility, and excessive dependence.

—Allowing patients as much mastery of their environment as possible—eg, letting them make choices as to lighting level or when to take pain medication—reassures and relaxes ICU patients.

—ICU nurses experience particularly high levels of anxiety, depression, job changes, and burnout.

D. Renal Dialysis

Renal patients have particular problems coping with their chronic, disabling, and limiting disease.

Table 21.1. Illness Associated with Psychosomatic Factors

Illness	Asssociated Psychological Factors
Cancer	Separation and loss, denial, repression
Coronary artery disease	Type A (competitive, driving) personality
Congestive heart failure	Exacerbated by emotional stress
Cardiac arrhythmias	Exacerbated by emotional trauma
Hypertension	Inhibited rage
Bronchial asthma	Excessive dependency needs
Infectious disease	Depression, anger, and stress
Peptic ulcer	Psychological stress, anxiety
Ulcerative colitis	Psychological stress
Rheumatoid arthritis	Psychological stress
Low back pain	Psychological trauma or stress
Migraine headache	Obsessional personality, stress
Tension headache	Anxiety, depression, type A personality, stress
Diabetes mellitus	Psychological stress
Hyperthyroidism	Psychological stress
Immune disorders	Psychological stress
Obesity	Oral fixation and regression
Pruritis (itching)	Repressed anger and anxiety

—On the renal dialysis unit, patients must come to terms with a chronic illness that requires dependency on others.

—Depression and suicide are not uncommon in dialysis patients.

—Sexual problems in dialysis patients often have both physical and psychological causes.

—Self-help groups and home dialysis units are associated with successful psychological adaptation to chronic renal disease.

E. Surgical Patients

—Surgical patients at relatively greater risk for developing psychological problems include patients who have unrealistic expectations regarding a surgical procedure, depressed patients who are convinced they will not survive surgery, and patients who deny that they are seriously worried preoperatively.

—When surgical patients are able to express their depression and anxiety and when they have a positive attitude toward the surgery, they are at relatively lower risk for morbidity and mortality.

—Other factors contributing to an improved outcome for surgical patients include knowing what to expect during and following the procedure in terms of pain, possible disorientation, tubes and machines, and presence of constructive family support.

IV. The Patient with Acquired Immunodeficiency Syndrome (AIDS)

A. Response to the Diagnosis

—Overwhelming anxiety is frequently the response to a diagnosis of AIDS.

—Hopelessness and suicidal depression may then develop.

—Patients respond well to reassurances that they will not be abandoned by the physician, family members, and friends.

Table 21.2. Ratings of Life Stressors

Life Event	Point Value
Death of a spouse	100
Divorce	73
Death of another close family member	63
Major illness or injury	53
Marriage	50
Retirement from work	45
Birth of a child	39
Child leaving home	29
Changing residence	20
Vacation	15
Christmas	12

Adapted from Holmes T: Life situations, emotions, and disease. *J Acad Psychosom Med* 1978;**19**:747.

B. Psychological Intervention

—Psychotherapy can help AIDS patients deal with the guilt they may have over their risk-taking behaviors that may have led to the disease.

—Counseling may help homosexual AIDS patients "come out" to family members.

—Individuals in high risk groups may be extremely anxious about getting AIDS despite negative test results.

—For these patients, insight-oriented psychotherapy may be useful.

—Health care workers dealing with dying AIDS patients may suffer from professional burnout and may benefit from grief therapy.

V. Stress and Illness

A. Psychosomatic Disorders

—Psychological factors may initiate or exacerbate a physical disorder (Table 21.1).

—Specific or nonspecific stress is associated with the development of psychosomatic disorders.

B. Effects of Stress on the Body

—**Hans Selye** described the stages that the body goes through in response to stress as the **general adaptation syndrome**.

—The general adaptation syndrome involves first the alarm reaction, followed by adaptation, and finally by exhaustion.

—According to Selye, stress to an individual results in emotional changes that in turn elicit the classic stress response of the endocrine system, which is characterized by rapid release of adrenocorticotropic hormone followed by release of corticosteroids.

—Corticosteroids in turn alter a variety of immune functions and usually suppress the immune response.

—Suppression of the immune system may be reflected in impaired lymphocyte function and lowered lymphocyte mitogen responses.

—Stress is also associated with increased heart rate, respiratory rate, blood pressure, body oxygen consumption, skin conductance, and resistance (as measured by galvanic skin response).

Table 21.3. DSM-III-R Severity of Psychosocial Stressor Scale

Stressor		Code	Severity
Adults	Children/Adolescents		
No immediate stressor	No immediate stressor	1	None
Child leaves home	School transfer	2	Mild
Marriage; separation; loss of employment; retirement; miscarriage	Suspension or removal from school; birth of sibling	3	Moderate
Divorce; birth of first child	Divorce of parents; unwanted pregnancy; trouble with law authorities	4	Severe
Death of spouse; serious physical illness; rape	Sexual or physical abuse; death of parent	5	Extreme
Death of child; suicide of spouse; overwhelming natural disaster	Death of both parents	6	Catastrophic

VI. Stress and Life Events

A. Interactions

—Correlations between life stress and both physical and emotional illness have been demonstrated.

—For external stress to cause mental or physical illness a combination of genetic and experiential factors must exist.

—Each person has a personal threshold of vulnerability to life stress and an innate ability to tolerate it.

B. Negative and Positive Stressors

—Stressful life events may be **negative**, such as death of a spouse, but may also be **positive**, such as the birth of a wanted child.

—Life stressors have been categorized according to a **point value** system, with 100 points being the highest stress (Table 21.2).

—In one study, about 80% of persons who accumulated 300 points in 1 year were at risk of illness within the next few years.

C. DSM-III-R Categories of Psychosocial Stressors

The DSM-III-R recognizes the importance of psychosocial stressors to psychological dysfunction.

—In the DSM-III-R categorization of mental disorders, there is a 6-point rating scale for coding psychosocial stressors—from 1 (no stress) to 6 (catastrophic stress)—as they affect the development or exacerbation of mental disorders.

—DSM-III-R ratings of psychosocial stressors for adults and children/adolescents differ (Table 21.3).

Review Test

PSYCHOLOGICAL REACTIONS TO ILLNESS

DIRECTIONS: For each of the questions or incomplete statements below, choose the answer that is **most correct.**

21.1. All of the following are true about life stress and illness EXCEPT:

A. Genetic factors are involved.
B. Experiential factors are involved.
C. Each individual has a threshold of vulnerability to life stress.
D. Only negative life events are likely to cause stress to the individual.
E. Death of a spouse is a very stressful life event for a married person.

21.2. Which of the following is considered the most catastrophic stressor for children and adolescents?

A. Divorce of parents
B. Change of school
C. Being arrested
D. Birth of a sibling
E. Receiving physical abuse

21.3. Asking for help from the physician and then not complying with his or her advice is characteristic of which of the following personality types?

A. Schizoid
B. Passive-aggressive
C. Paranoid
D. Histrionic
E. Dependent

21.4. All of the following are true about patients on the Intensive Care Unit (ICU) EXCEPT:

A. The initial emotion is frequently fear.
B. Excessive dependence is characteristic.
C. Hostility toward health care personnel may occur.
D. The nurses should relieve the patient of making any decisions.
E. Denial of serious illness is common.

21.5. Which of the following illnesses is/are associated with psychological factors?

A. Bronchial asthma
B. Coronary artery disease
C. Peptic ulcer
D. Low back pain
E. All of the above

21.6. All of the following are associated with the general adaptation syndrome as described by Hans Selye EXCEPT:

A. responses of the body to stress.
B. fight or flight.
C. alarm reaction.
D. adaptation.
E. exhaustion.

21.7. All of the following are physiologic consequences of stress EXCEPT:

A. decreased alpha waves on EEG.
B. release of ACTH.
C. suppression of the immune response.
D. increased body oxygen consumption.
E. increased skin conductance.

21.8. All of the following patients are at particular risk for psychological problems when physically ill EXCEPT:

A. patients with a history of psychosis.
B. patients with little control over their environment.
C. patients with deteriorating family relationships.
D. patients between the ages of 25 and 30.
E. patients with deteriorating relationships with the medical staff.

21.9. Surgical patients at relatively greater risk for developing psychological reactions include all of the following EXCEPT:

A. patients who believe they will not survive surgery.
B. patients who deny that they are seriously concerned about surgery.
C. patients who have unrealistic expectations of surgery.
D. patients in small voluntary hospitals.
E. patients without family support.

21.10. All of the following are true about psychiatric problems in medical inpatients EXCEPT:

A. Psychiatric problems are common in medical inpatients.
B. When psychotherapy is used, it is usually of the brief dynamic type.
C. The most common psychiatric disorder seen is schizophrenia.
D. Psychological problems can threaten a patient's life.
E. Behavior therapy may be used.

21.11. Which of the following is/are commonly experienced by nurses in the ICU?

A. Depression
B. Anxiety
C. Burnout
D. High job turnover
E. All of the above

21.12. All of the following are true about renal dialysis patients EXCEPT:

A. They must adapt to dependency on others.
B. Sexual problems frequently occur.
C. Self-help groups are useful.
D. Their lifestyles are rarely affected.
E. Use of home dialysis units is associated with successful psychological adaptation.

21.13. The first response of patients who have just received a diagnosis of AIDS is usually:

A. depression.
B. anxiety.
C. guilt.
D. hopelessness.
E. feelings of abandonment.

DIRECTIONS: For each of the numbered phrases below, choose the lettered personality type with which it is **most closely associated.**

A. Compulsive
B. Histrionic
C. Masochistic
D. Paranoid
E. Dependent

21.14. Fears loss of control

21.15. May view illness as a punishment

21.16. Fears loss of attractiveness

21.17. Has a strong need for personal care

21.18. Over sensitivity to any slight by the physician

DIRECTIONS: For each of the questions or incomplete statements below, **one** or **more** of the answers or completions given are correct. Choose answer:

A. if only **1, 2,** and **3** are correct.
B. if only **1** and **3** are correct.
C. if only **2** and **4** are correct.
D. if only **4** is correct.
E. if **all** are correct.

21.19. Which of the following characteristics of the patient influence(s) his or her expectations of the physician?

1. Personality
2. Experience with illness
3. Cultural background
4. Previous experience with doctors

21.20. The patient's psychological reactions to illness are dependent on his or her

1. social resources.
2. coping abilities.
3. concomitant psychiatric illness.
4. psychological resources.

21.21. Fears associated with physical illness include:
1. fear of separation from loved ones.
2. fear of strangers.
3. fear of injury to body parts.
4. fear of loss of control.

21.22. Which of the following is/are common problems dealt with by consultation-liaison psychiatrists?
1. Agitation
2. Noncompliance with medical advice
3. Sleep disorders
4. Disorientation

Answers and Explanations

PSYCHOLOGICAL REACTIONS TO ILLNESS

21.1. D. Positive as well as negative life events cause stress to the individual.

21.2. E. Sexual or physical abuse is a catastrophic stressor in the life of a child or adolescent.

21.3. B. The passive-aggressive personality type may ask for help from the physician and then not comply with the physician's advice.

21.4. D. Allowing patients some mastery over their environment, such as choosing when they will take their pain medication, can reassure patients on the ICU.

21.5. E. Bronchial asthma, coronary artery disease, and low back pain are associated with psychological factors.

21.6. B. The general adaptation syndrome involves an initial alarm reaction followed by adaptation and finally by exhaustion.

21.7. A. Physiologic consequences of stress include rapid release of ACTH followed by release of corticosteroids. Corticosteroids, in turn, can alter immune functions and may suppress the immune response. Stress is also associated with increased heart rate, respiratory rate, blood pressure, body oxygen consumption, and skin conductance and resistance.

21.8. D. Patients with prior history of psychotic decompensation or other psychiatric illness and patients with poor family or medical staff relationships are at particular risk for psychological problems when they are hospitalized.

21.9. D. Surgical patients at relatively higher risk for developing psychological problems include those who have unrealistic expectations about the surgery, those who are depressed and convinced that they will not survive the surgery, those who deny that they are seriously concerned about the surgery, and those without constructive family support.

21.10. C. Psychiatric problems are not uncommon in medical inpatients. Psychiatric disorders commonly seen in medical inpatients are depression, agitation, and sleep disorders.

21.11. E. All are correct.

21.12. D. The lifestyles of patients on renal dialysis are often severely affected by the disease and by the time required for dialysis.

21.13. B. Overwhelming anxiety is frequently the initial response to a diagnosis of AIDS.

21.14. A. The compulsive personality type may fear loss of control.

21.15. C. The masochistic personality type may view illness as a punishment.

21.16. B. The histrionic personality type may fear loss of attractiveness.

21.17. E. The dependent personality type may have a strong need for personal care.

21.18. D. The paranoid personality type may be over sensitive to any slight by the physician.

21.19. E. All are correct.

21.20. E. All are correct.

21.21. E. All are correct.

21.22. E. All are correct.

22

Epidemiology

I. Research Studies

A. Overview

Epidemiology involves the **statistical study** of the prevalence, incidence, and distribution of disease in a defined human population.

B. Incidence

The incidence and prevalence of an illness vary by age and sex.
Incidence is defined as the number of new cases occurring over a specific time period, most commonly 1 year.

—The **incidence rate** is the number of new persons developing the illness divided by the total number of persons at risk for the illness.

—**Lifetime expectancy** is the probability of an illness occurring during an individual's lifetime.

C. Prevalence

Prevalence is the number of cases of an illness that exist and may be classified as point, period, lifetime, or treated prevalence.

—**Point prevalence** is the number of individuals who have an illness at a specific point in time.

—**Period prevalence** is the number of individuals who have an illness during a specific time period.

—**Lifetime prevalence** is the number of individuals who have an illness at some point in time during their lives.

—**Treated prevalence** is the number of individuals being treated for an illness at a given time.

D. Frequency

—**Relative frequency** refers to the incidence or prevalence of a disorder in persons in a specific group (eg, old age, low socioeconomic status).

—**Sex-specific** and **age-specific rates** refer to the relative frequency of cases in each category.

E. Risk Factors

—Risk factors are variables that have been linked to the cause of a disease.

   —Ways of identifying risk factors include (1) association of the factor with only one disorder (specificity); (2) observation of the factor prior to the disorder (temporality); (3) demonstration of the presence of the factor

175

Table 22.1. Types of Reliability and Validity

Reliability

Interrater: test results can be reproduced when used by a different examiner.
Test-retest: test results can be reproduced when used on different occasions.

Validity

Criterion: results of one test are comparable to those of a test with known validity.
Content: test gathers data that can be interpreted or scored later.
Construct: test is designed to measure what it was intended to measure.
Face: test makes subjective sense to the examiner using it.

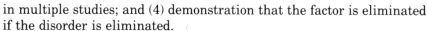

in multiple studies; and (4) demonstration that the factor is eliminated if the disorder is eliminated.

—**Relative risk** is the ratio of the incidence rate of a disorder among individuals exposed to a risk factor to the incidence rate of the disorder in unexposed individuals.

—**Attributable risk** is the arithmetic difference between the rate of incidence of the disorder in individuals exposed to a risk factor and the rate of incidence in those unexposed.

—Attributable risk is useful for determining what would happen if the risk factor was removed.

II. Assessment

A. Gathering Information

—Information about individuals can be collected from large data banks, from direct interviews, and from indirect surveys.

—Records in central data banks are called **case registers** and are more common in certain countries such as Sweden.

B. Interviews and Surveys

—**Interviews** are direct person to person interactions involving questions that may be in a structured or unstructured format.

—In **structured interviews**, an interviewer asks the same questions of all subjects.

—In **unstructured interviews**, there are no prepared questions; rather, answers to one question suggest the next subject based on the interviewer's clinical judgment.

—**Surveys** are indirect assessment methods that utilize structured self-report forms.

C. Assessment Instruments

To be effective, assessment instruments must be valid, reliable, bias-free, and sensitive.

—**Reliability** refers to the reproducibility of results.

—**Interrater** and **test-retest** are subtypes of reliability.

—**Validity** is a measure of whether the test assesses what it was designed to assess.

—**Criterion, content, construct,** and **face** are subtypes of validity (Table 22.1).

D. Bias

When a test is biased, it is constructed so that one outcome is more likely to occur.
—Bias can occur if the examiner knows how the results are expected to turn out, and it can flaw analytic studies.
—Bias is reduced if the sample is randomized, ie, each individual of the group has an equal chance of being chosen.

E. Sensitivity and Specificity

—**Sensitivity** of assessment instruments refers to the ability to detect the disorder being evaluated.
—**Specificity** of assessment refers to the ability of the test to evaluate only the disorder of interest, not to detect disorders that are not of interest.
—**False-positive results** occur if an instrument detects a disorder in someone who does not have the disorder.
—**False-negative results** occur if an instrument fails to detect a disorder in someone who has the disorder.
—**True-positive results** occur if an instrument detects a disease in a person with the disease.
—**True-negative results** occur if an instrument indicates the absence of a disorder in someone who does not have the disorder.
—The **predictive value** of a test indicates what percentage of test results match the actual diagnoses.

III. Types of Research Studies

A. Overview

Important types of research studies include longitudinal, cohort, cross-sectional, double-blind, and crossover studies.
—**Longitudinal studies** are carried out on the same individuals in a population over a long time period.
—A **cohort** is a specific group chosen from this population.
—**Cross-sectional studies** examine a group of individuals at one specific point in time.
—**Retrospective studies** are based on past events or data.
  —Retrospective studies that sample persons are **case history** studies (if the person has the disorder) or **case control** (if the person does not have the disorder) studies.
—**Prospective studies** are carried out using events as they occur.
—In **clinical treatment trials,** groups of patients who have received a treatment are compared with those who have not received a treatment.
  —To eliminate bias, double-blind, crossover, and randomized studies are used in clinical treatment trials.

B. Double-blind Studies

In a double-blind study, neither the subject nor the examiner knows what treatment the subject is receiving.
—The double-blind study design is used to eliminate the effects of both the subject's and experimenter's expectations of the outcome.

Table 22.2. Commonly Used Statistical Tests

Statistical Test	Used to Examine
t-test	Differences between means of two samples
Analysis of variance	Differences between means of more than two samples
Chi-square test	Differences between frequencies in a sample
Correlation	The mutual relationship between two variables
Regression	Whether one variable is dependent on another
Multivariate and factor analyses	Relationships among multiple variables

—In double-blind drug studies, a patient may receive a **placebo** (an inactive substance) rather than the active drug.

C. Placebo Responses

—The **placebo effect** is a response that is not due to a drug itself but rather to patient expectations of the drug's effects.

—Placebo responses indicate that what patients believe about a drug can influence the effect of the treatment with that drug.

D. Crossover Studies

—One variation of a double-blind study is a crossover study.

—In crossover studies, the treatment group receives the placebo and the control group receives the active drug at some time during the study.

—In this way, the treatment and control groups serve as controls for each other.

IV. Statistical Analyses

A. Statistics in Epidemiology

Statistics are used to analyze data from epidemiologic studies.
Statistical tests used frequently in medical epidemiology are listed in Table 22.2.

B. Variables

A variable is a quantity that can change under different experimental situations; variables may be independent or dependent.

—An **independent variable** is a characteristic that an experimenter can change, eg, giving a patient a drug to reduce blood pressure or a placebo.

—A **dependent variable** is a characteristic that reflects the effects of changing the independent variable, eg, blood pressure reading following treatment with the drug or placebo.

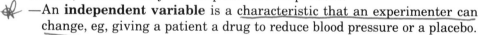

C. Variance

Variance is used to analyze the variation between factors such as subjects and treatment outcomes.

—**Analysis of variance** is a statistical technique used for determining how much variation in an experiment is due to the treatment in question and how much is due to chance.

D. Measures of Central Tendency

The mean, median, and mode are measures of central tendency in a group of numbers.

—The **mean** is the average and is derived by adding a group of numbers and dividing by the number of scores in the group.

—The **median** is the middle value in a group of numbers.

—The **mode** is the value that appears most often in a group of numbers.

E. **Normal Distribution**

A normal distribution is a theoretical distribution of scores that is symmetric and in which the mean, median, and mode are equal.

—The highest point in a distribution of scores is the **modal peak.**

—A **skewed distribution** means that the modal peak is off to one side (left or right).

F. **Standard Deviation and Standard Error**

—**Deviation** measures the difference between one score in a set of scores and the mean score in that set.

—**Standard deviation** measures variation and is obtained by squaring each deviation from the mean in a set of scores, averaging the squared deviations, and calculating the square root of the result.

—**Standard error** is the standard deviation divided by the square root of the number of scores in a set minus one.

G. **Correlation**

—The degree of relationship between two variables can be assessed using **correlation coefficients.**

—If variations in the two variables are in the same direction, the correlation coefficient is **positive**; if in opposite directions, the correlation coefficient is **negative**.

H. **Types of Error**

—The **null hypothesis** is an assumption that there is no significant difference between two sets of measures.

—A **type I** error occurs when the null hypothesis is rejected although it is true.

—A **type II** error occurs when the null hypothesis is accepted although it is false.

Review Test

EPIDEMIOLOGY

DIRECTIONS: For each of the questions or incomplete statements below, choose the answer that is **most correct.**

22.1. Point prevalence refers to:
A. the number of persons with a disorder at a specific time point.
B. the number of persons who have a disorder at some time during their lives.
C. the number of persons being treated for a disorder at a given time.
D. the number of new persons developing a disease over a 1-year period.
E. the probability of a person developing a disorder during his or her lifetime.

22.2. A test instrument does not detect a disorder. in someone who has the disorder. This is known as:
A. a false-positive result.
B. a false-negative result.
C. a true-positive result.
D. a true-negative result.
E. a predictive result.

22.3. A study is designed to determine how many people in the United States are smoking cigarettes at 11 AM on Monday, October 31, 1992. This type of study is:
A. a cohort study.
B. a longitudinal study.
C. a cross-sectional study.
D. a double-blind study.
E. a crossover study.

22.4. A study designed to determine how many patients were admitted to a large medical center with a diagnosis of ulcer over the period from July 1978 to July 1988 is:
A. a cohort study.
B. a cross-sectional study.
C. a retrospective study.
D. a prospective study.
E. a crossover study.

22.5. Twelve patients are given a drug that is supposed to lower blood pressure. The dependent variable in this study is:
A. the experimenter's bias.
B. giving the patients the drug.
C. giving the patients a placebo.
D. the patient's blood pressure following treatment with the drug.
E. the daily variability in the patient's blood pressure before the drug treatment.

22.6. Interrater reliability
A. refers to the reproducibility of the results of a test when the test is used on different occasions.
B. is an assessment instrument.
C. is a subtype of reliability.
D. refers to whether a test actually measures what it was designed to measure.
E. usually involves structured interviews.

22.7. All of the following are true about bias EXCEPT:
A. It favors one study outcome over another.
B. It can flaw analytic studies.
C. It can occur if the judgment of the examiner is influenced.
D. It is increased by randomization of the sample.
E. It is an error in construction.

22.8. All of the following are true about double-blind studies EXCEPT:
A. A crossover study is a type of double-blind study.
B. The examiner but not the subject knows what treatment is being given to the subject.
C. Placebos are used.
D. Double-blind studies are used to reduce the effects of experimenter expectations of the outcome.
E. Double-blind studies are used to reduce the effects of subject expectations of the outcome.

22.9. Test scores of 10, 10, 10, 20, 40, 70, and 90 are obtained by seven students:
A. The mean of the test scores is 50.
B. The median score on the test is 10.
C. The distribution of the test scores is completely normal.
D. The mode of the test scores is 10.
E. The modal peak is 20.

DIRECTIONS: For each of the numbered phrases below, choose the statistical test with which it is **most closely associated.**

A. *t*-test
B. Analysis of variance
C. Chi-square test
D. Correlation
E. Regression

22.10. Differences between means of three samples

22.11. Differences between frequencies in a sample

22.12. Differences between means of two samples

22.13. Whether one variable is dependent on another

22.14. The mutual relationship between two variables

DIRECTIONS: For each of the questions or incomplete statements below, **one** or **more** of the answers or completions given are correct. Choose answer:

A. if only **1, 2,** and **3** are correct.
B. if only **1** and **3** are correct.
C. if only **2** and **4** are correct.
D. if only **4** is correct.
E. if **all** are correct.

22.15. Ways to identify a risk factor include:
1. demonstrating that the factor appears in multiple studies.
2. associating the factor with only one disorder.
3. observing the factor prior to development of the disorder.
4. finding that when the factor is eliminated, the disorder disappears.

22.16. Which of the following is/are true?
1. Correlation coefficients measure the degree of relationship between two sets of measurements.
2. A skewed distribution means that the model peak is off to one side.
3. Square roots are used in determining standard deviation.
4. The standard deviation and the standard error of a set of scores are usually equal.

Answers and Explanations

EPIDEMIOLOGY

22.1. A. Point prevalence refers to the number of persons with a disorder at a specific point in time.

22.2. B. A false-negative result occurs if a test instrument fails to detect a disorder in someone who truly has the disorder.

22.3. C. A cross-sectional study is designed to examine a group at one point in time, ie, 11 AM, Monday, October 31st, 1992.

22.4. C. Retrospective studies are based on past events, ie, hospital admissions from July 1977 to July 1988.

22.5. D. The dependent variable is a measure of the outcome of an experiment. In this case, blood pressure following treatment with the drug or placebo is the outcome.

22.6. C. Interrator reliability, a subtype of reliability, states that test findings are reproducible when used by a different examiner.

22.7. D. Bias is decreased by randomization of the sample.

22.8. B. Both the examiner and subject are blind to the treatment in a double-blind study.

22.9. D. The mean of these test scores is 35.7, the median is 20, and the mode is 10. The distribution of these test scores is skewed to the left.

22.10. B. Analysis of variance is used to examine differences between means of more than two samples.

22.11. C. The chi-square test is used to examine differences between frequencies in a sample.

22.12. A. The *t*-test is used to examine differences between means of two samples.

22.13. E. Regression is used to examine whether one variable is dependent on another.

22.14. D. Correlation is used to examine the mutual relationship between two variables.

22.15. E. All are correct.

22.16. A. The standard error is the standard deviation divided by the square root of the number of scores in a set minus 1. The standard error is not equal to the standard deviation.

23

Systems of Health Care Delivery

I. Background

A. History

The major stimulus for the development of hospitals to provide health services came with the development of the **germ theory** in the mid 19th century.
—Prior to 1900, people generally died of acute respiratory or gastrointestinal infections.
—These problems were treated largely with preventive health measures.
—Since 1900, chronic diseases such as heart disease and cancer have been responsible for most deaths.

B. Current Health Care

—The number of hospitals in the United States has remained approximately the same from 1946 to 1982.
—There are about 7000 hospitals in the United States with a capacity of about 1,000,000 beds.
—There are about 19,000 nursing homes in the United States.
—Although the number of short-term care hospitals has remained the same, the number of long-term care hospitals has increased in recent years.

C. Levels of Health Care

The health care system in the United States can be classified into three levels—primary, secondary, and tertiary care (Table 23.1).

II. Hospitals

A. Hospitalization

—Approximately three-quarters of the adult population have been hospitalized at least once.
—Women are more likely to be hospitalized than men.
—As individuals get older, they are more likely to be hospitalized.
—Most general hospital stays average 7.8 days.
—There are currently 10% more hospital beds than are needed; urban areas, in particular, have an oversupply of beds.

B. Hospital Ownership

—Hospitals can be categorized as **for-profit** or **not-for-profit**.

Table 23.1. Levels in the Health Care System

Level	Facilities
Primary care	Hospital outpatient departments
	Community mental health centers
	School and industrial health centers
Secondary care	Hospital inpatient departments
	Hospital emergency rooms
Tertiary care	Specialty hospitals, eg, chronic disease and psychiatric hospitals

—**Investor-owned** hospitals total about 20% of the hospitals in the United States but constitute only 11% of the beds.

—Not-for-profit hospitals can be owned by the government or not.

—**Community hospitals**, which are public general hospitals, may be for-profit or not-for-profit.

—About 30% of community hospitals are owned by state or local governments.

—The largest component of hospital costs is the health care staff.

C. **Short-term and Long-term Care**

—Hospitals can also be divided into those providing **acute** (short-term) or **chronic** (long-term) care and as **general** or **specialized**.

—Usually, length of stay in a short-term hospital is less than 30 days; in a long-term hospital, it is more than 30 days.

—Stays in chronic disease and rehabilitation hospitals are generally long-term.

D. **General and Special Hospitals**

—**General hospitals** offer a wide range of medical and surgical services.

—**Special hospitals** offer care in one medical specialty, eg, pediatrics or psychiatry.

—There are about 872 short- and long-term special hospitals in the United States.

III. Nursing Homes

A. **Types of Nursing Homes**

Nursing homes provide long-term care and can be divided into groups according to the level of care offered.

—A **skilled nursing facility (SNF)** offers the services of both practical and registered nurses around the clock.

—An **intermediate care facility (ICF)** provides some nursing care; that is, restorative nursing care is available to all residents to help with self-care.

—A **residential care facility (RCF)** is basically a sheltered environment that does not provide nursing care.

—Few studies have been done of US nursing homes.

—A survey in 1977 showed that there were about 19,000 nursing homes: 3600 SNFs; 4600 combined SNFs and ICFs; 6000 ICFs; and 4700 RCFs.

B. **Related Care**

—An **extended care facility** of a hospital functions like an SNF or ICF for patients who do not need more than nursing care.

—**Halfway houses** and similar rehabilitation centers provide help for hospitalized patients to enter society.

IV. Other Health Care Delivery Systems

A. Health Maintenance Organizations

A health maintenance organization (HMO) is a grouping of facilities, physicians, and other health care personnel that provides medical services to a group of people who have paid a fixed amount in advance.

—The philosophy of HMOs stresses prevention rather than acute treatment.

—HMO subscribers pay an annual premium for health care benefits.

—Benefits of HMOs include hospitalization, physician services, preventive medicine services, and often dental, eye, and podiatric care.

—Currently, there are about 300 HMOs in the United States with an enrollment of 15 million people.

B. Independent Practice Associations and Preferred Provider Organizations

Variants of HMOs are the **independent practice associations (IPAs)** and **preferred provider organizations (PPOs)**.

—IPAs and PPOs are formed by groups of physicians that contract to provide services to specific groups of patients.

—In IPAs, a subscriber pays a **fixed** fee and uses the physicians in private office practice who participate in the IPA.

—In PPOs, a **third-party payor**, often a union trust fund or an insurance company, contracts with doctors and hospitals to provide medical services to its subscribers.

  —PPOs guarantee doctors a certain volume of patients and provide reduced costs for patients.

—There are about 10 PPOs in the United States.

C. Visiting Nurse Care

—Visiting nurse associations provide services in a patient's own home.

—Home care is a less expensive alternative to hospitalization or institutionalization.

—Approximately 30 million home health care visits were provided in 1982.

—Home care services include nursing, physical and occupational therapy, psychiatric nursing, and social work services.

D. Hospices

—Hospices provide supportive care to the terminally ill.

—The hospice concept developed in England in the 1960s and has become more common in the United States in the past few years.

—By the end of 1982, there were approximately 1000 hospice programs in the United States.

—In 1983, the federal government began to pay for hospice care under Medicare.

V. Physicians

A. Medical Education

—In 1963, the Health Professions Educational Assistance Act provided government support to undergraduate medical training.

—With this support the number of medical students doubled between 1965 and 1982.

—By 1982, there were 124 medical schools and 15 colleges of osteopathic medicine in the United States.

B. Distribution of Physicians

—There are about 500,000 physicians in the United States; about 20,000 of these are osteopathic physicians.

—Although high physician to patient ratios are typical of the Northeast and California, low ratios are common in the Southern and Mountain states.

—Medically underserved areas include the inner cities and rural areas.

—Attempts to even the geographical distribution of physicians generally have been unsuccessful.

C. Patient Consultations

—Most commonly, doctor-patient interaction occurs in the offices of individual physicians.

—When patient income increases, the number of doctor's office consultations increases and the number of visits to emergency rooms decreases.

—Seventy-five percent of the population see a physician in a given year.

—Patients tend to be very young, very old, or female.

—Patients average five physician visits per year.

—In order of frequency, the most common reasons for office visits are general physical examination, prenatal examination, throat problems, hypertension, and postoperative visits.

D. Medical Specialization

—Although in 1940 only about 20% of physicians were specialists, that percentage has increased to approximately 80%.

—Primary care physicians, which include family practitioners, internists, and pediatricians, comprise 35% of all doctors.

—It is projected that there will be a surplus of physicians in some specialties (surgery, neurology, ophthalmology, obstetrics/gynecology, internal medicine, and neurosurgery) and too few physicians in other specialties (psychiatry, emergency medicine, and preventive medicine) by the end of the century.

—Supply is expected to equal demand in family practice, dermatology, pediatrics, and otolaryngology.

VI. Other Health Care Personnel

A. Overview

—The ratio of other health care workers to physicians has increased 20-fold since 1900.

—Nonphysician health care personnel include nurses, nurse clinicians and nurse practitioners, physician's assistants, dentists, podiatrists, pharmacists, dieticians, physical and occupational therapists, radiologic technicians, and medical technologists.

—**Physician's assistants (PAs)** are certified by the National Commission on certification of PAs; however, in some states certification is not required.

—There are about 60 **dental schools** in the United States with a total enrollment of 22,000.

—There are approximately six colleges of **podiatry** (diseases of the foot) and about 9000 podiatrists in the United States.

B. Licensing of Paramedical Personnel

Paramedical personnel can be certified, registered, or licensed.

—**Licensing** of paramedical personnel is done by the states.

—**Certification** and **registration** of paramedical personnel generally are performed either by the state or by governing groups for each category of paramedical personnel.

Review Test

SYSTEMS OF HEALTH CARE DELIVERY

DIRECTIONS: For each of the questions or incomplete statements below, choose the answer that is **most correct.**

23.1. The percentage of physicians in the United States who are specialists is:

A. 20%.
B. 40%.
C. 50%.
D. 60%.
E. 80%.

23.2. All of the following are true about health care in the United States EXCEPT:

A. Prior to 1900, people generally died of infections.
B. Since 1900, heart disease and cancer have been responsible for most deaths.
C. There are currently about 7000 hospitals.
D. The number of hospitals increased substantially from 1946 to 1982.
E. There are about 1,000,000 hospital beds.

23.3. All of the following are primary care facilities EXCEPT:

A. school health centers.
B. hospital outpatient departments.
C. psychiatric hospitals.
D. industrial health centers.
E. community mental health centers.

23.4. Which of the following is true about hospitalization in the United States?

A. Men are hospitalized more often than women.
B. Approximately 10% of adults have been hospitalized at least once.
C. The average hospital stay is 2 days.
D. Rates of hospitalization increase with age.
E. There is presently an undersupply of hospital beds in urban areas.

23.5. All of the following are true about hospitals EXCEPT:

A. About 30% of community hospitals are owned by state or local government.
B. Not-for-profit hospitals may be owned by the federal government.
C. Twenty percent of hospitals in the United States are investor-owned.
D. Community hospitals are always not-for-profit.
E. The largest component of hospital costs is for health care staff.

23.6. All of the following are true about nursing homes EXCEPT:

A. A skilled nursing care facility has both practical and registered nurses.
B. An intermediate care facility provides some nursing care.
C. A residential care facility usually provides nursing care.
D. There are approximately 19,000 nursing homes in the United States.
E. Nursing homes generally provide long-term care.

23.7. All of the following are true about hospice care EXCEPT:

A. It has become increasingly popular in the United States in the past few years.
B. It was developed in England.
C. Medicare may cover the expenses incurred.
D. It provides care mainly to chronically ill people.
E. There were approximately 1000 hospice programs in the United States in the early 1980s.

23.8. Which of the following is true about visits to physicians?

A. Patient income is directly related to number of doctor's office consultations.
B. Patient income is directly related to the number of visits to emergency rooms.
C. Patients are more likely to be male than female.
D. Patients average 25 visits to physicians per year.
E. Most patients are middle-aged.

23.9. The most common reason for office visits to physicians is:

A. general physical examination.
B. prenatal examination.
C. postoperative visits.
D. hypertension.
E. throat problems.

23.10. All of the following specialties are likely to have a surplus of physicians by the end of the century EXCEPT:

A. psychiatry.
B. neurology.
C. ophthalmology.
D. neurosurgery.
E. surgery.

23.11. In which of the following medical specialties is supply expected to equal demand?

A. Surgery
B. Neurology
C. Ophthalmology
D. Pediatrics
E. Preventive medicine

DIRECTIONS: For each of the questions or incomplete statements below, **one** or **more** of the answers or completions given are correct. Choose answer:

A. if only **1, 2,** and **3** are correct.
B. if only **1** and **3** are correct.
C. if only **2** and **4** are correct.
D. if only **4** is correct.
E. if **all** are correct.

23.12. Health Maintenance Organizations (HMOs) may provide benefits for

1. optometrist's services.
2. preventive medicine services.
3. physician's services.
4. hospitalization.

23.13. In which of the following health care delivery systems do patients pay a fixed amount in advance rather than for medical need as it arises?

1. HMOs
2. Independent practice associations
3. Preferred provider organizations
4. Community-based hospitals

23.14. Which of the following is/are true about physicians in the United States?

1. High physician-patient ratios are typical of the Mountain states.
2. There are about 20,000 osteopathic physicians.
3. Overall, there are about 100,000 physicians.
4. Low physician-patient ratios are typical of the Southern states.

Answers and Explanations

SYSTEMS OF HEALTH CARE DELIVERY

23.1. E. About 80% of US physicians are specialists.

23.2. D. The number of hospitals in the United States has remained approximately the same from 1946 to 1982.

23.3. C. Primary care facilities include hospital outpatient departments, community mental health centers, and school and industrial health centers. Psychiatric hospitals are tertiary care facilities.

23.4. D. Women are hospitalized more often than men, approximately 75% of adults have been hospitalized at least once, and the average hospital stay is 7.8 days. Also, there is an oversupply of hospital beds in the United States, particularly in urban areas.

23.5. D. Community hospitals may be for-profit or not-for profit.

23.6. C. A residential care facility does not usually provide nursing care.

23.7. D. Hospice care provides services mainly to terminally ill people.

23.8. A. As patient income increases, the number of visits to the emergency room decreases. Patients average five visits to a physician per year.

23.9. A. The most common reason for office visits to physicians is for general physical examination.

23.10. A. It is expected that psychiatry, emergency medicine, and preventive medicine will have a shortage of physicians by the end of the century.

23.11. D. Supply of physicians is expected to equal demand in dermatology, family practice, pediatrics, and otolaryngology.

23.12. E. All are correct.

23.13. A. In HMOs, subscribers pay an annual premium for health care benefits. Independent practice associations and preferred provider organizations are variants of HMOs.

23.14. C. Low physician to patient ratios are typical of the Mountain as well as the Southern states. There are approximately 500,000 physicians in the United States.

24

Issues in Health Care Delivery

I. Health Care Costs

A. Paying the Costs

—Approximately $387 billion was spent on health care in 1984 in the United States; this represents just over 10% of the gross national product.

—With respect to **personal health care expenses**, the government pays about 40%, private health insurance pays 31%, direct private funds pay 28%, and industry and philanthropy pay 1%.

B. Where the Money Goes

—With respect to **health care expenditures**, hospitals represent 41%, physicians 20%, and nursing homes, drugs, and dental services the remaining percentages of the cost.

—Health care expenditures have been rising because of the increasing age of the American population, advances in medical technology, and ready availability of health care to old and indigent people through Medicare and Medicaid.

II. Health Insurance

A. Health Insurance Coverage

—About 85% of Americans have health insurance.

—Health insurance usually covers 80% of hospital costs and 60% of physician's services (except for psychiatry).

—Twenty-five percent of patient costs is for laboratory tests, and the remainder is for nursing, medication, administration, and support services.

B. Health Insurers

—Blue Cross/Blue Shield, a nonprofit private insurance carrier, is regulated by state insurance departments and insures about 50% of nongovernment employees.

—Individuals can also contract with commercial insurance companies to pay for hospital costs, physician's fees, and laboratory and diagnostic tests.

—These "self-pay" patients pay a specific amount based on a rating system.

C. Medicare

In 1965, the federal government established the federally funded health insurance programs **Medicare** and **Medicaid** as an amendment to the Social Security Act of 1935.

—**Medicare** provides hospital and medical costs for people eligible for social security, ie, over 65 or with permanent disabilities.

—Medicare is financed by tax moneys under the social security system.

—Medicare is comprised of two parts, Part A and Part B.

  —**Part A** of Medicare covers inpatient hospital care, home health care, nursing home care after hospitalization, and dialysis.

  —**Part B** is optional and is bought by the patient to cover therapy services, medical supplies, outpatient hospital care, doctor bills, and home health care.

—Medicare recipients must pay an annual deductible for physician services and 20% of other charges.

D. Medicaid

  Medicaid (Medi-Cal in California) is funded by both federal and state government and pays for health care needs including drugs and nursing home care for specific needy and low income people.

—There are no deductibles associated with Medicaid.

—Medicaid pays for inpatient and outpatient hospital care, nursing home care, home health care services, physician's services, and laboratory tests.

E. Payment of the Physician

—Physicians are commonly paid in the form of fee-for-service.

—Physicians may also be paid by salary when the physician is a member of an organization such as an HMO.

III. The Socioeconomics of Health Care

A. Lifestyle and Health

A variety of factors affect the health of the people and how health care is delivered to the population.

—Lifestyle and poor dietary and other personal habits account for about 70% of mental and physical illness; for example, cancer is frequently related to poor diet and to smoking tobacco.

B. Socioeconomic Status and Health

—Socioeconomic status is based on income, educational level, occupation, and how individuals spend their money.

—Persons in low socioeconomic groups are more likely to have poorer mental health, hypertension, arthritis, speech difficulties, eye diseases, upper respiratory illness, and decreased life expectancy.

—Increased rates of mental illness are seen in individuals in the inner city environment when compared with individuals in the suburbs.

C. Gender and Health

1. *Women*

  —Women visit physicians and are hospitalized more frequently than men.
  —Women are most often hospitalized for childbirth, cancer, and heart disease.

  —The rate of lung cancer in women has risen, as has the smoking rate.

—Leading chronic medical conditions in women are heart conditions, hypertension, and arthritis.

2. *Men*

—Men are most frequently hospitalized for heart disease, cancer, and fractures.
—Leading chronic conditions in men are heart conditions, arthritis, and impairment of the back or spine.

D. Age and Health

—The most common illnesses in all age groups are upper respiratory conditions, influenza, and injuries.
—Older (over age 65) and younger people (20 to 30 years) have more health problems and need more health care than people in middle adulthood.
—The incidence of illness increases with age; 86% of individuals over 65 years of age suffer from at least one chronic condition.
—In old age, the three leading medical conditions are arthritis, hypertension, and heart disease.
—The incidence of mental health problems also increases with age.

E. Race and Health

—Approximately 10 times as many visits to physicians were made by whites than by blacks.
—Blacks have higher rates of heart disease, hypertension, obesity, and diabetes than whites.

IV. Mortality Trends

A. Causes of Death in Adults

—The death rate per 100,000 people was lower in 1984 than in any previous year.
—In order of frequency, the three leading causes of death in 1983 were (1) heart disease, (2) cancer, and (3) stroke.
—Rates of the three leading causes of death were highest among black males.
—Women have lower mortality rates than men in all age groups, but this difference is decreasing.

B. Causes of Death in Children and Adolescents

—The most common causes of death in **infants** are congenital anomalies, respiratory distress syndrome, and sudden infant death syndrome, respectively.
—The mortality rate for black infants is twice that for white infants (19.2 vs. 9.7 per 1000).
—In order, the most common causes of death in **children under 14** are (1) accidents, (2) cancer, and (3) congenital anomalies.
—The most common causes of death in **adolescents** (ages 15 to 24) are accidents, homicide, and suicide.
—Approximately 75% of accidental deaths in adolescents occur as a result of automobile accidents.

C. Life Expectancy

—The average life expectancy in the United States is 74.7 years; however, this varies greatly with sex and race (Table 24.1).

Table 24.1. Life Expectancy (Years) in the United States by Sex and Race

	Overall	Black	White
Males	71.1	65.5	71.8
Females	78.3	73.7	78.8

—Differences in life expectancies by sex and race have been decreasing in recent years.

V. Legal Issues in Health Care

A. Overview

Legal issues in health care include **definition of death, malpractice,** and **informed consent**.

B. Death of a Patient

—When an individual dies, a physician must sign a death certificate attesting to the cause of death and whether the death is classified as natural, accidental, suicide, homicide, or due to unknown causes.

—If a physician is not present at the death, the body must be examined by the coroner, medical examiner, or pathologist to determine the cause of death.

C. Brain Death

—Brain death is defined as irreversible cessation of brain (including brain-stem) function.

—In 1986, the American Medical Association stated that life-prolonging medical treatment including food and water could be withheld from a brain-dead patient.

D. Malpractice

—Malpractice is generally defined as professional negligence.

—For a physician, professional negligence refers to deviation from normal standards of professional care.

—For a malpractice claim, a patient must be able to prove that the doctor demonstrated the four "D's"—**Dereliction** (negligence) of a **Duty Directly** causing **Damages** to the patient.

—Psychiatry ranks eighth among medical specialties in frequency of malpractice suits.

E. Informed Consent

The possibility of a malpractice suit can be reduced by the informed consent process.

—In informed consent, the patient signs a document of agreement prior to submitting to a procedure such as surgery.

—Informed consent, at least implied, must be obtained prior to any medical procedure.

—For informed consent, it is important that the patient understand the risks and benefits of a procedure.

—The patient must understand what will happen if he or she does not consent to the procedure.

—The patient must also be given the knowledge that he or she can withdraw consent at any time prior to the procedure.

Review Test

ISSUES IN HEALTH CARE DELIVERY

DIRECTIONS: For each of the questions or incomplete statements below, choose the answer that is **most correct.**

24.1. The percentage of the gross national product spent on health care in 1984 was about

A. 1%.
B. 3%.
C. 10%.
D. 20%.
E. 30%.

24.2. Which of the following pays the largest percentage of personal health care expenses?

A. The federal government
B. Private health insurance
C. Industry
D. Philanthropy
E. Direct payment of private funds

24.3. In the United States, most health care expenditures are for

A. physician's fees.
B. nursing homes.
C. hospitals.
D. drugs.
E. dental services.

24.4. All of the following are true about health care in the United States EXCEPT:

A. About 70% of mental and physical illness is due to poor personal habits and lifestyle.
B. The rate of lung cancer in women is decreasing.
C. Physical illness increases with age.
D. The incidence of mental illness increases with age.
E. Young people 20 to 30 years old have more health problems than people in middle adulthood.

24.5. All of the following are true EXCEPT:

A. Accidents are the most common cause of death in children under 14 years of age.
B. The most common cause of death in infants is congenital anomalies.
C. Approximately 75% of accidental deaths in adolescents are due to sports injuries.
D. The mortality rate for black infants is twice that for white infants.
E. Cancer is a common cause of death in children under 14 years of age.

24.6. All of the following are true in the United States EXCEPT:

A. The average life expectancy for all Americans is approximately 75 years.
B. The average life expectancy for white males is approximately 72 years.
C. The average life expectancy for black males is approximately 66 years.
D. The average life expectancy for white females is approximately 79 years.
E. The average life expectancy for black females is approximately 79 years.

24.7. All of the following are true about health insurance in the United States EXCEPT:

A. About 5% of patient costs are for laboratory tests.
B. It covers 60% of the costs of physician's services.
C. It covers 80% of hospital costs.
D. About 85% of Americans have health insurance.
E. Blue Cross/Blue Shield insures about 50% of nongovernment employees.

24.8. Which of the following is true about Medicare?

A. It is funded by individual states.
B. It is designed primarily for welfare recipients.
C. It is financed under the Social Security system.
D. It does not have deductibles.
E. It was established in 1985.

24.9. Medicare Part B generally covers all of the following EXCEPT:

A. inpatient hospital care.
B. medical supplies.
C. home health care.
D. doctor bills.
E. therapy services.

24.10. All of the following are true about Medicaid EXCEPT:

A. It has a $100 deductible for physician's services.
B. It is funded by both federal and state government.
C. It is designed primarily for people with low incomes.
D. It pays for outpatient hospital care.
E. It is called Medi-Cal in California.

24.11. The rates of all of the following conditions are higher among blacks than whites EXCEPT:

A. obesity.
B. bipolar illness.
C. diabetes.
D. heart disease.
E. hypertension.

DIRECTIONS: For each of the questions or incomplete statements below, **one** or **more** of the answers or completions given are correct. Choose answer:

A. if only **1, 2,** and **3** are correct.
B. if only **1** and **3** are correct.
C. if only **2** and **4** are correct.
D. if only **4** is correct.
E. if **all** are correct.

24.12. When compared with people in high socioeconomic groups, people in low socioeconomic groups are more likely to have:

1. arthritis.
2. eye diseases.
3. poor mental health.
4. hypertension.

24.13. Which of the following is/are leading chronic medical conditions in women in the United States?

1. Arthritis
2. Heart conditions
3. Hypertension
4. Spinal cord injuries

24.14. Which of the following is/are true about death in the United States?

1. The three leading causes are heart disease, cancer, and accidents.
2. The death rate per 100,000 people was higher in 1984 than in any previous year.
3. Rates of the three leading causes of death are lowest among black males.
4. Women have lower mortality rates than men in all age groups.

24.15. Which of the following is/are true about malpractice?

1. It is generally defined as professional negligence.
2. Psychiatry ranks first among medical specialities in frequency of malpractice suits.
3. A patient usually must be able to prove that the doctor caused damages in order to win a malpractice suit.
4. The four "D's" of malpractice are Damages, Dereliction, Denial, and Decision.

Answers and Explanations

ISSUES IN HEALTH CARE DELIVERY

24.1. C. Approximately 387 billion dollars were spent on health care in the United States in 1984. This represents 10.6% of the gross national product for that year.

24.2. A. The government pays about 40% of personal health care expenses; private insurance pays about 31%.

24.3. C. Hospital costs represent 41% of health care expenditures and physician costs represent 20%. Nursing home, drug, and dental service costs make up the remaining percentage.

24.4. B. The rate of lung cancer in women in the United States is increasing.

24.5. C. Approximately 75% of accidental deaths in adolescents (ages 15 to 24) occur in automobiles.

24.6. E. The average life expectancy for black females in the United States is 73.7 years. This figure is less than the 79-year life expectancy for white females.

24.7. A. About 25% of patient costs are for laboratory tests.

24.8. C. Medicare, established in 1965 and financed under the Social Security system, was primarily designed for people over 65 or for individuals with certain disabilities. Medicare recipients must pay an annual deductible for medical services.

24.9. A. Medicare Part B is optional medical insurance that covers doctor bills, medical supplies, home health care, outpatient hospital health care, and therapy services.

24.10. A. Medicaid has no deductibles.

24.11. B. Rates of obesity, diabetes, heart disease, hypertension, and arthritis are higher among blacks than whites.

24.12. E. All are correct.

24.13. A. Leading chronic medical conditions in women include arthritis, heart conditions, and hypertension.

24.14. D. The death rate per 100,000 people was lower in 1984 than in any other previous year. The three leading causes of death in the United States are heart disease, cancer, and stroke, in that order. The rates of the three leading causes of death are highest among black males. Women in all age groups have lower mortality rates than men.

24.15. B. Psychiatry ranks eighth among medical specialties in frequency of malpractice suits. The four D's of malpractice are *Dere-liction* of *Duty* *Directly* causing *Damages* to the patient.

Comprehensive Examination

Biological Bases of Behavior

The questions in this section relate to the material covered in Section I.

DIRECTIONS: For each of the questions or incomplete statements below, choose the answer that is **most correct.**

---

1. Which of the following has the highest risk of developing schizophrenia?
   A. The dizygotic twin of a schizophrenic patient
   B. The child of two schizophrenic parents
   C. The monozygotic twin of a schizophrenic patient
   D. The child of one schizophrenic parent
   E. A child raised in an institutional setting when neither biological parent was schizophrenic

2. Which of the following is true about affective disorders?
   A. A child with two bipolar parents has a 20% likelihood of having bipolar disorder in adulthood.
   B. The concordance rate for unipolar disorder is higher than that for bipolar disorder.
   C. The lifetime incidence of unipolar disorder is higher in men than in women.
   D. Markers on the X chromosome have been linked to mood disorders.
   E. The lifetime incidence of unipolar disorder is about 5% in women.

3. Which of the following conditions in which mental retardation occurs have a genetic component?
   A. Down's syndrome
   B. Klinefelter's syndrome
   C. Turner's syndrome
   D. Cri-du-chat syndrome
   E. All of the above

4. Which of the following is NOT a high potency antipsychotic?
   A. Chlorpromazine
   B. Haloperidol
   C. Perphenazine
   D. Trifluoperazine
   E. Haldol

5. All of the following are true about antianxiety agents EXCEPT:
   A. The most common side effect is drowsiness.
   B. They include meprobamate.
   C. They have abuse potential.
   D. Overdose may be lethal.
   E. The carbamates are less likely to cause dependence than the benzodiazepines.

DIRECTIONS: For each of the numbered items choose the **one** lettered heading with which it is **most closely associated.**

---

6. Increased pain perception

7. Sleep-arousal mechanism

8. Parkinson's disease

9. Klüver-Bucy syndrome

A. Reticular system

B. Temporal lobes

C. Thalamus

D. Basal ganglia

E. Hippocampus

DIRECTIONS: For each of the numbered items choose the **one** lettered heading with which it is **most closely associated.**

10. Schizophrenia

11. Depression

12. Anxiety

13. Alzheimer's disease

A. Serotonin

B. Dopamine

C. Acetylcholine

D. GABA

E. Histamine

DIRECTIONS: For each of the numbered items choose the **one** lettered heading with which it is **most closely associated.**

14. Most sedating

15. Least sedating

16. Least likely to cause orthostatic hypotension

17. Parkinsonian-like symptoms

A. Nortriptyline

B. Amoxapine

C. Desipramine

D. Imipramine

E. Amitriptyline

The Life Cycle

The questions in this section relate to the material covered in Section II.

DIRECTIONS: For each of the questions or incomplete statements below, choose the answer that is **most correct.**

18. The percentage of women who suffer postpartum blues following the birth of a child is approximately

A. 5 to 10%.
B. 25 to 30%.
C. 50 to 65%.
D. 75 to 85%.
E. 90 to 95%.

19. Which of the following developmental theorists described early infant development as the normal autistic phase?

A. Mahler
B. Freud
C. Erikson
D. Piaget
E. Harlowe

20. In the United States, the incidence of childhood physical abuse per year is approximately

A. 100,000.
B. 200,000.
C. 500,000.
D. 800,000.
E. 1,000,000.

21. All of the following are true about divorce EXCEPT:

A. Most divorced men and women marry again.
B. Children of divorce are more likely to be divorced.
C. Most single-parent families are headed by women.
D. Divorce is associated with marriage at an early age.
E. First marriages are more likely to end in divorce than second marriages.

22. All of the following are true about growing old in the United States EXCEPT:

A. Depression is more common in the elderly.
B. Anxiety caused by insecurity is common in the elderly.
C. Longevity is associated with being married.
D. Suicide is rarer in the elderly than in the general population.
E. Most elderly people have a positive feeling about their lives.

23. Characteristics of patients with Alzheimer's disease include:

A. severe memory loss.
B. personality changes.
C. apathy.
D. cognitive deficits.
E. all of the above.

DIRECTIONS: For each of the numbered items choose the **one** lettered heading with which it is **most closely associated.**

24. The favorite word is "no"

25. Imaginary companions

26. The capacity for logical thought

27. Identity consolidation versus role confusion

A. Infancy

B. Toddler years

C. Preschool

D. Latency

E. Adolescence

DIRECTIONS: For each of the numbered items choose the **one** lettered heading with which it is **most closely associated.**

28. "I will go to church every day if only I can get rid of this illness."

29. "The doctor is to blame for my illness."

30. "It can't be true that I am dying."

31. "I am ready to die."

A. Denial

B. Anger

C. Acceptance

D. Depression

E. Bargaining

Behavior of the Individual

The questions in this section relate to the material covered in Section III.

DIRECTIONS: For each of the questions or incomplete statements below, choose the answer that is **most correct.**

32. Which of the following is the least mature defense mechanism?

A. Altruism
B. Suppression
C. Sublimation
D. Humor
E. Denial

33. Which of the following functions to maintain a relationship to the external world?

A. The id
B. The ego
C. The superego
D. Defense mechanisms
E. Dream work

34. The pattern of reinforcment least resistant to extinction is:

A. fixed ratio.
B. fixed interval.
C. variable ratio.
D. variable interval.
E. continuous.

35. All of the following are true about biofeedback EXCEPT:

A. The patient must be motivated to learn.
B. It involves learning control over physiologic activities.
C. It is an extension of classical conditioning.
D. It has been used to treat peptic ulcer.
E. It has been used to treat tension headache.

36. Withdrawal of which of the following drugs is associated with the occurrence of delirium tremens?

A. Cocaine
B. Barbiturates
C. Alcohol
D. Amphetamines
E. Opioids

37. Caffeine is commonly found in all of the following EXCEPT:

A. tea.
B. cola.
C. nonprescription stimulants.
D. nonprescription diet drugs.
E. cough medicine.

38. All of the following are true about marijuana EXCEPT:

A. It is the most widely abused illegal drug in the United States.
B. Its effects include increased appetite.
C. Its effects include impaired memory.
D. Its effects include the amotivational syndrome.
E. Time perception is not affected by the drug.

39. Heroin addicts

A. are usually in their late 40s.
B. are more likely to be female than male.
C. are likely to die from sudden withdrawal of the drug.
D. can be treated with methadone because it is not addicting.
E. are given clonidine to block the heroin withdrawal syndrome.

40. All of the following are true about alcoholism EXCEPT:

A. It is more common in Asian Americans than in white Americans.
B. Sons are more vulnerable than daughters.
C. It is associated with about 50% of traffic fatalities.
D. Life expectancy is reduced.
E. Its occurrence is greatest in the Northeastern United States.

41. All of the following are associated with caffeine use EXCEPT:

A. Withdrawal is frequently accompanied by headaches.
B. It is found in nonprescription drugs.
C. Physical dependence is common.
D. Psychological dependence may occur with chronic use.
E. Withdrawal may be associated with lethargy.

42. Sawtooth waves are associated with which of the following sleep stages?

A. Stage 1
B. REM
C. Stage 2
D. Stage 3
E. Stage 4

43. Sleep disorders include:

A. insomnia.
B. hypersomnia.
C. sleep-wake schedule disorders.
D. sleep walking.
E. all of the above.

44. All of the following are true about sleep and affective disorders EXCEPT:

A. Manic patients may have a reduced need for sleep.
B. Depression is often associated with hypersomnia.
C. Long REM latency occurs in depression.
D. Premature morning awakenings may occur in unipolar depression.
E. Normal sleep onset is characteristic of unipolar depression.

DIRECTIONS: For each of the numbered items choose the **one** lettered heading with which it is **most closely associated.**

---

45. People are seen as being totally bad or totally good

46. Unacceptable feelings are expressed in actions

47. One's behavior is patterned after that of another person

48. An irrational feeling is made to appear reasonable

A. Rationalization
B. Acting out
C. Splitting
D. Identification
E. Displacement

DIRECTIONS: For each of the numbered items choose the **one** lettered heading with which it is **most closely associated.**

---

49. Adopting the behavior of someone admired or respected

50. Pairing an unwanted behavior with a painful stimulus

51. The conditioned response reappears in the absence of a stimulus

52. A nonreflex behavior serves as a reward or punishment

A. Operant conditioning
B. Aversive conditioning
C. Spontaneous recovery
D. Modeling
E. Stimulus generalization

Psychopathology

The questions in this section relate to the material covered in Section IV.

DIRECTIONS: For each of the questions or incomplete statements below, choose the answer that is **most correct.**

53. All of the following are true about schizophrenia EXCEPT:

A. The major neurotransmitter involved is dopamine.
B. Prodromal signs include peculiar behavior.
C. Prodromal signs include somatic complaints.
D. The most common type of hallucination is visual.
E. Approximately 50% of patients attempt suicide.

54. Positive symptoms of schizophrenia include:

A. flattening of affect.
B. hallucinations.
C. poverty of speech.
D. blocking.
E. social withdrawal.

55. All of the following are true about the use of antipsychotics EXCEPT:

A. Extrapyramidal neurologic signs are a common side effect.
B. Extrapyramidal signs are more common in men than in women.
C. Most antipsychotics are equally effective.
D. Schizophrenics usually are compliant about taking neuroleptic medication.
E. Tardive dyskinesia is a serious side effect of neuroleptic drugs.

56. Delusions of persecution are characteristic of which of the following types of schizophrenia?

A. Disorganized
B. Catatonic
C. Paranoid
D. Undifferentiated
E. Residual

57. All of the following are true about schizophrenia EXCEPT:

A. The differential diagnosis includes organic delirium.
B. The differential diagnosis includes manic-depressive illness.
C. The differential diagnosis includes brief reactive psychosis.
D. The frontal lobes have been implicated in its pathophysiology.
E. Decreased cerebrospinal fluid MHPG is seen in many schizophrenic patients.

58. Bipolar disorder

A. is more common in lower socioeconomic groups.
B. has a genetic component.
C. has a better prognosis than major depressive disorder.
D. is more common in African American patients than in white patients.
E. is characterized by chronic impairment between episodes.

59. In major depressive disorder

A. the frequency of episodes often increases with age.
B. the length of episodes often decreases with age.
C. treated episodes last for about 9 months.
D. premorbid problems are common.
E. patients usually commit suicide when at the most severe stage of depression.

60. Manic patients

A. usually show good judgment.
B. are frequently grandiose.
C. show psychomotor retardation.
D. usually lack energy.
E. are rarely assaultive.

61. Which of the following is true about the treatment of mood disorders?

A. Lithium is the drug of choice for patients with mania.
B. Carbamazepine may be used if lithium is not effective.
C. Psychotherapy can increase compliance with drug treatment in mood disorders.
D. Psychotherapy plus drug treatment is more beneficial than either treatment alone.
E. All of the above.

62. All of the following are true about the anxiety disorders EXCEPT:

A. The raphe nuclei are probably involved in their etiology.
B. Generalized anxiety disorder occurs more frequently in men.
C. Generalized anxiety disorder commonly develops at around age 25.
D. Physical manifestations include gastrointestinal problems.
E. Psychotherapy is used in treatment.

63. All of the following are true about panic attacks EXCEPT:

A. They fall under the heading of anxiety disorders.
B. They commonly occur twice per week.
C. The intense periods of anxiety commonly last 2 to 3 days.
D. They commonly first appear in young adulthood.
E. Symptoms include fainting.

64. Which of the following is true?

A. Dementia commonly progresses to delirium.
B. Slow onset is characteristic of delirium.
C. Clouding of consciousness commonly occurs in dementia.
D. Dementia is frequently reversible.
E. Delirium is commonly seen on medical hospital wards.

65. Pseudodementia

A. is not reversible.
B. is common in young adults.
C. is characterized by clouding of consciousness.
D. is characterized by depression.
E. has the same prognosis as dementia of the Alzheimer's type.

66. Anorexia nervosa

A. is most common in middle age.
B. is more common in lower socioeconomic groups.
C. has few serious medical consequences.
D. can be treated with family therapy.
E. has as its main feature loss of appetite.

67. An inferiority complex is characteristic of which of the following personality disorders?

A. Paranoid
B. Avoidant
C. Antisocial
D. Schizotypal
E. Schizoid

68. Which of the following is true about infantile autism?

A. More females are affected than males.
B. There is usually a family history of schizophrenia.
C. The onset is after 6 years of age.
D. There is no evidence of organic dysfunction.
E. It is a pervasive developmental disorder of childhood.

69. All of the following are true about attention deficit hyperactivity disorder EXCEPT:

A. Genetic factors have been implicated.
B. Emotional lability is common.
C. Benzodiazepines are the drugs of choice for treatment.
D. Irritability is common.
E. It is also called the hyperactive child syndrome.

Clinical Assessment

The questions in this section relate to the material covered in Section V.

DIRECTIONS: For each of the questions or incomplete statements below, choose the answer that is **most correct**.

70. Which of the following is used to test general intellectual ability in individuals 2 to 18 years old?
A. Halstead-Reitan Test Battery
B. Draw-a-Person Test
C. Stanford-Binet Scale
D. Bender-Gestalt Test
E. Rorschach Test

71. An individual with an IQ of 20 would be classified as:
A. mildly mentally retarded.
B. borderline.
C. moderately mentally retarded.
D. severely mentally retarded.
E. low average.

72. A test that requires a patient to construct a story based on pictures is the
A. MMPI.
B. Rorschach Test.
C. Draw-a-Person Test.
D. Thematic Apperception Test.
E. WAIS-R.

73. Memory is a function mainly of the
A. temporal lobes.
B. frontal lobes.
C. parietal lobes.
D. occipital lobes.
E. cerebellum.

74. Abnormal drowsiness is known as:
A. stupor.
B. coma.
C. delirium.
D. somnolence.
E. clouding of consciousness.

75. In taking a psychiatric history, which of the following areas are addressed?
A. Relationships with other people
B. Source of family income
C. Present drug and alcohol use
D. Past drug and alcohol use
E. All of the above

76. All of the following are true about the dexamethasone suppression test (DST) EXCEPT:
A. Dexamethasone is a synthetic glucocorticoid.
B. When given to a normal patient, dexamethasone suppresses the secretion of cortisol.
C. The DST may be used to confirm a diagnosis of mental depression.
D. Patients with a negative DST will have a good response to antidepressant drugs.
E. Patients with a positive DST will have a good response to electroconvulsive therapy.

77. All of the following are true about evoked potentials EXCEPT:
A. The response of the brain to sensory stimuli is measured.
B. They may be used in psychiatric evaluation.
C. They may be used to localize brain lesions.
D. They are absent during sleep.
E. They may differ between schizophrenic and normal patients.

Social Behavior

The questions in this section relate to the material covered in Section VI.

DIRECTIONS: For each of the questions or incomplete statements below, choose the answer that is **most correct.**

78. All of the following are true about the family in the United States EXCEPT:

A. Approximately 95% of the population marries at some time.
B. Approximately half of marriages will end in divorce.
C. Ten to 15% of couples are childless.
D. The nuclear family commonly includes parents and their children.
E. Approximately 10% of children live in families in which both parents work.

79. Which of the following involves a coalition of two family members against another family member?

A. Subsystem
B. Triangle
C. Emotional cutoff
D. Mutual accommodation
E. Multigenerational transmission process

80. Which of the following is true about Native American subcultures?

A. They have a lower rate of alcoholism.
B. They have a lower rate of suicide.
C. A sharp distinction is made between mental and physical illness.
D. They number about half a million individuals.
E. The federal government administers a separate medical care program for American Indians.

81. All of the following are true about immigrants to the United States EXCEPT:

A. They have a higher rate of psychiatric hospitalization.
B. Young immigrant women appear to be at greater risk for psychiatric problems than young immigrant men.
C. Immigrants show a higher incidence of paranoid symptoms.
D. Paranoid symptoms in immigrant groups have a good prognosis.
E. Paranoid symptoms in immigrant groups are often recurrent.

82. All of the following are true about sexual dysfunctions EXCEPT:

A. Premature ejaculation is common.
B. Sexual dysfunctions can develop after a period of normal functioning.
C. Sexual dysfunctions can have a combination of causes.
D. Primary impotence is common.
E. Secondary impotence is common.

83. All of the following are true about homosexuality EXCEPT:

A. The estimate of its occurrence in men is 3 to 6%.
B. Homosexual men generally have normal testosterone levels.
C. It is considered a sexual dysfunction in the DSM-III-R.
D. Alterations in prenatal hormones may be involved.
E. Cross-gender behavior during childhood commonly occurs.

84. In which of the following stages of the sexual response cycle does the tenting effect first occur?

A. The excitement phase
B. The plateau phase
C. Orgasm
D. Emission
E. The resolution phase

85. Which of the following is true about impotence associated with diabetes?

A. Five to 10% of diabetic men eventually become impotent.
B. Impotence usually occurs immediately upon the diagnosis of diabetes.
C. The major cause of impotence in diabetic men is psychological.
D. Poor metabolic control of diabetes is related to sexual problems.
E. The impotence associated with diabetes does not respond to treatment of any kind.

86. All of the following are true about aging and sexuality EXCEPT:

A. Menopause usually does not result in decreased libido in women.
B. Prolonged abstention from sex may lead more quickly to atrophy of the genital organs.
C. Sexual activity usually decreases with increasing age.
D. Approximately 93% of men aged 61 to 65 report having sexual interest.
E. Approximately 93% of women aged 61 to 65 report having sexual interest.

87. Which of the following groups of drugs is associated with the highest incidence of sexual problems?

A. Antihypertensives
B. Tranquilizers
C. Sedatives
D. Antipsychotics
E. Antidepressants

88. All of the following are true about the drugs of abuse and sexuality EXCEPT:

A. Marijuana enhances the enjoyment of sex primarily by physiologic means.
B. Marijuana use often results in an immediate increase in libido.
C. Cocaine use may be associated with priapism.
D. Use of amyl nitrate is associated with cardiovascular accidents.
E. Long-term use of alcohol is associated with decreased potency in men.

89. All of the following are true about rape EXCEPT:

A. It is frequently associated with the use of weapons.
B. Fifty-one percent of rapists are white.
C. Rapists tend to rape women of the same race.
D. Alcoholism is involved in at least one-third of rapes.
E. Most rapists are over 25 years of age.

90. Neurotransmitters linked to aggression include:

A. norepinephrine.
B. dopamine.
C. serotonin.
D. acetylcholine.
E. all of the above.

The Doctor-Patient Relationship

The questions in this section relate to the material covered in Section VII.

DIRECTIONS: For each of the questions or incomplete statements below, choose the answer that is **most correct**.

91. Compliance with medical advice is closely associated with:

A. marital status.
B. race.
C. religion.
D. educational level.
E. written instructions for taking medication.

92. All of the following are true about pain EXCEPT:

A. It is linked to depression.
B. The threshold is similar for most people.
C. Cultural factors are not related to the expression of pain.
D. Extreme sensitivity to pain is associated with anxiety.
E. Antidepressant drugs are used in the treatment of chronic pain.

93. Which of the following is true about the doctor-patient relationship?

A. Most individuals with symptoms visit physicians.
B. Chronically ill patients express the least skepticism about medical care.
C. Morbidity is higher in psychiatric populations.
D. Mortality is lower in psychiatric populations.
E. Patients rarely trust young physicians.

94. All of the following are true about hospitalized patients EXCEPT:

A. Common psychiatric problems include depression.
B. Approximately 5% of medical inpatients have psychiatric disorders.
C. Psychotherapy is used in hospitalized medical inpatients with psychological problems.
D. Behavioral therapy is used on hospitalized inpatients with psychological problems.
E. Patients with a history of psychiatric illness are at particular risk for psychological problems when hospitalized.

95. Surgical patients who are at relatively higher risk for morbidity and mortality include all of the following EXCEPT those who:

A. deny that they are seriously worried.
B. are convinced that they will not survive surgery.
C. have unrealistic expectations of the surgical procedure.
D. are not told what to expect during surgery.
E. are able to express their anxiety.

96. Psychological stress is associated with which of the following illnesses?

A. Hyperthyroidism
B. Diabetes mellitus
C. Immune disorders
D. Arthritis
E. All of the above

97. Which of the following is the least severe life stressor?

A. Divorce
B. Marriage
C. Retirement
D. Changing residences
E. Birth of a child

DIRECTIONS: For each of the numbered items choose the **one** lettered heading with which it is **most closely associated.**

---

98. "And then what happened?"

99. "You say that you felt the pain more in the evening?"

100. "Exactly where is the pain now?"

101. "That must have been terrifying for you."

102. "I understand that you must be really worried."

A. Empathy

B. Support

C. Direct question

D. Facilitation

E. Reflection

DIRECTIONS: For each of the numbered items choose the **one** lettered heading with which it is **most closely associated.**

103. Fears loss of attractiveness when ill		A.	Dependent
104. May view illness as a punishment		B.	Compulsive
105. Tends to blame others for the illness		C.	Histrionic
106. Has a need for personal care		D.	Masochistic
107. Fears loss of control in illness		E.	Paranoid

Health Care Delivery

The questions in this section relate to the material covered in Section VIII.

DIRECTIONS: For each of the questions or incomplete statements below, choose the answer that is **most correct.**

108. False-negative results occur if a test instrument
A. fails to detect a disorder in someone who has the disorder.
B. detects a disorder in someone who does not have the disorder.
C. detects things not being evaluated.
D. can detect the disorder being evaluated.
E. detects a disease in a person who has the disease.

109. Differences between frequencies in a sample are tested using
A. t-test.
B. analysis of variance.
C. chi-square test.
D. correlation.
E. regression.

110. All of the following are true about health care in the United States EXCEPT:
A. About 80% of physicians are specialists .
B. Prior to 1900, people generally died of infections.
C. There are about 19,000 nursing homes.
D. Men are hospitalized more often than women.
E. The largest component of hospital costs is for health care staff.

111. All of the following are true about visits to physicians EXCEPT:
A. As patient income increases, the number of visits to the emergency room decreases.
B. Each patient averages five visits to the physician per year.
C. Patients are more likely to be female than male.
D. The most common reason for a visit is general physical examination.
E. Most patients are middle aged.

112. In which of the following medical specialties is there expected to be a surplus of physicians by the turn of the century?
A. Dermatology
B. Family practice
C. Pediatrics
D. Psychiatry
E. Internal medicine

113. All of the following are true about health care expenses EXCEPT:

A. The percentage of the gross national product spent on health care in 1984 was about 1%.
B. The federal government pays about 40% of personal health care expenses.
C. Private insurance pays about 30% of personal health care expenses.
D. Hospital costs represent 41% of health care expenditures.
E. Physician costs make up 20% of health care expenditures.

114. All of the following are true EXCEPT:

A. The average life expectancy for white males is approximately 72 years.
B. One of the most common causes of death in infants is congenital anomalies.
C. The mortality rate for black infants is twice that for white infants.
D. The average life expectancy for black females is approximately 79 years.
E. The average life expectancy for white females is approximately 79 years.

115. All of the following are true about Medicare EXCEPT:

A. Part B covers doctor bills.
B. Part B covers home health care.
C. It was established in 1965.
D. It was designed primarily for welfare recipients.
E. There is an annual deductible.

Answers and Explanations

Section I. Biological Bases of Behavior

1. C. The monozygotic twin of a schizophrenic patient has a 35 to 58% chance of developing the disease. The child of one schizophrenic parent, the dizygotic twin of a schizophrenic patient, and the child of two schizophrenic parents have 10 to 12%, 9 to 26%, and 35 to 46% chances of developing the disease, respectively.

2. D. Markers on the X chromosome have been linked to mood disorders. A child with two bipolar parents has a 50 to 75% likelihood of developing the disease in adulthood. The concordance rate for bipolar disorder is higher than that for unipolar disorder, and the lifetime incidence of the latter illness is higher in women (about 20%) than in men (about 10%).

3. E. Down's, Klinefelter's, Turner's, and cri-du-chat are conditions that may result in mental retardation and that have a genetic component.

4. A. High potency antipsychotics include haloperidol (Haldol), perphenazine, and trifluoperazine. Chlorpromazine and thioridazine are low potency antipsychotics.

5. E. The carbamates, including meprobamate, have more abuse potential and are more likely to result in dependence than the benzodiazepines.

6. C. Increased pain perception may be associated with lesions of the thalamus.

7. A. Sleep-arousal mechanisms may be altered by damage to the recticular system.

8. D. Parkinson's disease is associated with damage to the basal ganglia.

9. B. Klüver-Bucy syndrome results from damage to the temporal lobes.

10. B. A hyperdopaminergic state may be involved in the etiology of schizophrenia.

11. A. Serotonin is involved in the pathophysiology of affective disorders.

12. D. Decreased GABA activity is thought to be involved in the pathophysiology of anxiety.

13. C. Degeneration of cholinergic neurons is involved in Alzheimer's disease.

14. E. Of the listed antidepressants, amitriptyline is the most sedating.

15. C. Of the listed antidepressants, desipramine is the least sedating.

16. A. Nortriptyline is the heterocyclic antidepressant least likely to cause orthostatic hypotension.

17. B. The heterocyclic amoxapine is associated with parkinsonian-like symptoms.

Section II. The Life Cycle

18. C. Following the birth of a child, approximately 50 to 65% of women suffer postpartum blues.

19. A. Margaret Mahler described early infant development as the normal autistic phase.

20. E. The incidence of childhood physical abuse per year in the United States is approximately 1,000,000.

21. E. Second marriages are more likely to end in divorce than first marriages.

22. D. Suicide is more common in the elderly than in the general population.

23. E. Characteristics of Alzheimer's disease include severe memory loss, personality changes, apathy, and cognitive deficits.

24. B. During the toddler years, the favorite word is "no."

25. C. Imaginary companions are common during the preschool years.

26. D. The child acquires the capacity for logical thought during latency.

27. E. A sense of independent self, Erikson's stage of identity consolidation versus role confusion, develops during adolescence.

28. E. This statement is an example of bargaining.

29. B. This statement is an example of anger.

30. A. This statement is an example of denial.

31. C. This statement is an example of acceptance.

Section III. Behavior of the Individual

32. E. Of the listed defense mechanisms, denial is the least mature.

33. B. The ego functions to maintain a relationship to the external world.

34. E. Continuous reinforcement is the pattern of reinforcement that is least resistant to extinction.

35. C. Biofeedback, which has been used to treat tension headaches, peptic ulcer, and other medical conditions, involves learning control over physiologic activities and is an extension of operant conditioning.

36. C. Withdrawal of alcohol is associated with the occurrence of delirium tremens.

37. E. Caffeine is commonly found in tea, cola, nonprescription stimulants, and nonprescription diet drugs.

38. E. Time perception is frequently affected by the use of marijuana.

39. E. Most heroin addicts are in their early 30s and are more likely to be male than female. Death from withdrawal of heroin is rare, and individuals may be given clonidine to block the heroin withdrawal syndrome. Like heroin, methadone causes physical dependence and tolerance.

40. A. Alcoholism is more common in white Americans than Asian Americans.

41. C. Although psychological dependence may occur with chronic use of caffeine, tolerance does not occur and physical dependence has not been well-documented with the use of this drug.

42. B. Sawtooth waves are associated with REM sleep.

43. E. Sleep disorders include insomnia, hypersomnia, sleep-wake schedule disorders, and sleep walking.

44. C. Insomnia in unipolar depression is characterized by normal sleep onset and premature morning awakenings. Although manic patients often have a reduced need for sleep, depression may be associated with hypersomnia. In depression, reduced slow wave sleep, short REM latency, and long first REM period may occur.

45. C. People are seen as being totally bad or totally good when an individual uses the defense mechanism of splitting.

46. B. When unacceptable feelings are expressed in actions, an individual is acting out.

47. D. When an individual uses the defense mechanism of identification, his or her behavior is patterned after that of another person.

48. A. An individual uses rationalization to make an irrational feeling appear reasonable.

49. D. In modeling, an individual adopts the behavior of someone admired or respected.

50. B. In aversive conditioning, an unwanted behavior is paired with a painful stimulus.

51. C. When the conditioned response reappears in the absence of a stimulus it is known as spontaneous recovery.

52. A. In operant conditioning, a nonreflex behavior serves as a reward or punishment.

Section IV. Psychopathology

53. D. The most common type of hallucinations seen in schizophrenia are auditory.

54. B. Positive symptoms of schizophrenia include loose associations, hallucinations, strange behavior, and talkativeness. Negative symptoms include flattening of affect, poverty of speech or speech content, thought blocking, poor grooming, lack of motivation, social withdrawal, and cognitive deficits.

55. D. In part because of the side effects of neuroleptic agents, schizophrenic patients may not comply with taking the drugs and may relapse.

56. C. Delusions of persecution are characteristic of paranoid schizophrenia.

57. E. Evidence of increased cerebrospinal fluid MHPG in some schizophrenic patients suggests that norepinephrine activity may be increased in schizophrenia.

58. B. Bipolar disorder has a genetic component, occurs with equal frequency in whites and blacks, may be more common in higher socioeconomic groups, and has a worse prognosis than major depressive disorder. In contrast to schizophrenia, bipolar patients do not usually show chronic impairment between episodes.

59. A. In major depressive disorder, both the frequency and the length of episodes often increase with advancing age. Although untreated episodes of depression last 6 to 13 months, treated episodes last only about 3 months. In depressed patients, suicide usually occurs when the patient is coming out of the severe depression.

60. B. Manic patients show poor judgment and may be grandiose, hyperactive, and assaultive.

61. E. In mood disorders, psychotherapy plus drug treatment is frequently more beneficial than either treatment alone. In addition, psychotherapy can increase compliance with drug treatment. Although lithium is the drug of choice for manic patients, carbamazepine may be used if lithium is not effective.

62. B. Generalized anxiety disorder occurs more frequently in women.

63. C. The intense periods of anxiety characteristic of panic attacks commonly last under 1 hour.

64. E. Delirium has a rapid onset and may progress to dementia if not treated. Clouding of consciousness is characteristic of the delirium commonly seen on medical hospital wards; it is frequently reversible.

65. D. Pseudodementia is common in older people, is characterized by depression, and, unlike Alzheimer's, can be reversed with treatment.

66. D. Anorexia nervosa occurs most commonly during late adolescence in higher socioeconomic groups. Although it has serious medical consequences, anorexia nervosa can be successfully treated. Methods of treatment include family therapy techniques.

67. B. An inferiority complex is characteristic of individuals with an avoidant personality disorder.

68. E. Infantile autism, a pervasive developmental disorder of childhood, affects more males than females and has an onset prior to 6 years of age. In infantile autism, there is evidence of organic dysfunction.

69. C. Genetic factors have been implicated in attention deficit hyperactivity disorder (ADHD). In this condition, emotional lability and irritability commonly occur. In the treatment of ADHD, central nervous system stimulants decrease motor activity and increase attention and the ability to concentrate.

Section V. Clinical Assessment

70. C. The Stanford-Binet Scale is used to test general intellectual ability in individuals 2 to 18 years of age.

71. D. An individual with an IQ of 20 would be classified as severely mentally retarded.

72. D. The Thematic Apperception Test requires a person to construct a story based on a series of pictures.

73. A. Memory is a function mainly of the temporal lobes.

74. D. Abnormal drowsiness is known as somnolence.

75. E. In taking a psychiatric history, relationships with other people, source of family income, and present and past drug and alcohol use are assessed.

76. D. Dexamethasone is a synthetic glucocorticoid that, when given to a normal patient, suppresses the secretion of cortisol. A positive dexamethasone suppression test indicates that a patient will have a good response to both antidepressant drugs and electroconvulsive therapy.

77. D. Evoked potentials are present during sleep.

Section VI. Social Behavior

78. E. In the United States, approximately 40% of children live in families in which both parents work.

79. B. A triangle is a rigid coalition between two family members against a third family member.

80. E. Native Americans have higher rates of both alcoholism and suicide. In Native American subcultures, which number approximately 1.4 million individuals, little distinction may be made between mental and physical illness.

81. B. Young immigrant men appear to be at greater risk for psychiatric problems than other sex and age groups.

82. D. Although secondary impotence is common, primary impotence is uncommon and occurs in only about 1% of men under 35 years of age.

83. C. Homosexuality is not considered a sexual dysfunction in the DSM-III-R.

84. A. The tenting effect first occurs during the excitement phase of the sexual response cycle.

85. D. Twenty-seven to 55% of diabetic men eventually become impotent. Although the major cause of impotence in diabetic men is physiologic, impotence does respond to psychological treatment. Treatment of impotence in diabetic men includes identification of interpersonal problems as well as surgical approaches such as penile implants. In addition, sexual problems associated with diabetes correspond with poor metabolic control of the disease.

86. E. Ninety-three percent of men but only 67% of women in the 61- to 65-year-old age group report having sexual interest.

87. A. Of the listed drugs, the antihypertensives are associated with the highest incidence of sexual problems.

88. A. Psychological, not physiologic, factors are probably responsible for the enhancement of the enjoyment of sex by marijuana.

89. E. Approximately 61% of rapists are under 25 years of age.

90. E. Neurotransmitters linked to aggression include norepinephrine, dopamine, serotonin, and acetylcholine.

Section VII. The Doctor-Patient Relationship

91. E. There is no clear association between compliance and a patient's sex, marital status, race, religion, socioeconomic status, intelligence, or educational level. However, compliance has been associated with a good doctor-patient relationship, older physician age, and written rather than verbal instructions for taking medication.

92. C. Cultural, ethnic, and religious factors may influence a patient's expression of pain and the responses of the patient's support systems to the pain.

93. C. Both morbidity and mortality are higher in psychiatric populations.

94. B. Up to 65% of medical inpatients have psychiatric disorders, most commonly anxiety, depression, and disorientation.

95. E. When surgical patients are able to express their depression and anxiety about the surgery, they are at relatively lower risk for morbidity and mortality.

96. E. Psychological stress is associated with a variety of illnesses, including hyperthyroidism, diabetes mellitus, immune disorders, and arthritis.

97. D. Of the listed life stressors, divorce is the most and changing residences the least severe.

98. D. "And then what happened?" is an example of the interviewing technique known as facilitation.

99. E. "You say that you felt the pain more in the evening?" is an example of the interviewing technique known as reflection.

100. C. "Exactly where is the pain now?" is an example of a direct question.

101. B. "That must have been terrifying for you" is an example of support.

102. A. In saying "I understand that you must be really worried," empathy is used to express the physician's concern for the patient.

103. C. The histrionic personality fears loss of attractiveness and may be dramatic and emotionally changeable during illness.

104. D. The masochistic personality type may view illness as a punishment and may prolong illnesses to receive love and attention.

105. E. The paranoid personality type often blames others, especially doctors, for the illness.

106. A. The dependent personality type fears being helpless and has a need to be cared for, resulting in demands for attention during illness.

107. B. The compulsive personality type fears loss of control and may become over controlling during illness.

Section VIII. Health Care Delivery

108. A. False-negative results occur when an instrument fails to detect a disorder in someone who has the disorder.

109. C. The chi-square test is used to examine differences between frequencies in a sample.

110. D. In the United States, women are hospitalized more often than men.

111. E. Most medical patients are either very young or very old.

112. E. By the turn of the century, there is expected to be a surplus of physicians in the fields of surgery, neurology, ophthalmology, obstetrics/gynecology, internal medicine, and neurosurgery.

113. A. Approximately $387 billion dollars, about 10.6% of the gross national product, was spent on health care in the United States in 1984.

114. D. While the average life expectancy for white females is approximately 79 years, the average life expectancy for black females is only about 74 years.

115. D. Medicare was designed primarily to provide hospital and medical costs for people eligible for Social Security. This group generally includes those over 65 or with disabilities. Medicaid was designed primarily to pay for health care needs for needy and low income people.

Suggested Readings

Enelow AJ, Swisher SN: *Interviewing and Patient Care*, 2nd ed. New York, Oxford University Press, 1979.

Kaplan HI, Sadock BJ: *Comprehensive Textbook of Psychiatry*, 5th ed. Baltimore, Williams & Wilkins, 1989.

Kaplan HI, Sadock BJ: *Synopsis of Psychiatry*, 5th ed. Baltimore, Williams & Wilkins, 1988.

Kolodny RC, Masters WH, Johnson VE: *Textbook of Sexual Medicine*. Boston, Little, Brown, 1979.

Rakich JS, Longest BB, Darr K: *Managing Health Services Organizations*, 2nd ed. Philadelphia, Saunders, 1985.

Simons RC: *Understanding Human Behavior in Health and Illness*, 3rd ed. Baltimore, Williams & Wilkins, 1985.

Waldinger RJ: *Psychiatry for Medical Students*. Washington, DC, American Psychiatric Press, 1984.

INDEX

Page numbers followed by "t" denote tables.